APJ Abdul Kalam
WINGS OF FIRE

**An Autobiography
with Arun Tiwari**

Universities Press

All rights reserved. No part of this book may be (i) modified, reproduced or utilised in any form, or by any means, electronic or mechanical, including photocopying, recording or by any information storage and retrieval system, in any form of binding or cover other than in which it is published, without permission in writing from the publisher; or (ii) used or reproduced in any manner for the purpose of training, development or operation of artificial intelligence (AI) technologies and systems, including generative AI technologies, without permission in writing from the copyright holder.

WINGS OF FIRE: AN AUTOBIOGRAPHY, NEW EDITION

Universities Press (India) Private Limited

Registered Office
3-6-747/1/A & 3-6-754/1, Himayatnagar, Hyderabad 500 029, Telangana, India
info@universitiespress.com; www.universitiespress.com

Distributed by
Orient Blackswan Private Limited

Registered Office
3-6-752 Himayatnagar, Hyderabad 500 029, Telangana, India
e-mail: centraloffice@universitiespress.com

Other Offices
Bengaluru / Chennai / Guwahati / Hyderabad / Kolkata / Mumbai / New Delhi / Noida / Patna

© The Authors 1999, 2026

First Edition published 1999. Seventy-first impression 2025
New Edition published 2026

ISBN: 978-93-49750-49-4

Cover and book design
© Universities Press (India) Private Limited 1999, 2026

Cover photograph: Courtesy *The Week*, a *Malayala Manorama* publication
Picture by B Jayachandran

'The Brahmos Missile' (adapted) published by Press Information Bureau on behalf of Ministry of Defence, Government of India, January 23, 2006. Ministry of Defence (GODL-India).

Typeset by
Orient BlackSwan, Hyderabad

Printed in India at
Rasi Graphics Pvt Ltd, Chennai 600 014

Published by
Universities Press (India) Private Limited
3-6-747/1/A & 3-6-754/1, Himayatnagar, Hyderabad 500 029, Telangana, India
info@universitiespress.com; www.universitiespress.com

To the memory of my parents

My Mother

Sea waves, golden sand, pilgrims' faith,
Rameswaram Mosque Street, all merge into one,
My Mother!
You come to me like heaven's caring arms.
I remember the war days when life was challenge and toil—
Miles to walk, hours before sunrise,
Walking to take lessons from the saintly teacher near the temple.
Again miles to the Arab teaching school,
Climb sandy hills to Railway Station Road,
Collect, distribute newspapers to temple city citizens,
Few hours after sunrise, going to school.
Evening, business time before study at night.
All this pain of a young boy,
My Mother, you transformed into pious strength
With kneeling and bowing five times
For the Grace of the Almighty only, My Mother.
Your strong piety is your children's strength,
You always shared your best with whoever needed the most,
You always gave, and gave with faith in Him.
I still remember the day when I was ten,
Sleeping on your lap to the envy of my elder brothers and sister
It was a full moon night, my world only you knew
Mother! My Mother!
When at midnight I woke with tears falling on my knee
You knew the pain of your child, My Mother.
Your caring hands, tenderly removing the pain
Your love, your care, your faith gave me strength
To face the world without fear and with His strength.
We will meet again on the great Judgement Day, My Mother!

APJ Abdul Kalam

Foreword

I embrace this task of writing the Foreword for the New Edition of *Wings of Fire*, not merely as a responsibility, but as a tribute to a life that had a deep impact on mine and that of many others. In the silent folds of my becoming, I have been shaped profoundly by Dr APJ Abdul Kalam in ways that lie beyond the grasp of my conscious intellect or measured reasoning.

In the early 1990s, I had the opportunity to work with Dr VS Arunachalam, the Scientific Adviser to the Defence Minister and the esteemed predecessor of Dr APJ Abdul Kalam. At that time, Dr Kalam was serving as the Director of the Defence Research and Development Laboratory (DRDL) in Hyderabad. He would frequently call Dr Arunachalam. After his characteristic, drawn-out "Hellooo..." and polite "May I speak to the SA?," I would instinctively respond with, "Who is speaking?"

While I am not always annoyed when people mispronounce my name, I have always wished they had taken the effort to get it right. I still remember my first conversation with Dr Kalam, during which he took a moment to clarify both the correct spelling and the pronunciation of my name. That small gesture meant a lot to me. What stood out was that Dr Kalam never made assumptions. If he was unsure about something, he asked questions and ensured that he got it right. After a couple of such calls, his distinctive voice became instantly recognizable. Dr Kalam would often inquire about my well-being, speak about the government, the weather, food, and a range of other everyday matters. The calls became unexpectedly personal.

When Dr Kalam was appointed as Scientific Adviser to the Defence Minister, a small gathering was arranged at the India International Centre (IIC) in New Delhi to welcome Dr Kalam and bid farewell to Dr Arunachalam. I was entrusted with the responsibility of bringing Dr Kalam to IIC from the DRDO Guest House in Asiad Village. In keeping with my usual practice, I arrived well ahead of schedule. Lost in the elegant surroundings of the Asiad Village, I almost missed Dr Kalam, who descended from the first floor to greet me. He got into the rear seat of the car, while I took the front seat (I had never travelled with an officer of his calibre before and had often seen junior staff members seated in the front when accompanying a senior official). I heard him say with a warm laugh, "You Guy, why are you sitting there?

There's space here!" Before I could respond, he called out again, "Come here, I say!" It felt wonderful to sit beside him and enjoy a warm chat.

In his affectionate way, he called me "My Guy." Everyone in our circle knew what it meant. To be known by him in that way is something I carry with gratitude to this day. I was also his "Funny Guy." It wasn't just about humour; it was about timing, trust and truth. I earned it when I accepted hard lessons or disagreed with reasons.

At one point when I briefly sported a beard, he looked at me with that familiar, thoughtful gaze and asked, "Why do you need one?" I had no good answer. He'd always seen me clean-shaven with a moustache, a look he felt reflected seriousness and self-respect. When I didn't take the hint, he simply said, "Remove it, I say," in a tone that blended command and affection. When my motorbike was stolen in 1995, Dr Kalam dropped me home almost every day for six months. He never once made it feel like an inconvenience. He seamlessly folded that long detour into his schedule. A father figure in the truest sense, not through authority, but through quiet action, steady presence and genuine care.

Dr Kalam's poetic temperament found a kindred spirit in his friend, Abbot Yu Hsi of Taiwan. Together, they championed poetry as a medium for peace, viewing poets as guardians of language and culture. Abbot Yu Hsi's vision of mobilizing 1,000 poets and 10,000 poems for global harmony resonated deeply with Dr Kalam. I had the privilege of accompanying Dr Kalam on his visit to Taiwan, where he attended the 30th World Congress of Poets, hosted by the Crane Summit 21st Century International Forum. This historic visit is still remembered, as Dr Kalam was the most distinguished Indian public figure to travel to Taiwan. At the Presidential Palace, President Ma Ying-jeou formed an instant rapport with Dr Kalam, expressing admiration for his scientific and literary achievements.

Once, on our travels, while we were waiting in a lounge, President Kalam noticed a young girl being questioned and held back by security outside. At his request, I inquired about it and learned that the girl simply wished to receive his blessings. Dr Kalam immediately instructed that she be allowed in, and he warmly gave her his blessings. I was struck by the moment, especially because, unlike many others who approached him, she neither asked for a photograph nor an autograph. In a world where chasing selfies and signatures is commonplace, her desire for nothing but Dr Kalam's blessing was deeply moving.

During our journeys together, Dr Kalam never liked to ask the ad hoc staff for favours, even when he was fully entitled to do so. I knew, for example, that he found it easier to eat oranges without the fibrous white strands of the endocarp getting caught in his dentures, but he would never ask anyone to separate the pulp for him. With me, however, he was completely at ease. He didn't mind when I quietly did it for him, and he'd enjoy the fruit with the simple delight of a child.

As we know, affluent individuals or people of a certain stature often had no hesitation in approaching Dr Kalam. However, ground staff, equipment operators, drivers, baggage handlers and others in similar roles often found it difficult to come forward even for a handshake, a kind word or a photo. Remarkably, Dr Kalam had an uncanny ability to notice such individuals. In many such instances, he would graciously take the initiative to start a conversation, often ending with an impromptu photo or a warm interaction that left a lasting memory for his admirers.

From my perspective, his presidential days were quite taxing. Dr Kalam often worked overtime, yet surprisingly, the words "tired" and "busy" didn't seem to exist in his vocabulary. There were nights when I had to carry time-sensitive files to his bedroom well past midnight. His initial reaction, on many occasions, was a gentle, "Tomorrow, I say." But before I could turn to leave, he would invite me in, review every file and clear them all without delay. For him, duty always came before comfort and the entire office bore witness to it.

President Kalam's office window overlooked the Mughal Gardens. Whenever he spotted peacocks dancing, he would immediately send word to the Rashtrapati Bhavan photographers, asking them to capture the moment without startling the birds. He was also particular about preserving the natural beauty of the surroundings. He disliked pruning branches, even for aesthetic reasons, believing that nature should be allowed to flourish freely.

Music was Dr Kalam's comfort zone. The soothing sounds of instrumental compositions by Ustad Bismillah Khan, Pandit Hariprasad Chaurasia or Pandit Shivkumar Sharma, and the soulful renderings of Mrs MS Subbulakshmi, would often fill his bedroom. He preferred playing them on his old cassette player, one of his mainstays, never quite taking to the CD player that he bought reluctantly after some persuasion during his time at Rashtrapati Bhavan. Whenever I gave him CDs of his favourite musicians, he would let me play them, gracious as always. Yet he remained delightfully old school, and he wore that trait with quiet charm.

At times, my mind is saturated with questions and doubts, bouncing between what was and what could have been. I keep wondering, "Should I have dropped everything and gone with him to Shillong? Would it have made a difference? Was the pain too much? Could I have helped, comforted, done something, anything, differently?" These questions have no answers. They only deepen the ache. The hardest part is living with the silence of all that remains unsaid, all that remains unknown.

Looking back, it is remarkable that at every stage of his journey, Dr Kalam remained unchanged and steadfast in his simplicity. Whether he was at DRDO, serving as the Principal Scientific Adviser to the Government of India, or leading the nation as the President of India, his lifestyle never changed with his rising stature. His needs were few. His approach was grounded. His mindset was unshaken by fame or power. From the food he ate to the clothes he wore, even the things he used every day, nothing was upgraded to be flaunted or for mere display. He lived a life of purpose, not possessions. His minimalism was not born out of any lack; it was second nature to him. Though he could afford luxuries, he chose to live by what was necessary.

Wings of Fire continues to inspire people of all ages and backgrounds. Dr Kalam's journey from humble beginnings to becoming a leading scientist serves as a powerful reminder that dreams backed by determination can shape a nation's destiny. His emphasis on self-reliance in technology and national strength resonates deeply with India's aspirations even today. The unwavering faith and gratitude expressed towards his mentors and colleagues reflect values that are timeless and universal. Beyond personal triumphs, this book beautifully captures the essence of the core values essential for a society to thrive, from the foundational bonds of family to the larger vision of national progress and global harmony.

Chapters 17 to 22 of this New Edition form a deeply personal and reflective continuation of Dr Kalam's extraordinary journey, chronicling his life from 1991 until his passing in 2015. These chapters are not merely historical records but heartfelt recollections from a close companion, Prof. Arun Tiwari. They capture the essence of a man who, even after holding the highest office in the country, remained devoted to the service of the nation and its youth. Through anecdotes, reflections and private conversations, these chapters bring to life the vision and boundless energy that defined Dr Kalam's legacy years. As such, they serve as both a tribute and an invitation to be inspired, to imagine boldly, and to act with righteousness and purpose.

This Foreword is a small, but heartfelt, gesture to honour the greatness of Dr Kalam. I'm deeply grateful to the publishers for allowing me to be part of this meaningful effort, one that will help keep his life, vision and values alive for generations to come.

Harry Sheridon
(Private Secretary to President Kalam)

Preface to the New Edition

Since its publication in 1999, *Wings of Fire* has been reprinted more than 70 times and has sold over 2 million copies in English and 22 other languages. It was also published in Braille and as an audiobook. This book has, thus, been cited, quoted and, above all, served as a source of inspiration to countless people.

At the time of publication, Dr Kalam was contemplating retirement. He dreamed of setting up a school where children could be imbued with his vision for India. However, he was called upon to serve the nation in more exalted roles.

Dr Kalam was appointed Scientific Adviser to the Defence Minister and Chief of DRDO. In this capacity, he attempted civilian spin-offs of defence technology, leading a national initiative for self-reliance. He was conferred the Bharat Ratna, and eventually became the President of India in 2002. His address to the European Parliament in 2007 became his much-loved and glorious swan song.

The First Edition of this book covered the period from Dr Kalam's birth to 1991. When I was asked to complete the narrative (for the period from 1991 to 2015), I was faced with two challenges. One pertained to how I could preserve the candidness and innocence with which Dr Kalam shared his life story, and the second dealt with how to elucidate the high-voltage narrative of nuclear tests and his public persona.

The 16 chapters of *Wings of Fire* have been left untouched. Part V, Dispersion, covers the period from 1991 to 2002, while the sixth and final part, titled Leading India, presents the events that occurred during 2002–2015. The earlier Epilogue has been retained at the end of Chapter 16 (the last chapter of the first edition), for it is timeless. India is expected to emerge as the fourth largest economy in the world in 2025, and "take our rightful place among the ranks of the developed nations," as Dr Kalam foretold.

It should be stressed that chapters 17–22 are my personal reminiscences. They comprise my recollections and reflections on the extraordinary second act of Dr Kalam – his post-ISRO period, the Presidential years and his demise – and are based on the numerous conversations I had with him. As such, these are a collection of personal stories and memories and should not be treated as factual, accurate or representative of the actual events described.

This New Edition is accompanied by more than 50 new photos that bring to life the many remarkable incidents in Dr Kalam's eventful life.

My relationship with Dr Kalam extended beyond *Wings of Fire* and we co-authored four more books, including his last one, *Transcendence*. I consider myself fortunate to be alive to see this book published in its expanded and complete form, and to have had the opportunity to contribute to it.

Arun Tiwari

Preface to the First Edition

I have worked under Dr APJ Abdul Kalam for over a decade. This might seem to disqualify me as his biographer, and I certainly had no notion of being one. One day, while speaking to him, I asked him if he had a message for young Indians. His message—don't crawl, fly—fascinated me. Later, I mustered the courage to ask him about his recollections so that I could pen them down before they were buried irretrievably under the sands of time.

We had a long series of sittings late into the night and early under the fading stars of dawn—all somehow stolen from his very busy schedule of eighteen hours a day. The profundity and range of his ideas mesmerized me. He had tremendous vitality and obviously received immense pleasure from the world of ideas. His conversation was not always easy to follow, but was always fresh and stimulating. There were complexities, subtleties, and intriguing metaphors and subplots in his narrative, but gradually the unfolding of his brilliant mind took the form of a continuous discourse.

When I sat down to write this book, I felt that it required greater skills than I possessed. But realising the importance of this task and regarding it an honour to have been permitted to attempt it, I prayed earnestly for the courage and calibre to complete it.

This book is written for the ordinary people of India for whom Dr Kalam has an immense affection, and of whom Dr Kalam is certainly one. He has an intuitive rapport with the humblest and simplest people, an indication of his own simplicity and innate spirituality.

For myself, writing this book has been like a pilgrimage. Through Dr Kalam, I was blessed with the revelation that the real joy of living can be found in only one way—in one's communion with an eternal source of hidden knowledge within oneself—which each individual is bidden to seek and find for himself or herself. Many of you may never meet Dr Kalam in person, but I hope you will enjoy his company through this book, and that he will become your spiritual friend.

I could include in this book only a few incidents among the many narrated to me by Dr Kalam. In fact, this book provides only a thumbnail sketch of Dr Kalam's life. It is quite possible that certain important incidents have been inadvertently dropped and that the contribution of some individuals to the projects co-ordinated by Dr Kalam has gone unrecorded. Since a quarter-century of professional life separates me from Dr Kalam, some important issues might also have remained unrecorded or have been distorted. I am solely responsible for such shortcomings, which are, of course, completely unintentional.

Arun Tiwari

Acknowledgements to the New Edition

The publishers would like to thank the following people and institutions for their invaluable assistance and encouragement in bringing this New Edition to fruition:

APJMJ Sheik Saleem, Dr Kalam's grand-nephew, for generously sharing previously unpublished photos of Dr Kalam from his archives.

Harry Sheridon, Dr Kalam's long-serving private secretary, for his unwavering support and assistance in obtaining new photos for this edition.

The Photo Cell, President's Secretariat, Rashtrapati Bhavan, for sharing the photos we requested, thus illuminating many of the events of Dr Kalam's Presidential years.

The Press Information Bureau (PIB), Government of India, for granting us permission to use two photos.

PV Manoranjan Rao, veteran space scientist, ISRO; **BN Suresh**, formerly, Director of VSSC and a member of the Space Commission; and **VP Balagangadharan**, formerly a scientist at VSSC, for granting us permission to re-use some photos from their book, *Ever Upwards: ISRO in Images*, published by Universities Press.

Acknowledgements to the First Edition

I wish to express my gratitude to all the people involved in the writing of this book, especially Mr YS Rajan, Mr A Sivathanu Pillai, Mr RN Agarwal, Mr Prahlada, Mr KVSS Prasada Rao and Dr SK Salwan, who were very generous in sharing their time and knowledge with me.

I am thankful to Prof. KAV Pandalai and Mr R Swaminathan, for critical reviews of the text. I thank Dr B Soma Raju for his tangible, but always unspoken, support for this project. My sincere thanks go to my wife and unsparing critic, Dr Anjana Tiwari, for her tough comments, accompanied with her gentle support.

It has been a pleasure to work with Universities Press, and the co-operation of the editorial and production staff is much appreciated.

There are many fine people, such as the photographer Mr. Prabhu, who have selflessly enriched me and this book in ways beyond measure. I thank them all.

And finally, my deepest gratitude to my sons, Aseem and Amol—for their unfailing emotional support during the writing, and because I seek in them that attitude towards life which Dr Kalam admired, and wanted this work to reflect.

Arun Tiwari

Contents

Foreword — v

Preface to the New Edition — ix

Preface to the First Edition — xi

Acknowledgements to the New Edition — xiii

Acknowledgements to the First Edition — xiv

Introduction — xvii

PART I: ORIENTATION (1931–1963) — 1

PART II: CREATION (1963–1980) — 27

PART III: PROPITIATION (1981–1989) — 85

PART IV: CONTEMPLATION (1990–1991) — 123

PART V: DISPERSION (1991–2002) — 141

PART VI: LEADING INDIA (2002–2015) — 155

INTRODUCTION

This book is being released at a time when India's technological endeavours, to assert its sovereignty and strengthen its security, are questioned by many in the world. Historically, people have always fought among themselves on one issue or another. Prehistorically, battles were fought over food and shelter. With the passage of time, wars were waged over religious and ideological beliefs; and now the dominant struggle of sophisticated warfare is for economic and technological supremacy. Consequently, economic and technological supremacy is equated with political power and world control.

A few nations who have grown very strong technologically, over the past few centuries, have wrested control, for their own purposes. These major powers have become the self-proclaimed leaders of the new world order. What does a country of one billion people, like India, do in such a situation? We have no other option but to be technologically strong. But, can India be a leader in the field of technology? My answer is an emphatic 'Yes'. And let me validate my answer by narrating some incidents from my life.

When I first began the reminiscences that have gone into this book, I was uncertain about which of my memories were worth narrating or were of any relevance at all. My childhood is precious to me, but would it be of interest to anyone else? Was it worth the reader's while, I wondered, to know about the tribulations and triumphs of a small-town boy? Of the straitened circumstances of my schooldays, the odd jobs I did to pay my school fees, and how my decision to become a vegetarian was partly due to my financial constraints as a college student—why should these be of any interest to the general public? In the end, I was convinced that these were relevant, if not for anything else but because they tell something of the story of modern India, as individual destiny and the social matrix in which it is embedded cannot be seen in isolation. Having been persuaded of this, it did seem germane to include the accounts of my frustrated attempt to become an Air Force pilot and of how I became, instead of the Collector my father dreamed I would be, a rocket engineer.

Finally, I decided to describe the individuals who had a profound influence on my life. This book is also by way of a submission of thanks, therefore, to my parents and immediate family, and to the teachers and preceptors I was fortunate to have had, both as a student and in my professional life. It is also a tribute to the unflagging enthusiasm and efforts of my young colleagues who helped to realize our collective dreams. The famous words of Isaac Newton about standing on the shoulders of giants are valid for every scientist and I certainly owe a great debt of knowledge and inspiration to the distinguished lineage of Indian scientists, that included Vikram Sarabhai, Satish Dhawan and Brahm Prakash. They played major roles in my life and in the story of Indian science.

I completed sixty years of age on 15 October 1991. I had decided to devote my retirement to fulfilling what I saw as my duties in the sphere of social service. Instead, two things happened simultaneously. First, I agreed to continue in government service for another three years and, next, a young colleague, Arun Tiwari, requested me to share my reminiscences with him, so that he could record them. He was someone who had been working in my laboratory since 1982, but I had never really known him well until the February of 1987 when I visited him at the Intensive Coronary Care Unit of the Nizam's Institute of Medical Sciences in Hyderabad. He was a mere 32 years old, but was fighting valiantly for his life. I asked him if there was anything he wanted me to do for him. "Give me your blessings, sir," he said, "so that I may have a longer life and can complete at least one of your projects."

The young man's dedication moved me and I prayed for his recovery all night. The Lord answered my prayers and Tiwari was able to get back to work in a month. He did an excellent job in helping to realize the *Akash* missile airframe from scratch within the short space of three years. He then took up the task of chronicling my story. Over the last year, he patiently transcribed the bits and pieces of my story and converted them into a fluent narrative. He also went through my personal library meticulously and selected from among the pieces of poetry those that I had marked while reading, and included them in the text.

This story is an account, I hope, not just of my personal triumphs and tribulations but of the successes and setbacks of the science establishment in modern India, struggling to establish itself in the technological forefront. It is the story of national aspiration and of co-operative endeavour. And, as I see it, the saga of India's search for scientific self-sufficiency and technological competence is a parable for our times.

Each individual creature on this beautiful planet is created by God to fulfil a particular role. Whatever I have achieved in life is through

His help, and an expression of His will. He showered His grace on me through some outstanding teachers and colleagues, and when I pay my tributes to these fine persons, I am merely praising His glory. All these rockets and missiles are His work through a small person called Kalam, in order to tell the several-million mass of India to never feel small or helpless. We are all born with a divine fire in us. Our efforts should be to give wings to this fire and fill the world with the glow of its goodness.

May God bless you!

APJ Abdul Kalam

I
ORIENTATION
[1931–1963]

This earth is His, to Him belong those vast and boundless skies;
Both seas within Him rest, and yet in that small pool He lies.

Atharva Veda
Book 4, Hymn 16.3

CHAPTER 1

I was born into a middle-class Tamil family in the island town of Rameswaram in the erstwhile Madras state. My father, Jainulabdeen, had neither much formal education nor much wealth; despite these disadvantages, he possessed great innate wisdom and a true generosity of spirit. He had an ideal helpmate in my mother, Ashiamma. I do not recall the exact number of people she fed every day, but I am quite certain that far more outsiders ate with us than all the members of our own family put together.

My parents were widely regarded as an ideal couple. My mother's lineage was the more distinguished, one of her forebears having been bestowed the title of 'Bahadur' by the British.

I was one of many children—a short boy with rather undistinguished looks, born to tall and handsome parents. We lived in our ancestral house, which was built in the middle of the nineteenth century. It was a fairly large pucca house, made of limestone and brick, on the Mosque Street in Rameswaram. My austere father used to avoid all inessential comforts and luxuries. However, all necessities were provided for, in terms of food, medicine or clothes. In fact, I would say mine was a very secure childhood, both materially and emotionally.

I normally ate with my mother, sitting on the floor of the kitchen. She would place a banana leaf before me, on which she then ladled rice and aromatic sambhar, a variety of sharp, home-made pickles and a dollop of fresh coconut *chutney*.

The famous Shiva temple, which made Rameswaram so sacred to pilgrims, was about a ten-minute walk from our house. Our locality was predominantly Muslim, but there were quite a few Hindu families too, living amicably with their Muslim neighbours. There was a very old mosque in our locality where my father would take me for evening prayers. I had not the faintest idea of the meaning of the Arabic prayers chanted, but I was totally convinced that they reached God. When my father came out of the mosque after the prayers, people of different religions would be sitting outside, waiting for him. Many of them offered bowls of water to my father who would dip his fingertips in them and say a prayer. This water was then carried home for invalids. I also remember people visiting our home to offer thanks after being cured. My father always smiled and asked them to thank Allah, the benevolent and merciful.

The high priest of Rameswaram temple, Pakshi Lakshmana Sastry, was a very close friend of my father's. One of the most vivid memories of my early childhood is of the two men, each in his traditional attire, discussing spiritual matters. When I was old enough to ask questions, I asked my father about the relevance of prayer. My father told me there was nothing mysterious about prayer. Rather, prayer made possible a communion of the spirit between people. "When you pray," he said, "you transcend your body and become a part of the cosmos, which knows no division of wealth, age, caste, or creed."

My father could convey complex spiritual concepts in very simple, down-to-earth Tamil. He once told me, "In his own time, in his own place, in what he really is, and in the stage he has reached—good or bad—every human being is a specific element within the whole of the manifest divine Being. So why be afraid of difficulties, sufferings and problems? When troubles come, try to understand the relevance of your sufferings. Adversity always presents opportunities for introspection."

"Why don't you say this to the people who come to you for help and advice?" I asked my father. He put his hands on my shoulders and looked straight into my eyes. For quite some time he said nothing, as if he was judging my capacity to comprehend his words. Then he answered in a low, deep voice. His answer filled me with a strange energy and enthusiasm:

> Whenever human beings find themselves alone, as a natural reaction, they start looking for company. Whenever they are in trouble, they look for someone to help them. Whenever they reach an impasse, they look to someone to show them the way out. Every recurrent anguish, longing, and desire finds its own special helper. For the people who come to me in distress, I am but a go-between in their effort to propitiate demonic forces with prayers and offerings. This is not a correct approach at all and should never be followed. One must understand the difference between a fear-ridden vision of destiny and the vision that enables us to seek the enemy of fulfilment within ourselves.

I remember my father starting his day at 4 a.m. by reading the *namaz* before dawn. After the *namaz*, he used to walk down to a small coconut grove we owned, about 4 miles from our home. He would return, with about a dozen coconuts tied together thrown over his shoulder, and only then would he have his breakfast. This remained his routine even when he was in his late sixties.

I have throughout my life tried to emulate my father in my own world of science and technology. I have endeavoured to understand the fundamental truths revealed to me by my father, and feel convinced that there exists a divine power that can lift one up from confusion, misery, melancholy and failure, and guide one to one's true place. And once an individual severs his emotional and physical bondage, he is on the road to freedom, happiness and peace of mind.

I was about six years old when my father embarked on the project of building a wooden sailboat to take pilgrims from Rameswaram to Dhanuskodi (also called Sethukkarai), and back. He worked at building the boat on the seashore, with the help of a relative, Ahmed Jallaluddin, who later married my sister, Zohara. I watched the boat take shape. The wooden hull and bulkheads were seasoned with heat from wood fires. My father was doing good business with the boat when, one day, a cyclone bringing winds of over 100 miles per hour carried away our boat, along with some of the landmass of Sethukkarai. The Pamban Bridge collapsed with a train full of passengers on it. Until then, I had only seen the beauty of the sea, now its uncontrollable energy came as a revelation to me.

By the time the boat met its untimely end, Ahmed Jallaluddin had become a close friend of mine, despite the difference in our ages. He was about 15 years older than I and used to call me Azad. We used to go for long walks together every evening. As we started from Mosque Street and made our way towards the sandy shores of the island, Jallaluddin and I talked mainly of spiritual matters. The atmosphere of Rameswaram, with its flocking pilgrims, was conducive to such discussion. Our first halt would be at the imposing temple of Lord Shiva. Circling around the temple with the same reverence as any pilgrim from a distant part of the country, we felt a flow of energy pass through us.

Jallaluddin would talk about God as if he had a working partnership with Him. He would present all his doubts to God as if He were standing nearby to dispose of them. I would stare at Jallaluddin and then look towards the large groups of pilgrims around the temple, taking holy dips in the sea, performing rituals and reciting prayers with a sense of respect towards the same Unknown, whom we treat as the formless Almighty. I never doubted that the prayers in the temple reached the same destination as the ones offered in our mosque. I only wondered whether Jallaluddin had any other special connection to God. Jallaluddin's schooling had been limited, principally because of his family's straitened circumstances. This may have been the reason why he always encouraged me to excel in my studies and enjoyed my success vicariously. Never did I find the slightest trace of resentment in Jallaluddin for his deprivation. Rather, he was always full of gratitude for whatever life had chosen to give him.

Incidentally, at the time I speak of, he was the only person on the entire island who could write in English. He wrote letters for almost anybody in need, be they letters of application or otherwise. Nobody among my acquaintance, either in my family or in the neighbourhood even, had Jallaluddin's level of education or any links of consequence with the outside world. Jallaluddin always spoke to me about educated people, of scientific discoveries, of contemporary literature, and of the achievements of medical science. It was he who made me aware of a "brave, new world" beyond our narrow confines.

In the humble environs of my boyhood, books were a scarce commodity. By local standards, however, the personal library of STR Manickam, a former 'revolutionary' or militant nationalist, was sizeable. He encouraged me to read all I could and I often visited his home to borrow books.

Another person who greatly influenced my boyhood was my first cousin, Samsuddin. He was the sole distributor for newspapers in Rameswaram. The newspapers would arrive at Rameswaram station by the morning train from Pamban. Samsuddin's newspaper agency was a one-man organization catering to the reading demands of the 1,000-strong literate population of Rameswaram town. These newspapers were mainly bought to keep abreast of current developments in the National Independence Movement, for astrological reference or to check the bullion rates prevailing in Madras. A few readers with a more cosmopolitan outlook would discuss Hitler, Mahatma Gandhi and Jinnah; almost all would finally flow into the mighty political current of Periyar EV Ramaswamy's movement against upper-caste Hindus. *Dinamani* was the most sought after newspaper. Since reading the printed matter was beyond my capability, I had to satisfy myself with glancing at the pictures in the newspaper before Samsuddin delivered them to his customers.

The Second World War broke out in 1939, when I was eight years old. For reasons I have never been able to understand, a sudden demand for tamarind seeds erupted in the market. I used to collect the seeds and sell them to a provision shop on Mosque Street. A day's collection would fetch me the princely sum of one *anna*. Jallaluddin would tell me stories about the war which I would later attempt to trace in the headlines in *Dinamani*. Our area, being isolated, was completely unaffected by the war. But soon India was forced to join the

Allied Forces and something like a state of emergency was declared. The first casualty came in the form of the suspension of the train halt at Rameswaram station. The newspapers now had to be bundled and thrown out from the moving train on the Rameswaram Road between Rameswaram and Dhanuskodi. That forced Samsuddin to look for a helping hand to catch the bundles and, as if naturally, I filled the slot. Samsuddin helped me earn my first wages. Half a century later, I can still feel the surge of pride in earning my own money for the first time.

Every child is born with some inherited characteristics into a specific socio-economic and emotional environment, and trained in certain ways by figures of authority. I inherited honesty and self-discipline from my father; from my mother, I inherited faith in goodness and deep kindness and so did my three brothers and sister. But it was the time I spent with Jallaluddin and Samsuddin that perhaps contributed most to the uniqueness of my childhood and made all the difference in my later life. The unschooled wisdom of Jallaluddin and Samsuddin was so intuitive and responsive to non-verbal messages, that I can unhesitatingly attribute my subsequently manifested creativity to their company in my childhood.

I had three close friends in my childhood—Ramanadha Sastry, Aravindan, and Sivaprakasan. All these boys were from orthodox Hindu Brahmin families. As children, none of us ever felt odd or othered because of our religious differences and upbringing. In fact, Ramanadha Sastry was the son of Pakshi Lakshmana Sastry, the high priest of the Rameswaram temple. Later, he took over the priesthood of the Rameswaram temple from his father; Aravindan went into the business of arranging transport for visiting pilgrims; and Sivaprakasan became a catering contractor for Southern Railways.

During the annual Shri Sita Rama Kalyanam ceremony, our family used to arrange boats with a special platform to carry idols of the Lord from the temple to the marriage site, situated in the middle of the pond called Rama Tirtha which was near our house. Events from the *Ramayana* and from the life of the Prophet were the bedtime stories my mother and grandmother would tell the children in our family.

One day when I was in the fifth standard at the Rameswaram Elementary School, a new teacher came to our class. I used to wear a cap which marked me as a Muslim, and I always sat in the front row next to Ramanadha Sastry, who wore a sacred thread. The new teacher could not stomach a Hindu priest's son sitting with a Muslim boy. In accordance with our social ranking as the new teacher saw it,

I was asked to go and sit on the back bench. I felt very sad, and so did Ramanadha Sastry. He looked utterly downcast as I shifted to my seat in the last row. The image of him weeping when I shifted to the last row left a lasting impression on me.

After school, we went home and told our respective parents about the incident. Lakshmana Sastry summoned the teacher, and, in our presence, told the teacher that he should not spread the poison of social inequality and communal intolerance in the minds of innocent children. He bluntly asked the teacher to either apologize or quit the school and the island. Not only did the teacher regret his behaviour, but the strong sense of conviction Lakshmana Sastry conveyed ultimately reformed this young teacher.

On the whole, the small society of Rameswaram was highly stratified and very rigid in terms of the segregation of different social groups. However, my science teacher, Sivasubramania Iyer, though an orthodox Brahmin with a very conservative wife, was something of a rebel. He did his best to break social barriers so that people from varying backgrounds could mingle easily. He used to spend hours with me and would say, "Kalam, I want you to develop so that you are on par with the highly educated people of the big cities."

One day, he invited me to his home for a meal. His wife was horrified at the idea of a Muslim boy being invited to dine in her ritually pure kitchen. She refused to serve me in her kitchen. Sivasubramania Iyer was not perturbed, nor did he get angry with his wife, but instead, served me with his own hands and sat down beside me to eat his meal. His wife watched us from behind the kitchen door. I wondered whether she had observed any difference in the way I ate rice, drank water or cleaned the floor after the meal. When I was leaving his house, Sivasubramania Iyer invited me to join him for dinner again the next weekend. Observing my hesitation, he told me not to get upset, saying, "Once you decide to change the system, such problems have to be confronted." When I visited his house the next week, Sivasubramania Iyer's wife took me inside her kitchen and served me food with her own hands.

Then the Second World War was over and India's freedom was imminent. "Indians will build their own India," declared Gandhiji. The whole country was filled with an unprecedented optimism. I asked my father's permission to leave Rameswaram and study at the district headquarters in Ramanathapuram.

He told me as if thinking aloud, "Abul! I know you have to go away to grow. Does the seagull not fly across the Sun, alone and without a nest? You must forego your longing for the land of your memories to move into the dwelling place of your greater desires; our love will not bind you nor will our needs hold you." He quoted Khalil Gibran to my hesitant mother, "Your children are not your children. They are the sons and daughters of Life's longing for itself. They come through you but not from you. You may give them your love but not your thoughts. For they have their own thoughts."

He took me and my three brothers to the mosque and recited the prayer *Al Fatiha* from the Holy Qur'an. As he put me on the train at Rameswaram station he said, "This island may be housing your body but not your soul. Your soul dwells in the house of tomorrow which none of us at Rameswaram can visit, not even in our dreams. May God bless you, my child!"

Samsuddin and Ahmed Jallaluddin travelled with me to Ramanathapuram to enrol me in Schwartz High School, and to arrange for my boarding there. Somehow, I did not take to the new setting. The town of Ramanathapuram was a thriving, factious town of some fifty thousand people, but the coherence and harmony of Rameswaram was absent. I missed my home and grabbed every opportunity to visit Rameswaram. The pull of educational opportunities at Ramanathapuram was not strong enough to nullify the attraction of *poli*, a South Indian sweet my mother made. In fact, she used to prepare twelve distinctly different varieties of it, bringing out the flavour of every single ingredient used in the best possible combinations.

Despite my homesickness, I was determined to come to terms with the new environment because I knew my father had invested great hopes in my success. My father visualized me as a Collector in the making and I thought it my duty to realize my father's dream, although I desperately missed the familiarity, security and comforts of Rameswaram.

Jallaluddin used to speak to me about the power of positive thinking and I often recalled his words when I felt homesick or dejected. I tried hard to do as he said, which was to strive to control my thoughts and my mind and, through these, to influence my destiny. Ironically, that destiny did not lead me back to Rameswaram, but rather, swept me farther away from the home of my childhood.

CHAPTER 2

Once I settled down at the Schwartz High School in Ramanathapuram, the enthusiastic fifteen-year-old within me re-emerged. My teacher, Iyadurai Solomon, was an ideal guide for an eager young mind that was yet uncertain of the possibilities that lay before it. He made his students feel very comfortable in class with his warm and open-minded attitude. He used to say that a good student could learn more from a bad teacher than a poor student from even a skilled teacher.

During my stay in Ramanathapuram, my relationship with him grew beyond that of teacher and pupil. In his company, I learnt that one could exercise enormous influence over the events of one's own life. Iyadurai Solomon used to say, "To succeed in life and achieve results, you must understand and master three mighty forces—desire, belief, and expectation." Iyadurai Solomon, who later became a Reverend, taught me that before anything I wanted could happen, I had to desire it intensely and be absolutely certain it would happen. To take an example from my own life, I had been fascinated by the mysteries of the sky and the flight of birds from early childhood. I used to watch cranes and seagulls soar into flight and longed to fly. Simple, provincial boy though I was, I was convinced that one day I, too, would soar up into the skies. Indeed, I *was* the first child from Rameswaram to fly.

Iyadurai Solomon was a great teacher because he instilled in all the children a sense of their own worth. Solomon raised my self-esteem to a high point and convinced me, the son of parents who had not had the benefits of education, that I too could aspire to become whatever I wished. "With faith, you can change your destiny," he would say.

One day, when I was in the fourth form, my mathematics teacher, Ramakrishna Iyer, was teaching another class. Inadvertently, I wandered into that classroom and in the manner of an old-fashioned despot, Ramakrishna Iyer caught me by the neck and caned me in front of the whole class. Many months later, when I scored full marks in mathematics, he narrated the incident to the entire school at morning assembly. "Whomsoever I cane becomes a great man! Take my word, this boy is going to bring glory to his school and to his teachers." His praise quite made up for the earlier humiliation!

By the time I completed my education at Schwartz, I was a self-confident boy determined to succeed. The decision to go in for further education was taken without a second thought. To us, in those days, the awareness of the possibilities for a professional education did not exist; higher education simply meant going to college. The nearest college was at Tiruchchirappalli, spelled Trichinopoly those days, and called Trichi for short.

In 1950, I arrived at St. Joseph's College, Trichi, to study for the Intermediate examination. I was not a bright student in terms of examination grades but, thanks to my two buddies back in Rameswaram, I had acquired a practical bent of mind.

Whenever I returned to Rameswaram from Schwartz, my elder brother, Mustafa Kamal, who ran a provision store on the railway station road, would call me in to help him and then vanish for hours together, leaving the shop in my charge. I sold oil, onions, rice and everything else. The fastest moving items, I found, were cigarettes and bidis. I used to wonder what made poor people smoke away their hard-earned money. When spared by Mustafa, I would be put in charge of his kiosk by my younger brother, Kasim Mohammed. There I sold novelties made of seashells.

At St. Joseph's, I was lucky to find a teacher like the Rev. Father TN Sequeira. He taught us English and was also our hostel warden. We were about a hundred boys living in the three-storeyed hostel building. Rev. Father used to visit each boy every night with a Bible in his hand. His energy and patience were amazing. He was a very considerate person who took care of even the most minute requirements of his students. On Deepavali, on his instructions, the Brother in charge of the hostel and the mess volunteers would visit each room and distribute good gingelly oil for the ritual bath.

I stayed on the St. Joseph's campus for four years and shared my room with two others. One was an orthodox Iyengar from Srirangam and the other a Syrian Christian from Kerala. The three of us had a wonderful time together. When I was made secretary of the vegetarian mess during my third year in the hostel, we invited the Rector, Rev. Father Kalathil, over for lunch one Sunday. Our menu included the choicest preparations from our diverse backgrounds. The result was rather unexpected, but Rev. Father was lavish in his praise of our efforts. We enjoyed every moment with Rev. Father Kalathil, who participated in our unsophisticated conversation with childlike enthusiasm. It was a memorable event for us all.

My teachers at St. Joseph's were the true followers of Kanchi Paramacharya, who evoked people to "enjoy the action of giving". The vivid memory of our mathematics teachers, Prof. Thothathri Iyengar and Prof. Suryanarayana Sastry, walking together on the campus inspires me to this day.

When I was in my final year at St. Joseph's, I acquired a taste for English literature. I began to read the great classics, Tolstoy, Scott and Hardy being special favourites despite their exotic settings, and then I moved on to some works in philosophy. It was around this time that I developed a great interest in physics.

The lessons on subatomic physics at St. Joseph's by my physics teachers, Prof. Chinna Durai and Prof. Krishnamurthy, introduced me to the concept of the half-life period and matters related to the radioactive decay of substances. Sivasubramania Iyer, my science teacher at Rameswaram, had never taught me that most subatomic particles are unstable and that they disintegrate after a certain time into other particles. All this I was learning for the first time. But when he taught me to strive with diligence because decay is inherent in all compounded things, was he not talking of the same thing? I wonder why some people tend to see science as something which takes man away from God. As I look at it, the path of science can always wind through the heart. For me, science has always been the path to spiritual enrichment and self-realization.

Even the rational thought-matrices of science have been home to fairy tales. I am an avid reader of books on cosmology and enjoy reading about celestial bodies. Many friends, while asking me questions related to space flights, sometimes slip into astrology. Quite honestly, I have never really understood the reason behind the great importance attached by people to the faraway planets in our solar system. As an art, I have nothing against astrology, but if it seeks acceptance under the guise of science, I reject it. I do not know how these myths evolved about planets, star constellations, and even satellites—that they can exercise power on human beings. The highly complicated calculations manipulated around the precise movements of celestial bodies to derive highly subjective conclusions appear illogical to me. As I see it, the Earth is the most powerful and energetic planet. As John Milton puts it so beautifully in *Paradise Lost*, Book VIII:

> . . . *What if the Sun*
> *Be centre to the World, and other stars . . . . .*
> *The planet Earth, so steadfast though she seem,*
> *Insensibly three different motions move?*

Wherever you go on this planet, there is movement and life. Even apparently inanimate things like rocks, metal, timber, clay are full of intrinsic movement—with electrons dancing around each nucleus. This motion originates in their response to the confinement imposed on them by the nucleus, by means of electric forces which try to hold them as close as possible. Electrons, just like any individual with a certain amount of energy, detest confinement. The tighter the electrons are held by the nucleus, the higher their orbital velocity will be: in fact, the confinement of electrons in an atom results in enormous velocities of about 1000 km per second! These high velocities make the atom appear a rigid sphere, just as a fast-moving fan appears like a disc. It is very difficult to compress atoms more strongly—thus giving matter its familiar solid aspect. Everything solid, thus, contains much empty space within and everything stationary contains great movement within. It is as though the great dance of Shiva is being performed on Earth during every moment of our existence.

When I joined the B.Sc. degree course at St. Joseph's, I was unaware of any other option for higher education. Nor did I have any information about career opportunities available to a student of science. Only after obtaining a B.Sc. did I realize that physics was not my subject. I had to go into engineering to realize my dreams. I could have joined the engineering course long ago, right after finishing my Intermediate course. Better late than never, I told myself as I made the detour, applying for admission into the Madras Institute of Technology (MIT), regarded as the crown jewel of technical education in South India at that time.

I managed to be on the list of selected candidates, but admission to this prestigious institution was an expensive affair. Around a thousand rupees was required, and my father could not spare that much money. At that time, my sister, Zohara, stood behind me, mortgaging her gold bangles and chain. I was deeply touched by her determination to see me educated and by her faith in my abilities. I vowed to release her bangles from mortgage with my own earnings. The only way before me to earn money at that point of time was to study hard and get a scholarship. I went ahead at full steam.

What fascinated me most at MIT was the sight of two decommissioned aircraft displayed there for the demonstration of the various subsystems of flying machines. I felt a strange attraction towards them, and would sit near them long after other students had gone back to the hostel, admiring man's will to fly free in the sky, like a bird. After completing my first year, when I had to opt for a specific branch, I almost spontaneously chose aeronautical engineering. The goal was very clear in my mind now; I was going to fly aircraft. I was convinced of this, despite being aware of my lack of assertiveness, which probably came about because of my humble background. Around this time, I made special efforts to try and communicate with different kinds of people. There were setbacks, disappointments and distractions, but my father's inspiring words anchored me in those periods of nebulous drift. "He who knows others is learned, but the wise one is the one who knows himself. Learning without wisdom is of no use."

In the course of my education at MIT, three teachers shaped my thinking. Their combined contributions formed the foundation on which I later built my professional career. These three teachers were Prof. Sponder, Prof. KAV Pandalai and Prof. Narasingha Rao. Each of them had a very distinct personality, but they shared a common impulse—the capacity to feed their students' intellectual hunger by sheer brilliance and untiring zeal.

Prof. Sponder taught me technical aerodynamics. He was an Austrian with rich practical experience in aeronautical engineering. During the Second World War, he had been captured by the Nazis and imprisoned in a concentration camp. Understandably, he had developed a very strong dislike for Germans. Incidentally, the aeronautical department was headed by a German, Prof. Walter Repenthin. Another well-known professor, Dr Kurt Tank, was a distinguished aeronautical engineer who had designed the German Focke-Wulf FW 190 single-seater fighter plane, an outstanding combat aircraft of the Second World War. Dr Tank later joined Hindustan Aeronautics Limited (HAL) in Bangalore and was responsible for the design of India's first jet fighter, the HF-24 Marut.

Notwithstanding these irritants, Prof. Sponder preserved his individuality and maintained high professional standards. He was always calm, energetic and in total control of himself. He kept abreast of the latest technologies and expected his students to do the same. I consulted him before opting for aeronautical engineering. He told me that one should never worry about one's future prospects: instead, it was more important to lay sound foundations, to have sufficient enthusiasm and an accompanying passion for one's chosen field of study. The trouble with Indians, Prof. Sponder used to observe, was not that they lacked educational opportunities or industrial infrastructure— the trouble was in their failure to discriminate between disciplines and to rationalize their choices. Why aeronautics? Why not electrical engineering? Why not mechanical engineering? I myself would like to tell all novitiate engineering students that when they choose their specialization, the essential point to consider is whether the choice articulates their inner feelings and aspirations.

Prof. KAV Pandalai taught me aero-structure design and analysis. He was a cheerful, friendly and enthusiastic teacher, who brought a fresh approach to every year's teaching course. It was Professor Pandalai who opened up the secrets of structural engineering to us. Even today I believe that everyone who has been taught by Prof. Pandalai would agree that he was a man of great intellectual integrity and scholarship—but with no trace of arrogance. His students were free to disagree with him on several points in the classroom.

Prof. Narasingha Rao was a mathematician, who taught us theoretical aerodynamics. I still remember his method of teaching fluid dynamics. After attending his classes, I began to prefer mathematical physics to any other subject. Often, I have been told I carry a "surgical knife" to aeronautical design reviews. If it had not been for Prof. Rao's kind and persistent advice on picking up proofs to equations of aerodynamic flow, I would not have acquired this metaphorical tool.

Aeronautics is a fascinating subject, containing within it the promise of freedom. The great difference between freedom and escape, between motion and movement, between slide and flow are the secrets of this science. My teachers revealed these truths to me. Through their meticulous teaching, they created within me an excitement for aeronautics. Their intellectual fervour, clarity of thought and passion for perfection helped me to launch into a serious study of fluid dynamics-modes of compressible medium motion, development of shock waves and shock, induced flow separation at increasing speeds, shock stall and shockwave drag.

Slowly, a great amalgamation of information took place in my mind. The structural features of aeroplanes began to gain new meanings—biplanes, monoplanes, tailless planes, canard configured planes, delta-wing planes, all these began to assume increasing significance for me. The three teachers, all of them authorities in their different fields, helped me to mould a composite knowledge.

My third and last year at MIT was a year of transition and was to have a great impact on my later life. In those days, a new climate of political enlightenment and industrial effort was sweeping across the country. I had to test my belief in God and see if it could fit into the matrix of scientific thinking. The accepted view was that a belief in scientific methods was the only valid approach to knowledge. If so, I wondered, was matter alone the ultimate reality and were spiritual phenomena but a manifestation of matter? Were all ethical values relative, and was sensory perception the only source of knowledge and truth? I wondered about these issues, attempting to sort out the vexing question of "scientific temper" and my own spiritual interests. The value system in which I had been nurtured was profoundly religious. I had been taught that true reality lay beyond the material world in the spiritual realm, and that knowledge could be obtained only through inner experience.

Meanwhile, when I had finished my course work, I was assigned a project to design a low-level attack aircraft together with four other colleagues. I had taken up the responsibility of preparing and drawing the aerodynamic design. My team mates distributed among themselves the tasks of designing the propulsion, structure, control and instrumentation of the aircraft. One day, my design teacher, Prof. Srinivasan, then the Director of the MIT, reviewed my progress and declared it dismal and disappointing. I offered a dozen excuses for the delay, but none of them impressed Prof. Srinivasan. I finally pleaded for a month's time to complete the task. The professor looked at me for some time and said, "Look, young man, today is Friday afternoon. I give you three days' time. If by Monday morning I don't get the configuration drawing, your scholarship will be stopped." I was dumbstruck. The scholarship was my lifeline and I would be quite helpless if it was withdrawn. I could see no other way out but to finish the task as I had been instructed. That night, I remained at the drawing board, skipping dinner. Next morning, I took only an hour's break to freshen up and eat a little food. On Sunday morning, I was very near completion, when suddenly I felt someone else's presence in the room. Prof. Srinivasan was watching me from a distance. Coming straight from the gymkhana, he was still in his tennis outfit and had dropped in to see my progress. After examining my work, Prof. Srinivasan hugged me affectionately and patted my back in appreciation. He said, "I knew I was putting you under stress and asking you to meet an impossible deadline. I never expected you to perform so well."

During the rest of the period of the project, I participated in an essay competition organized by the MIT Tamil Sangam (Literary Society). Tamil is my mother tongue and I am proud of its origins, which have been traced back to Sage Agastya in the pre-*Ramayana* period; its literature dates back to the fifth century BC. It is said to be a language moulded by lawyers and grammarians and is internationally acclaimed for its clear-cut logic. I was very enthusiastic about ensuring that science did not remain outside the purview of this wonderful language. I wrote an article entitled "Let Us Make Our Own Aircraft" in Tamil. The article evoked much interest and I won the competition, taking the first prize from 'Devan', the editor of the popular Tamil weekly, *Ananda Vikatan*.

My most touching memory of MIT is related to Prof. Sponder. We were posing for a group photograph as part of a farewell ritual. All the graduating students had lined up in three rows with the professors seated in the front. Suddenly, Prof. Sponder got up and looked for me. I was standing in the third row. "Come and sit with me in the front," he said. I was taken aback by Prof. Sponder's invitation. "You are my best student and hard work will help you bring a great name for your teachers in future." Embarrassed by the praise but honoured by the recognition, I sat with Prof. Sponder for the photograph. "Let God be your hope, your stay, your guide and provide the lantern for your feet in your journey into the future," said the introverted genius, bidding me adieu.

From MIT, I went to Hindustan Aeronautics Limited (HAL) at Bangalore as a trainee. There I worked on engine overhauling as part of a team. Hands-on work on aircraft engine overhauling was very educative. When a principle learnt in the classroom is borne out by practical experience, it creates a strange sense of excitement—akin to unexpectedly running into an old friend among a crowd of strangers. At HAL, I worked on the overhauling of both piston and turbine engines. The hazy concepts of gas dynamics and diffusion processes in the working principle of *after burning* came into sharper focus in my mind. I was also trained in radial engine-cum-drum operations.

I learned how to check a crankshaft for wear and tear, and a connecting rod and crankshaft for twist. I did calibrations of a fixed-pitch fan fitted to a super-charged engine. I opened up pressure and acceleration-cum-speed control systems, and air starter supply systems of turbo-engines. Getting to understand feathering, unfeathering and reversing of propeller engines was very interesting. The demonstration of the delicate art of *beta* (blade angle control) by HAL technicians still lingers in my memory. They had neither studied in major universities, nor were they merely implementing what their engineer-in-charge was suggesting. They had been working hands-on for years and this had given them something like an intuitive feel for the work.

Two alternative opportunities for employment, both close to my long-standing dream of flying, presented themselves before me when

I came out of HAL as a graduate aeronautical engineer. One was a career in the Air Force and another was a job at the Directorate of Technical Development and Production, DTD&P(Air), at the Ministry of Defence. I applied for both. The interview calls arrived from both the places almost simultaneously. I was asked to reach Dehra Dun by the Air Force recruitment authorities and Delhi by DTD&P(Air). The boy from the Coromandel Coast took a train to the North of India. My destination was more than 2000 km away, and was to be my first encounter with the vastness of my motherland.

CHAPTER 3

Through the window of the compartment, I watched the countryside slip past. From a distance, the men in the fields in their white dhotis and turbans, and the womenfolk in bright splashes of colour against the green background of paddy fields, seemed to inhabit some beautiful painting. I sat glued to the window. Almost everywhere, people were engaged in some activity which had a rhythm and tranquillity about it—men driving cattle, women fetching water from streams. Occasionally, a child would appear and wave at the train.

It is astonishing how the landscape changes as one moves northwards. The rich and fertile plains of the river Ganga and its numerous tributaries have invited invasion, turmoil, and change. Around 1500 BC, fair-skinned Aryans swept in through the mountain passes from the far north-west. The tenth century brought Muslims, who later mingled with the local people and became an integral part of this country. One empire gave way to another. Religious conquests continued. All this time, the part of India south of the Tropic of Cancer remained largely untouched, safe behind the shield of the Vindhya and Satpura mountain ranges. The Narmada, Tapti, Mahanadi, Godavari, and Krishna rivers had woven a net of almost unassailable protection for the tapering Indian peninsula. To bring me to Delhi, my train had crossed all these geographical impediments through the power of scientific advancement.

I halted for a week in Delhi, the city of the great Sufi saint Hazrat Nizamuddin, and appeared for the interview at DTD&P(Air). I did well at the interview. The questions were of a routine nature, and did not challenge my knowledge of the subject. Then I proceeded to Dehra Dun for my interview at the Air Force Selection Board. At the Selection Board, the emphasis was more on "personality" than on intelligence. Perhaps they were looking for physical fitness and an articulate manner. I was excited but nervous, determined but anxious, confident but tense. I could only finish ninth in the batch of 25 examined to select eight officers for commissioning in the Air Force. I was deeply disappointed. It took me some time to comprehend that the opportunity to join the Air Force had just slipped through my fingers. I dragged myself out of the Selection Board and stood at the edge of a cliff. There was a lake far below. I knew that the days ahead would be difficult. There were questions to be answered and a plan of action to be prepared. I trekked down to Rishikesh.

I bathed in the Ganga and revelled in the purity of its water. Then, I walked to the Sivananda Ashram situated a little way up the hill. I could feel intense vibrations when I entered. I saw a large number of *sadhus* seated all around in a state of trance. I had read that *sadhus* were psychic people—people who know things intuitively and, in my dejected mood, I sought answers to the doubts that troubled me.

I met Swami Sivananda—a man who looked like a Buddha, wearing a snow-white dhoti and wooden slippers. He had an olive complexion and black, piercing eyes. I was struck by his irresistible, almost childlike smile and gracious manner. I introduced myself to the Swamiji. My Muslim name aroused no reaction in him. Before I could speak any further, he inquired about the source of my sorrow. He offered no explanation of how he knew that I was sad and I did not ask.

I told him about my unsuccessful attempt to join the Indian Air Force and my long-cherished desire to fly. He smiled, washing away all my anxiety almost instantly. Then he said in a feeble, but very deep voice,

> Desire, when it stems from the heart and spirit, when it is pure and intense, possesses awesome electromagnetic energy. This energy is released into the ether each night, as the mind falls into the sleep state. Each morning it returns to the conscious state reinforced with the cosmic currents. That which has been imagined will surely and certainly be manifested. You can rely, young man, upon this ageless promise as surely as you can rely upon the eternally unbroken promise of sunrise... and of Spring.

When the student is ready, the teacher will appear—How true! Here was the teacher to show the way to a student who had nearly gone astray! "Accept your destiny and go ahead with your life. You are not destined to become an Air Force pilot. What you are destined to become is not revealed now but it is predetermined. Forget this failure, as it was essential to lead you to your destined path. Search, instead, for the true purpose of your existence. Become one with yourself, my son! Surrender yourself to the wish of God," Swamiji said.

I returned to Delhi and enquired at the DTD&P(Air) about the outcome of my interview. In response, I was handed my appointment letter. I joined the next day as Senior Scientific Assistant on a basic salary of Rs 250/- per month. If this was to be my destiny, I thought, let it be so. Finally, I was filled with mental peace. No more did I feel any bitterness or resentment at my failure to enter the Air Force. All this was in 1958.

At the Directorate, I was posted at the Technical Centre (Civil Aviation). If I was not flying aeroplanes, I was at least helping to make them airworthy. During my first year in the Directorate, I carried out a design assignment on supersonic target aircraft with the help of the officer-in-charge, R Varadharajan, and won a word of praise from the Director, Dr Neelakantan. To gain shop-floor exposure to aircraft maintenance, I was sent to the Aircraft and Armament Testing Unit (A&ATU) at Kanpur. At that time, they were involved in a tropical evaluation of Gnat Mk 1 aircraft. I participated in the performance assessment of its operation systems.

Even in those days, Kanpur was a very populous city. It was my first experience of living in an industrial town. The cold weather, crowds, noise and smoke were in total contrast to what I was used to in Rameswaram. I was particularly troubled by the ubiquitous presence of potatoes on the dining table, right from breakfast to dinner. To me, it seemed that a feeling of loneliness pervaded the city. The people on the streets had come from their villages in search of jobs in factories, leaving behind the smell of their soil and the protection of their families.

On my return to Delhi, I was informed that the design of a *DART* target had been taken up at the DTD&P(Air) and that I had been included in the design team. I completed this task with the other team members. Then, I undertook a preliminary design study on a Human Centrifuge. I later carried out the design and development of a Vertical Takeoff and Landing Platform. I was also associated with the development and construction of the Hot Cockpit. Three years passed. Then the Aeronautical Development Establishment (ADE) was born in Bangalore and I was posted to the new establishment.

Bangalore as a city was in direct contrast to Kanpur. In fact, I feel our country has an uncanny way of bringing out extremes in her people. I suppose it is because Indians have been both afflicted and enriched by centuries of migrations. Loyalty to different rulers has dulled our capacity for a single allegiance. Instead, we have developed an extraordinary ability to be compassionate and cruel, sensitive and callous, deep and fickle, all at the same time. To the untrained eye, we may appear colourful and picturesque; to the critical eye, we are but shoddy imitations of our various masters. In Kanpur, I saw *paan-*

chewing imitations of Wajid Ali Shah, and in Bangalore it was replaced by dog-walking sahibs. Here too, I longed for the depth and calmness of Rameswaram. The relationship between the heart and the head of an earthy Indian has been eroded by the divided sensibilities of our cities. I spent my evenings exploring the gardens and shopping plazas of Bangalore.

The workload at ADE during the first year of its inception was quite light. In fact, I had to generate work for myself at first, until the tempo gradually built up. Based on my preliminary studies on ground-handling equipment, a project team was formed to design and develop an indigenous hovercraft prototype as a ground equipment machine (GEM). The team was a small working group, comprising four persons at the level of Scientific Assistant. Dr OP Mediratta, Director of the ADE, asked me to lead the team. We were given three years to launch the engineering model.

The project was, by any standards, bigger than our collective capabilities. None of us had any experience in building a machine, let alone a flying machine. There were no designs or standard components available to begin with. All we knew was that we had to make a successful heavier-than-air flying machine. We tried to read as much literature as we could find on hovercrafts, but there was not much available. We tried to consult people knowledgeable in this area, but could find none. One day, I simply took the decision to proceed with the limited information and resources available.

This endeavour to produce a wingless, light, swift machine opened the windows of my mind. I was quick to see at least a metaphorical connection between a hovercraft and an aircraft. After all, the Wright Brothers made the first aeroplane after fixing bicycles for seven years! I saw in the GEM project great opportunities for ingenuity and growth. We went straight into hardware development after spending a few months on the drawing board.

There is always the danger that a person with my kind of background—rural or small-town, middle-class, whose parents had limited education—will retreat into a corner and remain there struggling for bare existence, unless some great turn of circumstance propels him into a more favourable environment. I knew I had to create my own opportunities.

Part by part, subsystem by subsystem, stage by stage, things started moving. Working on this project, I learned that once your mind stretches to a new level it never goes back to its original dimension.

At that time VK Krishna Menon was the Defence Minister. He was keenly interested in the progress of our small project, which he envisioned as the beginning of the indigenous development of India's defence equipment. Whenever he was in Bangalore, he always found some time to review the progress of our project. His confidence in our ability ignited our enthusiasm. I would enter the assembly shop leaving my other problems outside, just as my father used to enter the mosque for prayer, leaving his shoes outside.

But not everyone accepted Krishna Menon's opinion about GEM. Our experiments with the available parts and components did not exactly delight my senior colleagues. Many even called us a group of eccentric inventors in pursuit of an impossible dream. I, being the leader of the "navvies", was a particularly inviting target. I was regarded as yet another country bumpkin who believed that riding the air was his domain. The weight of opinion against us buttressed my ever-optimistic mind. The comments of some of the senior scientists at ADE made me recall John Trowbridge's famous satirical poem on the Wright Brothers, published in 1896:

> . . . . *with thimble and thread*
> *And wax and hammer, and buckles and screws,*
> *And all such things as geniuses use;* —
> *Two bats for patterns, curious fellows!*
> *A charcoal-pot and a pair of bellows.*

When the project was about a year old, Defence Minister Krishna Menon made one of his routine visits to ADE. I escorted him into our assembly shop. Inside, on a table lay the GEM model broken down into sub-assemblies. The model represented the culmination of one year's untiring efforts to develop a practical hovercraft for battlefield applications. The minister fired one question after another at me, determined to ensure that the prototype would go into test flight within the coming year. He told Dr Mediratta, "GEM flight is possible with the gadgets Kalam now possesses".

The hovercraft was christened *Nandi*, after the bull ridden by Lord Shiva. For a prototype, its form, fit and finish was beyond our expectation, given the rudimentary infrastructure we possessed. I told my colleagues, "Here is a flying machine, not constructed by a bunch of cranks but by engineers of ability. Don't look at it—it is not made to look at, but to fly with."

Defence Minister Krishna Menon flew in the *Nandi*, overruling the accompanying officials' concern for his safety. A Group Captain in the minister's troupe, who had logged in many thousands of flying hours, even offered to fly the machine to save the minister from the potential danger of flying with an inexperienced civilian pilot like myself and gestured to me to come out of the machine. I was sure about my competence in flying the machine I had made, and therefore shook my head in negation. Observing this wordless communication, Krishna Menon dismissed the insulting suggestion of the Group Captain with a laugh and signalled to me to start the machine. He was very happy. "You have demonstrated that the basic problems of hovercraft development are solved. Go for a more powerful prime mover and call me for a second ride," Krishna Menon told me. The sceptical Group Captain (now Air Marshal) Golay later became a good friend of mine.

We completed the project ahead of schedule. We had a working hovercraft with us, moving on an air cushion of about 40 mm with a load of 550 kg, including the tare weight. Dr Mediratta was visibly pleased with the achievement. But by this time, Krishna Menon was out of office and could not take his promised second ride. In the new order, not many people shared his dream with regard to military applications of an indigenous hovercraft. In fact, even today, we import hovercrafts. The project was mired in controversies and was finally shelved. It was a new experience for me. So far, I had believed that the sky was the limit, but now it appeared that the limits were much closer. There are boundaries that dictate life: you can only lift so much weight; you can only learn so fast; you can only work so hard; you can only go so far!

I was unwilling to face reality. I had put my heart and soul into *Nandi*. That it would not be used was something beyond my comprehension. I was disappointed and disillusioned. In this period of confusion and uncertainty, memories from my childhood came back to me and I discovered new meanings in them.

Pakshi Sastry used to say, "Seek the truth, and the truth shall set you free." As the Bible says, "Ask and you shall receive." It did not happen immediately, but it happened nevertheless. One day, Dr Mediratta called me. He inquired about the state of our hovercraft. When told that it was in perfect condition to be flown, he asked me to organize a demonstration for an important visitor the next day. No VIP was scheduled to visit the laboratory during the next week as far as I knew. However, I communicated Dr Mediratta's instructions to my colleagues and we felt a new surge of hope.

The next day Dr Mediratta brought a visitor to our hovercraft—a tall, handsome, bearded man. He asked me several questions about the machine. I was struck by the objectivity and clarity of his thinking. "Can you give me a ride in the machine?" he enquired. His request filled me with joy. Finally, here was someone who was interested in my work.

We took a ten-minute ride in the hovercraft, a few centimetres above the ground. We were not flying, but were definitely floating in the air. The visitor asked me a few questions about myself, thanked me for the ride and departed. But not before introducing himself—he was Prof. MGK Menon, Director of the Tata Institute of Fundamental Research (TIFR). After a week, I received a call from the Indian Committee for Space Research (INCOSPAR) to attend an interview for the post of Rocket Engineer. All I knew about INCOSPAR at that time was that it was formed out of the TIFR talent pool at Bombay (now Mumbai) to organize space research in India.

I went to Bombay to attend the interview. I was unsure about the type of questions I would have to face at the interview. There was hardly any time to read up or talk to any experienced person. Lakshmana Sastry's voice quoting from the *Bhagawad Gita* echoed in my ears:

> *All beings are born to delusion . . . overcome by the dualities which arise from wish and hate . . . . But those men of virtuous deeds in whom sin has come to an end, freed from the delusion of dualities, worship Me steadfast in their vows.*

I reminded myself that the best way to win was to not need to win. The best performances are accomplished when you are relaxed and free of doubt. I decided to take things as they came. Since neither Prof. MGK Menon's visit nor the call for an interview had been of my making, I decided this was the best attitude to take.

I was interviewed by Dr Vikram Sarabhai along with Prof. MGK Menon and Mr Saraf, then the Deputy Secretary of the Atomic Energy Commission. As I entered the room, I sensed their warmth and friendliness. I was almost immediately struck by Dr Sarabhai's warmth. There was none of the arrogance or the patronizing attitudes which interviewers usually display when talking to a young and vulnerable candidate. Dr Sarabhai's questions did not probe my existing knowledge or skills; rather they were an exploration of the possibilities I was filled with. He was looking at me as if in reference to a larger whole. The entire encounter seemed to me a total moment of truth, in which my dream was enveloped by the larger dream of a bigger person.

I was advised to stay back for a couple of days. However, the next evening I was told about my selection. I was to be absorbed as a rocket engineer at INCOSPAR. This was a breakthrough a young man like myself dreamed of.

My work at INCOSPAR commenced with a familiarization course at the TIFR Computer Centre. The atmosphere here was remarkably different from that at DTD&P(AIR). Labels mattered very little. There was no need for anyone to justify his position or to be at the receiving end of the others' hostility.

Some time in the latter half of 1962, INCOSPAR took the decision to set up the Equatorial Rocket Launching Station at Thumba, a sleepy fishing village near Trivandrum (now Thiruvananthapuram) in Kerala. Dr Chitnis of the Physical Research Laboratory, Ahmedabad, had spotted it as a suitable location as it was very close to the Earth's magnetic equator. This was the quiet beginning of modern rocket-based research in India. The site selected at Thumba lay between the railway line and the sea coast, covering a distance of about 2.5 km and measuring about 600 acres. Within this area, stood a large church, whose site had to be acquired. Land acquisition from private parties is always a difficult and time-consuming process, especially in densely populated places like Kerala. In addition, there was the delicate matter of acquiring a site of religious significance. The Collector of Trivandrum then, K Madhavan Nair, executed this task in a most tactful, peaceful and expeditious manner, with the blessings and cooperation of Right Rev. Dr Dereira, who was the Bishop of Trivandrum in 1962. Soon RD John, the executive engineer of the Central Public Works Department (CPWD), had transformed the entire area. The St. Mary Magdalene church housed the first office of the Thumba Space Centre. The prayer room was my first laboratory, the Bishop's room was my design and drawing office. To this day, the church is maintained in its full glory and, at present, houses the Indian Space Museum.

Very soon after this, I was asked to proceed to America for a six-month training programme on sounding rocket launching techniques, at the National Aeronautics and Space Administration (NASA) work centres. I took some time off before going abroad and went to Rameswaram. My father was very pleased to learn about the opportunity that had come my way. He took me to the mosque and organized a special *namāz* in thanksgiving. I could feel the power of God flowing in a circuit through my father to me and back to God; we were all under the spell of the prayer.

One of the important functions of prayer, I believe, is to act as a stimulus to creative ideas. Within the mind are all the resources required for successful living. Ideas are present in the consciousness, which when released and given scope to grow and take shape, can lead to successful events. God, our Creator, has stored within our minds and personalities great potential strength and ability. Prayer helps us to tap and develop these powers.

Ahmed Jallaluddin and Samsuddin came to see me off at Bombay airport. It was their first exposure to a big city like Bombay, just as I myself was about to have my first exposure to a mega city like New York. Jallaluddin and Samsuddin were self-reliant, positive, optimistic men who undertook their work with the assurance of success. It is from these two persons that I drew the core creative power of my mind. My sentiments could not be contained, and I could feel the mist of tears in my eyes. Then, Jallaluddin said, "Azad, we have always loved you, and we believe in you. We shall always be proud of you". The intensity and purity of their faith in my capabilities broke my last defences, and tears welled up in my eyes.

II
CREATION
[1963–1980]

CHAPTER 4

I started my work at NASA at the Langley Research Center (LRC) in Hampton, Virginia. This is primarily an R&D centre for advanced aerospace technology. One of my most vivid memories of LRC is of a piece of sculpture depicting a charioteer driving two horses, one representing scientific research and the other technological development, metaphorically encapsulating the interconnection between research and development.

From LRC I went to the Goddard Space Flight Center (GSFC) at Greenbelt, Maryland. This Center develops and manages most of NASA's Earth-orbiting science and applications satellites. It operates NASA's tracking networks for all space missions. Towards the end of my visit, I went to the Wallops Flight Facility at Wallops Island in East Coast, Virginia. This place was the base for NASA's sounding rocket programme. Here, I saw a painting prominently displayed in the reception lobby. It depicted a battle scene with a few rockets flying in the background. A painting with this theme should be the most commonplace thing at a Flight Facility, but the painting caught my eye because the soldiers on the side launching the rockets were not white, but dark-skinned, with the racial features of people found in South Asia. One day, my curiosity got the better of me, drawing me towards the painting. It turned out to be Tipu Sultan's army fighting the British. The painting depicted a fact forgotten in Tipu's own country but commemorated here on the other side of the planet. I was happy to see an Indian glorified by NASA as a hero of warfare rocketry.

My impression of the American people can be summarized by a quotation from Benjamin Franklin, "Those things that hurt, instruct!" I realized that people in this part of the world meet their problems head on. They attempt to get out of them rather than suffer them.

My mother had once narrated an incident from the Holy Book—after God created man, he asked the angels to prostrate themselves before Adam. Everybody prostrated themselves except Iblis, or Satan, who refused. "Why did you not prostrate yourself?" Allah asked. "You created me of fire and him of clay. Does not that make me nobler than Adam?" Satan contended. God said, "Be gone from paradise! This is no place for your contemptuous pride." Satan obeyed, but not before cursing Adam with the same fate. Soon Adam followed suit by becoming a transgressor after eating the forbidden fruit. Allah said, "Go hence and may your descendants live a life of doubt and mistrust."

What makes life in Indian organizations difficult is the wide-spread prevalence of this very contemptuous pride. It stops us from listening to our juniors, subordinates and people down the line. You cannot expect a person to deliver results if you humiliate him, nor can you expect him to be creative if you abuse him or despise him. The line between firmness and harshness, between strong leadership and bullying, between discipline and vindictiveness is very fine, but it has to be drawn. Unfortunately, the only line prominently drawn in our country today is between the 'heroes' and the 'zeros'. On one side are a few hundred 'heroes' keeping nine hundred and fifty million people down on the other side. This situation has to change.

As the process of confronting and solving problems often requires hard work and is painful, we have endless procrastination. Actually, problems can be the cutting edge that actually distinguish between success and failure. They draw out innate courage and wisdom.

As soon as I returned from NASA, India's first rocket launch took place on 21 November 1963. It was a sounding rocket, called Nike-Apache, made at NASA. The rocket was assembled in the church building at Thumba that I have referred to earlier. The only equipment available to transport the rocket was a truck and a manually operated hydraulic crane. The assembled rocket was to be shifted from the church building to the launch pad by truck. When the rocket was lifted by the crane and was about to be placed on the launcher, it started tilting, indicating a leak in the hydraulic system of the crane. As we were fast approaching the launch time, 6 p.m., any repairs to the crane had to be ruled out. Fortunately, the leak was not large and we managed to lift the rocket manually, using our collective muscle power, and finally place it on the launcher.

In the maiden Nike-Apache launch, I was in charge of rocket integration and safety. Two of my colleagues who played a very active and crucial role in this launch were D Easwardas and R Aravamudan. Easwardas undertook the rocket assembly and arranged the launch. Aravamudan, whom we called Dan, was in charge of radar, telemetry and ground support. The launch was smooth and problem-free. We obtained excellent flight data and returned with a sense of pride and accomplishment.

When we were relaxing the next evening at the dinner table, we received news of the assassination of President John F Kennedy in Dallas,

Texas. We were appalled. The Kennedy years were a significant era in America, when young men were at the helm of affairs. I used to read with interest about Kennedy's moves in the missile crisis of late 1962. The Soviet Union built missile sites in Cuba, from which it would have been possible to launch attacks on American cities. Kennedy imposed a blockade or 'quarantine', barring the introduction of any offensive missiles to Cuba. America also threatened to respond to any Soviet nuclear attack from Cuba on any country in the Western Hemisphere by retaliating against the USSR. After fourteen days of intense drama, the crisis was resolved by the Soviet Premier Khrushchev ordering that the Cuban bases be dismantled and the missiles returned to Russia.

The next day, Prof. Sarabhai had a detailed discussion with us on future plans. He was creating a new frontier in the field of science and technology in India. A new generation, scientists and engineers in their 30s and early 40s, was being charged with an unprecedented dynamism. Our biggest qualifications at INCOSPAR were not our degrees and training, but Prof. Sarabhai's faith in our capabilities. After the successful launch of Nike-Apache, he chose to share with us his dream of an Indian Satellite Launch Vehicle.

Prof. Sarabhai's optimism was highly contagious. The very news of his coming to Thumba would electrify people and all laboratories, workshops and design offices would hum with unceasing activity. People would work virtually round the clock because of their enthusiasm to show Prof. Sarabhai something new, something that had not been done before in our country—be it a new design or a new method of fabrication or even an out-of-the-way administrative procedure. Prof. Sarabhai would often assign multiple tasks to a single person or a group. Though some of those tasks would appear totally unrelated in the beginning, they would, at a later stage, emerge as deeply interconnected. When Prof. Sarabhai was talking to us about the Satellite Launch Vehicle (SLV), he asked me, almost in the same breath, to take up studies on a rocket-assisted take-off system (RATO) for military aircraft. The two things had no apparent connection except in the mind of this great visionary. I knew that all I had to do was to remain alert and focussed on my purpose, and sooner or later, an opportunity to do a challenging job would enter my laboratory.

Prof. Sarabhai was ever-willing to try out novel approaches and liked to draw in young people. He had the wisdom and judgement which enabled him to realize not only if something was well done, but also when it was time to stop. In my opinion, he was an ideal experimenter and innovator. When there were alternative courses of action before us, whose outcome was difficult to predict, or to reconcile varying perspectives, Prof. Sarabhai would resort to experimentation to resolve the issue. This was precisely the situation at INCOSPAR in 1963. A bunch of young, inexperienced, but nevertheless energetic and enthusiastic persons was given the task of fleshing out the spirit of self-reliance in the field of science and technology in general, and of space research in particular. It was a great example of leadership by trust.

The rocket launch site later blossomed into the Thumba Equatorial Rocket Launch Station (TERLS). TERLS was established through active collaboration with France, USA and USSR. The leader of the Indian space programme—Prof. Vikram Sarabhai—had comprehended the full implications of the challenge and had not balked at taking it on. Right from the day INCOSPAR was formed, he was aware of the need to organize an integrated national space programme, with the equipment for the manufacture of rockets and launch facilities developed and produced indigenously.

With this in view, a wide-ranging programme for scientific and technological development in rocket fuels, propulsion systems, aeronautics, aerospace materials, advanced fabrication techniques, rocket motor instrumentation, control and guidance systems, telemetry, tracking systems and scientific instruments for experimentation in space were launched at the Space Science and Technology Centre and the Physical Research Laboratory at Ahmedabad. Incidentally, this laboratory has produced a large number of Indian space scientists of extremely high calibre over the years.

The real journey of the Indian aerospace programme, however, had begun with the Rohini Sounding Rocket (RSR) programme. What is it that distinguishes a sounding rocket from a Satellite Launch Vehicle (SLV) and from a missile? In fact, they are three different kinds of rockets. Sounding rockets are normally used for probing the near-Earth environment, including the upper regions of the atmosphere. While they can carry a variety of scientific payloads to a range of altitudes, they cannot impart the final velocity needed to orbit the payload. On the other hand, a launch vehicle is designed to inject into orbit a technological payload or satellite. The final stage of a launch vehicle provides the necessary velocity for a satellite to enter an orbit. This is a complex operation requiring on-board guidance and control systems. A missile, though belonging to the same family, is a still more complex system. In addition to the large terminal velocity and on-board guidance and control, it must have the capability to home onto targets. When the targets are fast-moving and capable of manoeuvring, a missile is also required to carry out target-tracking functions.

The RSR programme was responsible for the development and fabrication of sounding rockets and their associated on-board systems for scientific investigations in India. Under this programme, a family of operational sounding rockets were developed. These rockets had wide ranging capabilities, and to date several hundreds of these rockets have been launched for various scientific and technological studies.

I still remember that the first Rohini rocket consisted of a single solid propulsion motor weighing a mere 32 kg. It lifted a nominal 7 kg payload to an altitude of about 10 km. It was soon followed by another, to which one more solid propellant stage was added to dispatch multi-experiment payloads weighing nearly 100 kg to an altitude of over 350 km.

The development of these rockets had resulted in a fully indigenous capability in the production of sounding rockets as well as their propellants. This programme had brought into the country technology for the production of very-high-performance solid propellants, like those based on polyurethane and polybutane polymer. It later resulted in the setting up of a Propellant Fuel Complex (PFC) to manufacture strategic chemicals required for rocket engines, and a Rocket Propellant Plant (RPP) to produce propellants.

The development of Indian rockets in the twentieth century can be seen as a revival of the eighteenth century dream of Tipu Sultan. When Tipu Sultan was killed, the British captured more than 700 rockets and subsystems of 900 rockets in the battle of Turukhanahally in 1799. His army had 27 brigades, called Kushoons, and each brigade had a company of rocket men, called Jourks. These rockets had been taken to England by William Congreve and were subjected by the British to what we call 'reverse engineering' today. There were, of course, no GATT, IPR Act, or patent regime. With the death of Tipu, Indian rocketry also met its demise—at least for 150 years.

Meanwhile, rocket technology made great strides abroad. Konstantin Tsiolkovsky in Russia (1903), Robert Goddard in USA (1914) and Hermann Oberth in Germany (1923) gave rocketry new dimensions. In Nazi Germany, Wernher von Braun's group produced V-2 short-range ballistic missiles and showered fire on the Allied Forces. After the war, both USA and the USSR captured their share of German rocket technology and rocket engineers. With this booty, they started to run their deadly arms race with missiles and warheads.

Rocketry was reborn in India thanks to the technological vision of Prime Minister Jawaharlal Nehru. Prof. Sarabhai took the challenge of giving physical dimensions to this dream. Very many individuals with myopic vision questioned the relevance of space activities in a newly independent nation which was finding it difficult to feed its population. But neither Prime Minister Nehru nor Prof. Sarabhai had any ambiguity of purpose. Their vision was very clear: if Indians were to play a meaningful role in the community of nations, they must be second to none in the application of advanced technologies to their real-life problems. They had no intention of using it merely as a means to display our might.

CHAPTER 5

During his frequent visits to Thumba, Prof. Sarabhai would openly review the progress of work with the entire team. He never gave directions. Rather, through a free exchange of views, he led us forward into new terrain which often revealed an unforeseen solution. Perhaps he was aware that though a particular goal might be clear to himself, and he could give adequate directions for its accomplishment, his team members might have resisted working towards a goal that made no sense to them. He considered the collective understanding of the problem the main attribute of effective leadership. He once told me, "Look, my job is to make decisions; but it is equally important to see to it that these decisions are accepted by my team members."

In fact, Prof. Sarabhai took a series of decisions that were to become the life-mission of many. We would make our own rockets, our own Satellite Launch Vehicles (SLVs) and our own satellites. And this would not be done one-by-one but concurrently, in a multi-dimensional fashion. In the development of payloads for the sounding rockets, instead of getting a certain payload and then engineering it to fit into the rocket, we discussed the matter threadbare with the payload scientists working in different organizations and at different locations. I may even say that the most significant achievement of the sounding rocket programme was to establish and maintain nation-wide mutual trust.

Perhaps realizing that I preferred to persuade people to do as they were told rather than use my legitimate authority, Prof. Sarabhai assigned me the task of providing interface support to payload scientists. Almost all physical laboratories in India were involved in the sounding rocket programme, each having its own mission, its own objective and its own payload. These payloads were required to be integrated to the rocket structure so as to ensure their proper functioning and endurance under flight conditions. We had *X*-ray payloads to look at stars; payloads fitted with radio frequency mass spectrometers to analyse the gas composition of the upper atmosphere; sodium payloads to find out wind conditions, its direction and velocity. We also had ionospheric payloads to explore different layers of the atmosphere. I not only had to interact with scientists from TIFR, National Physical Laboratory (NPL), and Physical Research Laboratory (PRL), but also with payload scientists from USA, USSR, France, Germany and Japan.

I often read Khalil Gibran, and always find his words full of wisdom. "Bread baked without love is a bitter bread that feeds but half a man's hunger,"—those who cannot work with their hearts achieve but a hollow, half-hearted success that breeds bitterness all around. If you are a writer who would secretly prefer to be a lawyer or a doctor, your written words will feed but half the hunger of your readers; if you are a teacher who would rather be a businessman, your instructions will meet but half the need for knowledge of your students; if you are a scientist who hates science, your performance will satisfy but half the needs of your mission. The personal unhappiness and failure to achieve results that comes from being a round peg in a square hole is not, by any means, new. But there are exceptions to this, like Prof. Oda and Sudhakar, who bring to their work a personal touch of magic based upon their individual character, personality, inner motives, and perhaps the dreams crystallized within their hearts. They become so emotionally involved with their work that any dilution of the success of their effort fills them with grief.

Prof. Oda was an X-ray payload scientist from the Institute of Space and Aeronautical Sciences (ISAS), Japan. I remember him as a diminutive man with a towering personality and eyes that radiated intelligence. His dedication to his work was exemplary. He would bring X-ray payloads from ISAS, which along with the X-ray payloads made by Prof. UR Rao, would be engineered by my team to fit into the nose cone of the Rohini Rocket. At an altitude of 150 km, the nose cone would be separated by explosion of pyros triggered by an electronic timer. With this, the X-ray sensors would be exposed to space for collecting the required information about the emissions from stars. Together, Prof. Oda and Prof. Rao were a unique blend of intellect and dedication, which one rarely sees. One day, when I was working on the integration for Prof. Oda's payload with my timer devices, he insisted on using the timers he had brought from Japan. To me they looked flimsy, but Prof. Oda stuck to his stand that the Indian timers be replaced by the Japanese ones. I yielded to his suggestion and replaced the timers. The rocket took off elegantly and attained the intended altitude. But the telemetry signal reported mission failure on account of timer malfunction. Prof. Oda was so upset that tears welled up in his eyes. I was stunned by the emotional intensity of Prof. Oda's response. He had clearly put his heart and soul into his work.

Sudhakar was my colleague in the Payload Preparation Laboratory. As part of the pre-launch schedule, we were filling and remotely pressing the hazardous sodium and thermite mix. As usual, it was a hot and humid day at Thumba. After the sixth such operation, Sudhakar and

I went into the payload room to confirm the proper filling of the mix. Suddenly, a drop of sweat from his forehead fell onto the sodium, and before we knew what was happening, there was a violent explosion which shook the room. For a few paralysed seconds, I did not know what to do. The fire was spreading, and water would not extinguish the sodium fire. Trapped in this inferno, Sudhakar, however, did not lose his presence of mind. He broke the glass window with his bare hands and literally threw me out to safety before jumping out himself. I touched Sudhakar's bleeding hands in gratitude, he was smiling through his pain. Sudhakar spent many weeks in the hospital recuperating from the severe burns he had received.

At TERLS, I was involved with rocket preparation activities, payload assembly, testing and evaluation besides building subsystems like payload housing and jettisonable nose cones. Working with the nose cones led me, as a natural consequence, into the field of composite materials.

It is interesting to know that the bows found, during archaeological excavations at different sites in the country, reveal that Indians used composite bows made of wood, sinew, and horn as early as the eleventh century, at least 500 years before such bows were made in medieval Europe. The versatility of composites, in the sense that they possess very desirable structural, thermal, electrical, chemical and mechanical properties, fascinated me. I was so enthused with these man-made materials that I was in a hurry to know everything about them almost overnight. I used to read up everything available on related topics. I was particularly interested in the glass and carbon Fibre Reinforced Plastic (FRP) composites.

An FRP composite is composed of an inorganic fibre woven into a matrix that encloses it and gives the component its bulk form. In February 1969, Prime Minister Indira Gandhi visited Thumba to dedicate TERLS to the International Space Science Community. On this occasion, she commissioned the country's first filament winding machine in our laboratory. This event brought my team, which included CR Satya, PN Subramanian and MN Satyanarayana, great satisfaction. We made high-strength glass cloth laminates to build non-magnetic payload housings and flew them in two-stage sounding rockets. We also wound and test-flew rocket motor casings of up to 360 mm diameter.

Slowly, but surely, two Indian rockets were born at Thumba. They were christened Rohini and Menaka, after the two mythological dancers in the court of Indra, the king of the sky. The Indian payloads no longer needed to be launched by French rockets. Could this have been done but for the atmosphere of trust and commitment which Prof. Sarabhai had created at INCOSPAR? He brought into use each person's knowledge and skills. He made every man feel directly involved in problem solving. By the very fact of the team members' participation, the solutions became genuine and earned the trust of the entire team, resulting in total commitment towards implementation.

Prof. Sarabhai was matter-of-fact and never tried to hide his disappointment. He used to talk with us in an honest and objective manner. Sometimes I found him making things look more positive than they actually were, and then charming us by his almost magical powers of persuasion. When we were at the drawing board, he would bring someone from the developed world for a technical collaboration. That was his subtle way of challenging each one of us to stretch our capabilities.

At the same time, even if we failed to meet certain objectives, he would praise whatever we had accomplished. Whenever he found any one of us going over his head and attempting a task for which he did not have the capability or skill, Prof. Sarabhai would reassign activity in such a way so as to lower pressure and permit better quality work to be performed. By the time the first Rohini-75 rocket was launched from TERLS on 20 November 1967, almost each one of us was in his own groove.

Early next year, Prof. Sarabhai wanted to see me urgently in Delhi. By now I was accustomed to Prof. Sarabhai's working methods. He was always full of enthusiasm and optimism. In such a state of mind, sudden flashes of inspiration were almost natural. On reaching Delhi, I contacted Prof. Sarabhai's secretary for an appointment and was asked to meet him at 3.30 a.m. at Hotel Ashoka. Delhi being a slightly unfamiliar place, with an unfriendly climate for someone like me, conditioned to the warm and humid climate of South India, I decided to wait in the hotel lounge after finishing my dinner.

I have always been a religious person in the sense that I maintain a working partnership with God. I was aware that the best work required more ability than I possessed and therefore I needed help that only God could give me. I made a true estimate of my own ability, then raised it by 50 per cent and put myself in God's hands. In this partnership, I have always received all the power I needed, and in fact have actually felt it flowing through me. Today, I can affirm that God is within you in the form of this power, to help achieve your goals and realize your dreams.

There are many different types and levels of experience that turn this internal power reaction critical. Sometimes, when we are ready, the gentlest of contacts with Him fills us with insight and wisdom. This could come from an encounter with another person, from a word, a question, a gesture or even a look. Many a time, it could come even through a book, a conversation, some phrase, even a line from a poem or the mere sight of a picture. Without the slightest warning, something new breaks into your life and a secret decision is taken, a decision that you may be completely unconscious of, to start with.

I looked around the elegant lounge. Somebody had left a book on a nearby sofa. As if to fill the small hours of that cold night with some warm thoughts, I picked up the book and started browsing. I must have turned only a few pages of the book, about which I do not remember a thing today.

It was some popular book related to business management. I was not really reading it, only skimming over paragraphs and turning pages. Suddenly, my eyes fell on a passage in the book, it was a quotation from George Bernard Shaw. The gist of the quote was that all reasonable men adapt themselves to the world. Only a few unreasonable ones persist in trying to adapt the world to themselves. All progress in the world depends on these unreasonable men and their innovative and often non-conformist actions.

I started reading the book from the Bernard Shaw passage onwards. The author was describing certain myths woven around the concept and the process of innovation in industry and business. I read about the myth of strategic planning. It is generally believed that substantial strategic and technological planning greatly increases the odds of a 'no surprises' outcome. The author was of the opinion that it is essential for a project manager to learn to live with uncertainty and ambiguity. He felt that it was a myth to hold that the key to economic success is computability. A quotation from General George Patton was given as a counterpoint to this myth—that a good plan violently executed right now is far better than a perfect plan executed next week. It is a myth that to win big one must strive to optimize, the author felt. Optimization wins only on paper, but would invariably lose later in the real world, the book said.

Waiting in the hotel lobby at 1 a.m. for an appointment two hours later was certainly not a reasonable proposition, neither for me nor for Prof. Sarabhai. But then, Prof. Sarabhai had always exhibited a strong component of unorthodoxy in his character. He was running the show of space research in the country—under-staffed, overworked—nevertheless in a successful manner.

Suddenly, I became aware of another man who came and sat down on the sofa opposite mine. He was a well-built person with an intelligent look and refined posture. Unlike me—always disorderly in my dress—this man was wearing elegant clothes. Notwithstanding the odd hours, he was alert and vivacious.

There was a strange magnetism about him which derailed the train of my thoughts on innovation. And before I could get back to the book, I was informed that Prof. Sarabhai was ready to receive me. I left the book on the nearby sofa from where I had picked it up. I was surprised when the man sitting on the opposite sofa was also asked to come inside. Who was he? It was not long before my question was answered. Even before we sat down, Prof. Sarabhai introduced us to each other. He was Group Captain VS Narayanan from Air Headquarters.

Prof. Sarabhai ordered coffee for both of us and unfolded his plan of developing a rocket-assisted take-off system (RATO) for military aircraft. This would help our warplanes to take off from short runways in the Himalayas. Hot coffee was served over small talk. It was totally uncharacteristic of Prof. Sarabhai. But as soon as we finished the coffee, Prof. Sarabhai rose and asked us to accompany him to Tilpat Range on the outskirts of Delhi. As we were passing through the lobby, I threw a cursory glance at the sofa where I had left the book. It was not there.

It was about an hour's drive to the Range. Prof. Sarabhai showed us a Russian RATO. "If I get you the motors of this system from Russia, could you do it in eighteen months' time?" Prof. Sarabhai asked us. "Yes, we can!" Both Gp Capt VS Narayanan and I spoke almost simultaneously. Prof. Sarabhai's face beamed, reflecting our fascination. I recalled what I had read, "He will bestow on you a light to walk in."

After dropping us back at Hotel Ashoka, Prof. Sarabhai went to the Prime Minister's house for a breakfast meeting. By that evening, the news of India taking up the indigenous development of a device to help short-run take-offs by high-performance military aircraft, with myself heading the project, was made public. I was filled with many emotions—happiness, gratitude, a sense of fulfilment and these lines from a little-known poet of the nineteenth century crossed my mind:

For all your days prepare
And meet them ever alike
When you are the anvil, bear –
When you are the hammer, strike.

RATO motors were mounted on aircraft to provide the additional thrust required during the take-off run under certain adverse operating conditions like partially bombed-out runways, high-altitude airfields, more than the prescribed load, or very high ambient temperatures. The Air Force was in dire need of a large number of RATO motors for their S-22 and HF-24 aircraft.

The Russian RATO motor shown to us at the Tilpat Range was capable of generating a 3000 kg thrust with a total impulse of 24500 kg-seconds. It weighed 220 kg and had a double base propellant encased in steel. The development work was to be carried out at the Space Science and Technology Centre with the assistance of the Defence Research and Development Organization (DRDO), HAL, DTD&P(Air) and Air Headquarters.

After a detailed analysis of the available options, I chose a fibreglass motor casing. We decided in favour of a composite propellant which gives a higher specific impulse and aimed at a longer burning time to utilize it completely. I also decided to take additional safety measures by incorporating a diaphragm which would rupture if the chamber pressure for some reason exceeded twice the operating pressure.

Two significant developments occurred during the work on RATO. The first was the release of a 10 year profile for space research in the country, prepared by Prof. Sarabhai. This profile was not merely an activity plan laid down by the top man for his team to comply with, it was a theme paper meant for open discussions, to be later transformed into a programme. In fact, I found it was the romantic manifesto of a person deeply in love with the space research programme in his country.

The plan mainly centred around the early ideas which had been born at INCOSPAR; it included utilization of satellites for television and developmental education, meteorological observations and remote sensing for management of natural resources. To this had been added the development and launch of satellite launch vehicles.

The active international cooperation dominant in the early years was virtually eased out in this plan and the emphasis was on self-reliance and indigenous technologies. The plan talked about the realization of an SLV for injecting lightweight satellites into a low Earth orbit, upgrading of Indian satellites from laboratory models to space entities and development of a wide range of spacecraft subsystems like the apogee and booster motors, momentum wheel, and solar panel deployment mechanism. It also promised a wide range of technological spin-offs like the gyros, various types of transducers, telemetry, adhesives, and polymers for non-space applications. Over and above, there was the dream of an adequate infrastructure that would be capable of supporting R&D in a variety of engineering and scientific disciplines.

The second development was the formation of a Missile Panel in the Ministry of Defence. Both Narayanan and I were inducted as members. The idea of making missiles in our own country was exciting, and we spent hours on end studying the missiles of various advanced countries.

The distinction between a tactical missile and a strategic missile is often a fine one. Generally, by 'strategic', it is understood that the missile will fly thousands of kilometres. However, in warfare, this term is used to denote the kind of target rather than its distance from missile launch. Strategic missiles are those that strike at the enemy's heartland, either in counter force attacks on their strategic forces or in counter-value attacks on the society, which in essence means its cities. Tactical weapons are those that influence a battle, and the battle may be on land, sea or air, or on all three together. This categorization now appears nonsensical, as the US Air Force's ground-launched Tomahawk is used in a tactical role, notwithstanding its range of some 3000 km. In those days, however, strategic missiles were synonymous with intermediate range ballistic missiles (IRBMs) with ranges in the order of 1500 nautical miles or 2780 km and inter-continental ballistic missiles (ICBMs) with a capability of going even further.

Gp Capt Narayanan had an ineffable enthusiasm for indigenous guided missiles. He was a great admirer of the strong-arm approach of the Russian Missile Development Programme. "When it could be done there, why not here, where space research has already prepared the soil for a bonanza of missile technology?" Narayanan used to needle me.

The bitter lessons of the two wars in 1962 and 1965 had left the Indian leadership with little choice in the matter of achieving self-reliance in military hardware and weapon systems. A large number of Surface-to-Air Missiles (SAMs) were obtained from the USSR to guard strategic locations. Gp Capt Narayanan passionately advocated the development of these missiles in the country.

While working together on RATO motors and on the Missile Panel, Narayanan and I played the roles of student and teacher interchangeably wherever required. He was very eager to learn about rocketry and I was very curious to know about airborne weapon systems. The depth of Narayanan's conviction and his force of application were inspiring. Right from the day of our pre-dawn visit to the Tilpat Range with Prof.

Sarabhai, Narayanan was always busy with his RATO motor. He had arranged everything that was required before being asked. He obtained funding of Rs 75 lakhs with a further commitment towards any unforeseen costs. "You name the thing and I will get it for you, but do not ask for time," he said. At times, I often laughed at his impatience, and read for him these lines from T.S. Eliot's *Hollow Men*:

> *Between the conception*
> *And the creation*
> *Between the emotion*
> *And the response*
> *Falls the Shadow.*

Defence R&D at that time was heavily dependent on imported equipment. Virtually nothing indigenous was available. Together, we made a long shopping list and drew up an import plan. But this made me unhappy—was there no remedy or alternative? Was this nation doomed to live with screwdriver technology? Could a poor country like India afford this kind of development?

One day, while working late in the office, which was quite routine after I took up the RATO projects, I saw a young colleague, Jaya Chandra Babu going home. Babu had joined us a few months ago and the only thing I knew about him was that he had a very positive attitude and was articulate. I called him into my office and did a bit of thinking aloud. "Do you have any suggestions?" I then asked him. Babu remained silent for a while, and then asked for time until the next evening to do some homework before answering my question.

The next evening, Babu came to me before the appointed time. His face was beaming with promise. "We can do it, sir! The RATO system can be made without imports. The only hurdle is the inherent inelasticity in the approach of the organization towards procurement and sub-contracting, which would be the two major thrust areas to avoid imports." He gave me seven points, or, rather, asked for seven liberties—financial approval by a single person instead of an entire hierarchy, air travel for all people on work irrespective of their entitlement, accountability to only one person, lifting of goods by air-cargo, sub-contracting to the private sector, placement of orders on the basis of technical competence, and expeditious accounting procedures.

These demands were unheard of in government establishments, which tend to be conservative, yet I could see the soundness of his proposition. The RATO project was a new game and there was nothing wrong if it was to be played with a new set of rules. I weighed all the pros and cons of Babu's suggestions for a whole night and finally decided to present them to Prof. Sarabhai. Hearing my plea for administrative liberalization and seeing the merits behind it, Prof. Sarabhai approved the proposals without a second thought.

Through his suggestions, Babu had highlighted the importance of business acumen in developmental work with high stakes. To make things move faster within existing work parameters, you have to pump in more people, more material and more money. If you can't do that, change your parameters! Instinctive businessman that he was, Babu did not remain long with us and left ISRO for greener pastures in Nigeria. I could never forget Babu's common sense in financial matters.

We had opted for a composite structure for the RATO motor casing using filament fibreglass/epoxy. We had also gone in for a high-energy composite propellant and an event-based ignition and jettisoning system in real-time. A canted nozzle was designed to deflect the jet away from the aircraft. We conducted the first static test of RATO in the twelfth month of the project initiation. Within the next four months, we conducted 64 static tests. And we were just about 20 engineers working on the project!

CHAPTER 6

The future satellite launch vehicle (SLV) had also been conceived by this time. Recognizing the immense socio-economic benefits of space technology, Prof. Sarabhai decided in 1969, to go full-steam ahead with the task of establishing indigenous capability in building and launching our own satellites. He personally participated in an aerial survey of the east coast for a possible site for launching satellite launch vehicles and large rockets.

Prof. Sarabhai was concentrating on the east coast in order to let the launch vehicle take full advantage of the Earth's west to east rotation. He finally selected the Sriharikota island, 100 km north of Madras (now Chennai), and thus the SHAR Rocket Launch Station was born. The crescent-shaped island has a maximum width of 8 km and lies alongside the coastline. The island is as big as Madras city. The Buckingham Canal and the Pulicat lake form its western boundary.

In 1968, we had formed the Indian Rocket Society. Soon after, INCOSPAR was reconstituted as an advisory body under the Indian National Science Academy (INSA) and the Indian Space Research Organization (ISRO) was created under the Department of Atomic Energy (DAE) to conduct space research in the country.

By this time, Prof. Sarabhai had already hand-picked a team to give form to his dream of an Indian SLV. I consider myself fortunate to have been chosen to be a project leader. Prof. Sarabhai gave me the additional responsibility of designing the fourth stage of the SLV. Dr VR Gowarikar, MR Kurup and AE Muthunayagam were given the tasks of designing the other three stages.

What made Prof. Sarabhai pick a few of us for this great mission? One reason seemed to be our professional background. Dr Gowarikar was doing outstanding work in the field of composite propellants. MR Kurup had established an excellent laboratory for propellants, propulsion and pyrotechnics. Muthunayagam had proved himself in the field of high-energy propellants. The fourth stage was to be a composite structure and called for a large number of innovations in fabrication technology; perhaps that was why I was brought in.

I laid the foundation for Stage IV on two rocks—sensible approximation and unawed support. I have always considered the price of perfection prohibitive and allowed mistakes as a part of the learning process. I prefer a dash of daring and persistence to perfection. I have always supported learning on the part of my team members by paying vigilant attention to each of their attempts, be they successful or unsuccessful.

In my group, progress was recognized and reinforced at every tiny step. Although I provided access to all the information that my co-workers in Stage IV needed, I found I could not spend enough time to be a useful facilitator and a source of support. I wondered if there was something wrong with the way in which I managed my time. At this stage, Prof. Sarabhai brought a French visitor to our work centre to point out the problem to me. This gentleman was Prof. Curien, President of CNES (Centre Nationale de Etudes Spatiales), our counterpart in France. They were then developing the Diamont launch vehicles. Prof. Curien was a thorough professional. Together, Prof. Sarabhai and Prof. Curien helped me set a target. While they discussed the means by which I could reach it, they also cautioned me about the possibilities of failure. While I arrived at a better awareness of Stage IV problems through the supportive counselling of Prof. Curien, Prof. Sarabhai's catalytic intervention led Prof. Curien to reinterpret his own progress in the Diamont programme.

Prof. Curien advised Prof. Sarabhai to relieve me of all the minor jobs which posed little challenge and to give me more opportunities for achievement. He was so impressed by our well-planned efforts that he inquired if we could make the Diamont's fourth stage. I recall how this brought a subtle smile to Prof. Sarabhai's face.

As a matter of fact, the Diamont and SLV airframes were incompatible. The diameters were quite different and to attain interchangeability, some radical innovations were required. I wondered where I should start. I decided to look around for solutions among my own colleagues. I used to carefully observe my colleagues to see if their daily routine reflected their desire to constantly experiment. I also started asking and listening to anyone who showed the slightest promise. Some of my friends cautioned me about what they termed as my naivete. I made it an unfailing routine to make notes on individual suggestions and gave handwritten notes to colleagues in engineering and design, requesting concrete follow-up action within five or ten days.

This method worked wonderfully well. Prof. Curien testified, while reviewing our progress, that we had achieved in a year's time what our counterparts in Europe could barely manage in three years. Our plus point, he noted, was that each of us worked with those below and above in the hierarchy. I made it a point to have the team meet at least once every week. Though it took up time and energy, I considered it essential.

How good is a leader? No better than his people and their commitment and participation in the project as full partners! The fact that I got them all together to share whatever little development had been achieved—results, experiences, small successes, and the like—seemed to me worth putting all my energy and time into. It was a very small price to pay for that commitment and sense of teamwork, which could in fact be called trust. Within my own small group of people I found leaders, and learned that leaders exist at every level. This was another important aspect of management that I learned.

We had modified the existing SLV-IV Stage design to suit the Diamont airframe. It was reconfigured and upgraded from a 250 kg, 400-mm-diameter stage to a 600 kg, 650-mm-diameter stage. After two years' effort, when we were about to deliver it to CNES, the French suddenly cancelled their Diamont BC programme. They told us that they did not need our Stage IV anymore. It was a great shock, making me relive the earlier disappointments at Dehra Dun, when I failed to get into the Air Force, and at Bangalore, when the *Nandi* project was aborted at ADE.

I had invested great hope and effort in the fourth stage, so that it could be flown with a Diamont rocket. The other three stages of SLV, involving enormous work in the area of rocket propulsion were at least five years away. However, it did not take me long to shelve the disappointment of Diamont BC Stage IV. After all, I had thoroughly enjoyed working on this project. In time, RATO filled the vacuum created in me by the Diamont BC Stage.

When the RATO project was underway, the SLV project slowly started taking shape. Competence for all major systems of a launch vehicle had been established in Thumba by now. Through their outstanding efforts, Vasant Gowarikar, MR Kurup and Muthunayagam prepared TERLS for a big leap in rocketry.

Prof. Sarabhai was an exemplar in the art of team-building. On one occasion, he had to identify a person who could be given the responsibility for developing a telecommand system for the SLV. Two men were competent to carry out this task—one was the seasoned and sophisticated UR Rao and the other was a relatively unknown experimenter, G Madhavan Nair. Although I was deeply impressed by Madhavan Nair's dedication and abilities, I did not rate his chances as very good. During one of Prof. Sarabhai's routine visits, Madhavan Nair boldly demonstrated his improvised but highly reliable telecommand system. Prof. Sarabhai did not take much time to back the young experimenter in preference to an established expert. Madhavan Nair not only lived up to the expectations of his leader but even went beyond them. He was to later become the project director of the Polar Satellite Launch Vehicle (PSLV).

SLVs and missiles can be called first cousins: they are different in concept and purpose, but come from the same bloodline of rocketry. A massive missile development project had been taken up by DRDO at the Defence Research & Development Laboratory (DRDL), Hyderabad. As the pace of this surface-to-air missile development project increased, the frequency of the Missile Panel meetings and my interaction with Gp Capt Narayanan also increased.

In 1968, Prof. Sarabhai came to Thumba on one of his routine visits. He was shown the operation of the nose-cone jettisoning mechanism. As always, we were all anxious to share the results of our work with Prof. Sarabhai. We requested Prof. Sarabhai to formally activate the pyro system through a timer circuit. Prof. Sarabhai smiled, and pressed the button. To our horror, nothing happened. We were dumbstruck. I looked at Pramod Kale, who had designed and integrated the timer circuit. In a flash each of us mentally went through an analysis of the failure. We requested Prof. Sarabhai to wait for a few minutes, then we detached the timer device, giving direct connection to the pyros. Prof. Sarabhai pressed the button again. The pyros were fired and the nose cone was jettisoned. Prof. Sarabhai congratulated Kale and me; but his expression suggested that his thoughts were elsewhere. We could not guess what was on his mind. The suspense did not last for long and I got a call from Prof. Sarabhai's secretary to meet him after dinner for an important discussion.

Prof. Sarabhai was staying at the Kovalam Palace Hotel, his usual home whenever he was in Trivandrum. I was slightly perplexed by the summons. Prof. Sarabhai greeted me with his customary warmth. He talked of the rocket launching station, envisaging facilities like launch pads, block houses, radar, telemetry and so on—things which are taken for granted in Indian space research today. Then he brought up the incident that had occurred that morning. This was exactly what I had feared. My apprehension of a reproach from my leader, however, was unfounded. Prof. Sarabhai did not conclude that the failure of the pyro timer circuit was the outcome of insufficient knowledge and lack of skill on the part of his people or of faulty understanding at the direction stage. He asked me instead, if we were unenthused by a job that did not pose sufficient challenge. He also asked me to consider if my work was possibly being affected by any problem of which I was hitherto unaware. He finally put his finger on the key issue. We lacked a single roof to carry out system integration of all our rocket stages and rocket systems. Electrical and mechanical integration work was going on with a significant phase difference—both in time and in space. There was little effort to bring together the disparate work on electrical and mechanical integration. Prof. Sarabhai spent the next hour in redefining our tasks, and, in the small hours of the morning, the decision to set up a Rocket Engineering Section was taken.

Mistakes can delay or prevent the proper achievement of the objectives of individuals and organizations, but a visionary like Prof. Sarabhai can use errors as opportunities to promote innovation and the development of new ideas. He was not especially concerned with the mistake in the timer circuit, least of all with pinning the blame for it. Prof. Sarabhai's approach to mistakes rested on the assumption that they were inevitable but generally manageable. It was in the handling of the crises that arose as a consequence that talent could often be revealed. I later realized by experience that the best way to prevent errors was to anticipate them. But this time, by a strange twist of fate, the failure of the timer circuit led to the birth of a rocket engineering laboratory.

It was my usual practice to brief Prof. Sarabhai after every Missile Panel Meeting. After attending one such meeting in Delhi on 30 December 1971, I was returning to Trivandrum. Prof. Sarabhai was visiting Thumba that very day to review the SLV design. I spoke to him on the telephone from the airport lounge about the salient points that had emerged at the panel meeting. He instructed me to wait at Trivandrum Airport after disembarking from the Delhi flight, and to meet him there before his departure for Bombay the same night.

When I reached Trivandrum, a pall of gloom hung in the air. The aircraft ladder operator Kutty told me in a choked voice that Prof. Sarabhai was no more. He had passed away a few hours ago, following a cardiac arrest. I was shocked to the core; it had happened within an hour of our conversation. It was a great blow to me and a huge loss to Indian science. That night passed in preparations for airlifting Prof. Sarabhai's body for the cremation in Ahmedabad.

For five years, between 1966 and 1971, about 22 scientists and engineers had worked closely with Prof. Sarabhai. All of them were later to take charge of important scientific projects. Not only was Prof. Sarabhai a great scientist, but also a great leader. I still remember him reviewing the bi-monthly progress of the design projects of SLV-3 in June 1970. Presentations on Stages I to IV were arranged. The first three presentations went through smoothly. Mine was the last presentation.

I introduced five of my team members who had contributed in various ways to the design. To everybody's surprise, each of them presented his portion of the work with authority and confidence. The presentations were discussed at length and the conclusion was that satisfactory progress had been made.

Suddenly, a senior scientist who worked closely with Prof. Sarabhai turned to me and enquired, "Well, the presentations for your project were made by your team members based on their work. But what did you do for the project?" That was the first time I saw Prof. Sarabhai really annoyed. He told his colleague, "You ought to know what project management is all about. We just witnessed an excellent example. It was an outstanding demonstration of team work. I have always seen a project leader as an integrator of people and that is precisely what Kalam is." I consider Prof. Sarabhai as the Mahatma Gandhi of Indian science—generating leadership qualities in his team and inspiring them through both ideas and example.

After an interim arrangement with Prof. MGK Menon at the helm, Prof. Satish Dhawan was given the responsibility of heading ISRO. The whole complex at Thumba, which included TERLS, the Space Science and Technology Centre (SSTC), the RPP, the Rocket Fabrication Facility (RFF), and the Propellant Fuel Complex (PFC) were merged together to form an integrated space centre and christened the Vikram Sarabhai Space Centre (VSSC) as a tribute to the man to whom it owed its existence. The renowned metallurgist, Dr Brahm Prakash, took over as the first Director of VSSC.

The RATO system was successfully tested on 8 October 1972 at Bareilly Air Force station in Uttar Pradesh, when a high performance Sukhoi-16 jet aircraft became airborne after a short run of 1200 m, as against its usual run of 2 km. We used the 66th RATO motor in the test. The demonstration was watched by Air Marshal Shivdev Singh and Dr BD Nag Chaudhury, then the Scientific Adviser to the Defence Minister. This effort was said to have saved approximately Rs 4 crores in foreign exchange. The vision of the industrialist scientist had finally borne fruit.

Before taking up the responsibility of organizing space research in India and becoming the chairman of INCOSPAR, Prof. Sarabhai had established a number of successful industrial enterprises. He was aware that scientific research could not survive in isolation, away from industry. Prof. Sarabhai founded Sarabhai Chemicals, Sarabhai Glass, Sarabhai Geigy Limited, Sarabhai Merck Limited, and the Sarabhai Engineering Group. His Swastik Oil Mills did pioneering work in the extraction of oil from oilseeds, manufacture of synthetic detergents and of cosmetics. He geared Standard Pharmaceuticals Limited to enable large-scale manufacture of penicillin, which was imported from abroad at astronomical cost at that time. Now with the indigenization of RATO, his mission had acquired a new dimension—independence in the manufacture of military hardware and the potential saving of crores of rupees in foreign exchange. I recalled this on the day of the successful trial of the RATO system. Including trial expenses, we spent less than Rs. 25 lakhs on the entire project. The Indian RATO could be produced at Rs.17,000 apiece, and it replaced the imported RATO, which cost Rs. 33,000.

At the Vikram Sarabhai Space Centre, work on the SLV went on at full swing. All the subsystems had been designed, technologies identified, processes established, work centres selected, manpower earmarked and schedules drawn. The only hitch was the lack of a management structure to effectively handle this mega-project and coordinate activities which were spread over a large number of work centres with their own ways of working and management.

Prof. Dhawan, in consultation with Dr Brahm Prakash, picked me for this job. I was appointed the Project Manager—SLV, and reported directly to the Director, VSSC. My first task was to work out a project management plan. I wondered why I was selected for this task when there were stalwarts like Gowarikar, Muthunayagam, and Kurup around. With organizers like Easwardas, Aravamudan, and SC Gupta available, how would I do better? I articulated my doubts to Dr Brahm Prakash. He told me not to focus on what I saw as other people's strengths compared to my own, but instead, to attempt to expand their abilities.

Dr Brahm Prakash advised me to take care of the performance degraders and cautioned me against outrightly seeking optimal performance from the participating work centres. "Everyone will work to create their bit of SLV; your problem is going to be your dependency on others in accomplishing the total SLV. The SLV mission will be accomplished with, and through, a large number of people. You will require a tremendous amount of tolerance and patience," he said. It reminded me of what my father used to read to me from the Holy Qur'an on the distinction between right and wrong: "We have sent no apostle before you who did not eat or walk about the market squares. We test you by means of one another. Will you not have patience?"

I was aware of the contradiction that often occurred in such situations. People heading teams often have one of the following two orientations: for some, work is the most important motivation; for others, their workers are the all-consuming interest. There are many others who fall either between these two positions or outside them. My job was going to be to avoid those who were interested neither in the work nor in the workers. I was determined to prevent people from taking either extreme, and to promote conditions where work and workers went together. I visualized my team as a group in which each member worked to enrich the others in the team and experience the enjoyment of working together.

The primary objectives of the SLV Project were design, development and operation of a standard SLV system, SLV-3, capable of reliably and expeditiously fulfilling the specified mission of launching a 40 kg satellite into a 400 km circular orbit around the Earth.

As a first step, I translated the primary project objectives into some major tasks. One such task was the development of a rocket motor system for the four stages of the vehicle. The critical problems in the completion of this task were: making an 8.6 tonne propellant grain and a high-mass-ratio apogee rocket motor system which would use high-energy propellants. Another task was vehicle control and guidance. Three types of control systems were involved in this task—aerodynamic surface control, thrust vector control and reaction control for the first, second and third stages and the spin-up mechanism for the fourth stage. Inertial reference for control systems and guidance through inertial measurement was also imperative. Yet another major task was the augmentation of launch facilities at SHAR with systems integration and checkout facilities and development of launch support systems such as launchers and vehicle assembly fixtures. A target of 'all line' flight test within 64 months was set in March 1973.

I took up the executive responsibility of implementing the project within the framework of policy decisions taken, the approved management plan, and the project report; and also within the budget and through the powers delegated to me by the Director, VSSC. Dr Brahm Prakash formed four Project Advisory Committees to advise me on specialized areas like rocket motors, materials and fabrication, control and guidance, electronics, and mission and launching. I was assured of the guidance of outstanding scientists like DS Rane, Muthunayagam, TS Prahlad, AR Acharya, SC Gupta, and CL Amba Rao, to name a few.

The Holy Qur'an says: "We have sent down to you revelations showing you an account of those who have gone before you and an admonition to righteous men." I sought to share the wisdom of these extremely brilliant people. "Light upon light. Allah guides to His light whom He will. He has knowledge of all things."

We made three groups to carry out the project activities—a Programme Management Group, an Integration and Flight Testing Group and a Subsystems Development Group. The first Group was made responsible for looking after the overall executive aspects of SLV-3: project management, including administration, planning and evaluation, subsystems specifications, materials, fabrication, quality assurance and control. The Integration and Flight Testing Group was assigned the tasks of generation of facilities required for integration and flight testing of SLV-3. They were also asked to carry out the analysis of the vehicle, including mechanical and aerodynamic interface problems. The Subsystems Development Group was given the job of interacting with various divisions of VSSC and was made responsible for ensuring that all technological problems in the development of various subsystems were overcome by creating a synergy amongst the available talent in these divisions.

I projected a requirement of 275 engineers and scientists for SLV-3 but could get only about 50. If it had not been for synergistic efforts, the whole project would have remained a non-starter. Some young engineers like MSR Dev, G Madhavan Nair, S Srinivasan, US Singh, Sunderrajan, Abdul Majeed, Ved Prakash Sandlas, Namboodiri, Sasi Kumar, and Sivathanu Pillai developed their own ground rules designed to help them work efficiently as a project team, and produced outstanding individual and team results. These men were in the habit of celebrating their successes together—in a sort of mutual appreciation club. This boosted morale, and helped them a great deal to accept setbacks and to revitalize themselves after periods of intense work.

Each member of the SLV-3 project team was a specialist in his own field. It was natural therefore that each one of them valued his independence. To manage the performance of such specialists the team leader has to adopt a delicate balance between the hands-on and the hands-off approach. The hands-on approach takes an active interest on a very regular basis in the members' work. The hands-off approach trusts team members and recognizes their need for autonomy to carry out their roles, as they see fit. It hinges on their self-motivation. When the leader goes too far with the hands-on approach, he is seen as an anxious and interfering type. If he goes too far hands-off, he is seen as abdicating his responsibility or not being interested. Today, the members of the SLV-3 team have grown to lead some of the country's most prestigious programmes. MSR Dev heads the Augmented

Satellite Launch Vehicle (ASLV) project, Madhavan Nair is the chief of the Polar Satellite Launch Vehicle (PSLV) project and Sandlas and Sivathanu Pillai are Chief Controllers in DRDO Headquarters. Each one of these men rose to his present position through consistent hard work and rock-like will power. It was indeed an exceptionally talented team.

CHAPTER 7

Having taken up the leadership of executing the SLV-3 project, I faced urgent and conflicting demands on my time—for committee work, material procurement, correspondence, reviews, briefings, and for the need to be informed on a wide range of subjects.

My day would start with a stroll of about 2 km around the lodge I was living in. I used to prepare a general schedule during my morning walk, and emphasize two or three things I would definitely like to accomplish during the day, including at least one thing that would help achieve long-term goals.

Once in the office, I would clean the table first. Within the next ten minutes, I would scan all the papers and quickly divide them into different categories: those that required immediate action, low priority ones, ones that could be kept pending, and reading material. Then I would put the high priority papers in front of me and everything else out of sight.

Coming back to SLV-3, about 250 sub-assemblies and 44 major subsystems were conceived during the design. The list of materials went up to over 1 million components. A project implementation strategy had become essential to achieve sustained viability of this complex programme of seven to ten years' duration. From his side, Prof. Dhawan came up with a clear statement that all the manpower and funds at VSSC and SHAR would have to be directed to us. From our side, we evolved a matrix type of management to achieve productive interfacing with more than 300 industries. The target was that our interaction with them must lead to their technology empowerment. Three things I stressed before my colleagues—importance of design capability, goal setting and realization, and the strength to withstand setbacks. Now, before I dwell on the finer aspects of the management of the SLV-3 project, let me talk about the SLV-3 itself.

It is interesting to describe a launch vehicle anthropomorphically. The main mechanical structure may be visualized as the body of a human being, the control and guidance systems with their associated electronics constitute the brain. The musculature comes from propellants. How are they made? What are the materials and techniques involved?

A large variety of materials go into the making of a launch vehicle—both metallic and non-metallic, which include composites and ceramics. In metals, different types of stainless steel, alloys of aluminium, magnesium, titanium, copper, beryllium, tungsten and molybdenum are used. Composite materials are composed of a mixture or combination of two or more constituents which differ in form and material composition and which are essentially insoluble in one another. The materials which combine may be metallic, organic or inorganic. While other material combinations possible are virtually unlimited, the most typical composites in launch vehicles are made of structural constituents, embedded in a matrix. We used a large variety of glass fibre reinforced plastic composites and opened avenues for the entry of Kevlar, polyamides and carbon-carbon composites. Ceramics are special types of baked clay used for microwave transparent enclosures. We considered using ceramics, but had to reject the idea then due to technological limitations.

Through mechanical engineering, these materials are transformed into hardware. In fact, of all the engineering disciplines which feed directly into the development of rocketry, mechanical engineering is perhaps the most intrinsic one. Be it a sophisticated system like a liquid engine or a piece of hardware as simple as a fastener, its ultimate fabrication calls for expert mechanical engineers and precision machine tools. We decided to develop important technologies like welding techniques for low-alloy stainless steel, electroforming techniques, and ultra-precision process tooling. We also decided to make some important machines in-house, like the 254-litre vertical mixer and the groove machining facility for our third and fourth stages. Many of our subsystems were so massive and complex that they implied sizeable financial outlays. Without any hesitation, we approached industries in the private sector and developed contract management plans which later became blueprints for many government-run science and technology business organizations.

Coming to the life part of the SLV, there is the complex electrical circuitry, which sets the mechanical structure in motion. This vast spectrum of activities, encompassing simple electrical power IV supplies to sophisticated instrumentation as well as guidance and control systems is collectively referred to in aerospace research as 'Avionics'. Development efforts in avionic systems had already been initiated at VSSC in the field of digital electronics, microwave radars and radar transponders, and inertial components and systems. It is very important to know the state of the SLV when it is in flight. SLV brought a new surge of activity in the development of a variety of transducers for measurement of physical parameters like pressure, thrust, vibration, acceleration, etc. The transducers convert the physical parameters of the vehicle into electrical signals. An on-board telemetry system processes these signals suitably and transmits them in the form of radio signals to the ground stations, where they are received and deciphered back to the original information collected by the transducers. If the systems work according to design there is little cause for concern; but in case something goes wrong, the vehicle must be destroyed to stop it from making any unexpected moves. To ensure safety, a special telecommand system was made to destroy the rocket in case it malfunctions, and an interferometer system was developed to determine the range and position of the SLV, as a added means to the radar system. The SLV project also initiated the indigenous production of sequencers which time the various events, such as ignition, stage separation, vehicle altitude programmers which store the information for the rocket manoeuvres, and auto-pilot electronics which take appropriate decisions to steer the rocket along its predetermined path.

Without the energy to propel the whole system, a launch vehicle remains grounded. A propellant is usually a combustible substance that produces heat and supplies ejection particles in a rocket engine. It is both a source of energy and a working substance for expanding energy. Because the distinction is more decisive in rocket engines, the term propellant is used primarily to describe chemicals carried by rockets for propulsive purposes.

It is customary to classify propellants as either solids or liquids. We concentrated on solid propellants. A solid propellant consists essentially of three components: the oxidizer, the fuel and the additives. Solid propellants are further classified into two types: composite and double base. The former consists of an oxidizer or inorganic material (like ammonium perchlorate) in a matrix of organic fuel (like synthetic rubber). Double base propellants were distant dreams those days but nevertheless we dared to dream about them.

All this self sufficiency and indigenous manufacture came gradually, and not always without pain. We were a team of almost self-trained engineers. In retrospect I feel the unique blend of our untutored talent, character, and dedication suited SLV development the most. Problems surfaced regularly and almost consistently. But my team members never exhausted my patience. I recall writing after winding up a late night shift:

Beautiful hands are those that do
Work that is earnest and brave and true
Moment by moment
The long day through.

Almost parallel to our work on SLV, the DRDO was preparing itself for developing an indigenous surface-to-air missile. The RATO project was abandoned because the aircraft for which it was designed became obsolete. The new aircraft did not need RATO. With the project called off, Narayanan was DRDO's logical choice to lead the team for making the missile. Unlike us at ISRO, they preferred the philosophy of one-to-one substitution rather than technology development and performance upgrading. The Surface-to-Air Missile SA-2 of Russian origin was chosen to acquire detailed knowledge of all the design parameters of a proven missile and to establish, thereby, the necessary infrastructure required in the organization. It was thought that once one-to-one indigenization was established, further advances in the sophisticated field of guided missiles would be a natural fallout. The project was sanctioned in February 1972 with the code name *Devil* and funding of about Rs. 5 crore was made available for the first three years. Almost half of it was to go in foreign exchange.

By now promoted to Air Commodore, Narayanan took over as Director, DRDL. He mobilized this young laboratory located in the south-eastern suburbs of Hyderabad to take up this enormous task. The landscape dotted with tombs and old buildings started reverberating with new life. Narayanan was a man of tremendous energy—a man always in the boost phase. He gathered around him a strong group of enthusiastic people, drawing many service officers into this predominantly civilian laboratory. Totally preoccupied with SLV affairs, my participation in the Missile Panel meetings gradually dwindled, and then stopped altogether. However, stories about Narayanan and his *Devil* were beginning to reach Trivandrum. A transformation of an unprecedented scale was taking place there.

During my association with Narayanan in the RATO project, I had discovered that he was a hard taskmaster—one who went all out for control, mastery and domination. I used to wonder if managers like him, who aim at getting results no matter what the price, would face a rebellion of silence and non-cooperation in the long run.

New Year's day, 1975, brought with it an opportunity to have a first-person assessment of the work going on under Narayanan's leadership. Prof. MGK Menon, who was working then as Scientific

Adviser to the Defence Minister and was head of the DRDO, appointed a review committee under the chairmanship of Dr Brahm Prakash to evaluate the work carried out in the *Devil* project. I was taken into the team as a rocket specialist to evaluate the progress made in the areas of aerodynamics, structure and propulsion of the missile. On the propulsion aspects, I was assisted by BR Somasekhar and by Wing Commander P Kamaraju. The committee members included Dr RP Shenoy and Prof. IG Sarma who were to review the work done on the electronic systems.

We met at DRDL on 1 and 2 January 1975, followed by a second session after about six weeks. We visited the various development work centres and held discussions with the scientists there. I was greatly impressed by the vision of AV Ranga Rao, the dynamism of Wing Commander R Gopalaswami, the thoroughness of Dr I Achyuta Rao, the enterprise of G Ganesan, S Krishnan's clarity of thought and R Balakrishnan's critical eye for detail. The calm of JC Bhattacharya and Lt Col R Swaminathan in the face of immense complexities was striking. The zeal and application of Lieutenant Colonel VJ Sundaram was conspicuous. They were a brilliant, committed group of people—a mix of service officers and civilian scientists—who had trained themselves in the areas of their own interest out of their driving urge to fly an Indian missile.

We had our concluding meeting towards the end of March 1975 at Trivandrum. We felt that the progress in the execution of the project was adequate in respect of hardware fabrication to carry out the philosophy of one-to-one substitution of missile subsystems except in the liquid rocket area, where some more time was required to succeed. The committee was of the unanimous opinion that DRDL had achieved the twin goals of hardware fabrication and system analysis creditably in the design and development of the ground electronics complex assigned to them.

We observed that the one-to-one substitution philosophy had taken precedence over the generation of design data. Consequently, many design engineers had not been able to pay adequate attention to the necessary analysis which was the practice followed by us at VSSC. The system analysis studies carried out up to then had also been only of a preliminary nature. In all, the results accomplished were outstanding, but we still had a long way to go. I recalled a school poem:

Don't worry and fret, fainthearted,
The chances have just begun,

*For the best jobs haven't been started,
The best work hasn't been done.*

The committee made a strong recommendation to the Government to give *Devil* a further go-ahead. Our recommendation was accepted and the project proceeded.

Back home at VSSC, SLV was taking shape. In contrast to the DRDL which was sprinting ahead, we were moving slowly. Instead of following the leader, my team was trekking towards success on several individual paths. The essence of our method of work was an emphasis on communication, particularly in the lateral direction, among the teams and within the teams. In a way, communication was my *mantra* for managing this gigantic project: To get the best from my team members, I spoke to them frequently on the goals and objectives of the organization, emphasizing the importance of each member's specific contribution towards the realization of these goals. At the same time, I tried to be receptive to every constructive idea emanating from my subordinates and to relay it in an appropriate form for critical examination and implementation. I had written somewhere in my diary of that period:

*If you want to leave your footprints
On the sands of time
Do not drag your feet.*

Most of the time, communication gets confused with conversation. In fact, the two are distinctly different. I was (and am) a terrible conversationalist but consider myself a good communicator. A conversation full of pleasantries is most often devoid of any useful information, whereas communication is meant only for the exchange of information. It is very important to realize that communication is a two-party affair which aims at passing on or receiving a specific piece of information.

While working on the SLV, I used communication to promote understanding and to come to an agreement with colleagues in defining the problems that existed and in identifying the action necessary to be taken to solve them. Authentic communication was one of the tools skilfully used in managing the project. How did I do that? To begin with, I tried to be factual and never sugar-coated the bitter pill of facts. At one of the Space Science Council (SSC) review meetings, frustrated by the procurement delays, I erupted into an agitated complaint against the indifference and retape tactics of the controller of accounts and financial adviser of VSSC. I insisted that the systems of work followed by the accounts staff had to change and demanded the delegation of their functions to the project team. Dr Brahm Prakash was taken aback by the bluntness of my submission. He stubbed out his cigarette and walked out of the meeting.

I spent the whole night regretting the pain my harsh words had caused Dr Brahm Prakash. However, I was determined to fight the inertia built into the system before I found myself being dragged down with it. I asked myself a practical question: could one live with these insensitive bureaucrats? The answer was a big no. Then I asked myself a private question: what would hurt Dr Brahm Prakash more, my seemingly harsh words now, or the burial of the SLV at a later stage? Finding my head and heart agreeing, I prayed to God for help. Fortunately for me, Dr Brahm Prakash delegated financial powers to the project the next morning.

Anyone who has taken up the responsibility to lead a team can be successful only if he is sufficiently independent, powerful and influential in his own right to become a person to reckon with. This is perhaps also the path to individual satisfaction in life, for freedom with responsibility is the only sound basis for personal happiness. What can one do to strengthen personal freedom? I would like to share with you two techniques I adopt in this regard.

First, by building your own education and skills. Knowledge is a tangible asset, quite often the most important tool in your work. The more up-to-date the knowledge you possess, the freer you are. Knowledge cannot be taken away from anyone except by obsolescence. A leader can only be free to lead his team if he keeps abreast of all that is happening around him—in real time. To lead, in a way, is to engage in continuing education. In many countries, it is normal for professionals to go to college several nights every week. To be a successful team leader, one has to stay back after the din and clutter of a working day to emerge better-equipped and ready to face a new day.

The second way is to develop a passion for personal responsibility. The sovereign way to personal freedom is to help determine the forces that determine you. Be active! Take on responsibility! Work for the things you believe in. If you do not, you are surrendering your fate to others. The historian, Edith Hamilton, wrote of ancient Greece, "When the freedom they wished for most was freedom from responsibility, then Athens ceased to be free and was never free again". The truth is that there is a great deal that most of us can individually do to increase our freedom. We can combat the forces that threaten to oppress us. We can fortify ourselves with the qualities and conditions that promote individual freedom. In doing so, we help to create a stronger organization, capable of achieving unprecedented goals.

As work on the SLV gained momentum, Prof. Dhawan introduced the system of reviewing progress with the entire team involved in the project. Prof. Dhawan was a man with a mission. He would effortlessly pull together all the loose ends to make work move smoothly. At VSSC the review meetings presided over by Prof. Dhawan used to be considered major events. He was a true captain of the ISRO ship—a commander, navigator, housekeeper, all rolled into one. Yet, he never pretended to know more than he did. Instead, when something appeared ambiguous, he would ask questions and discuss his doubts frankly. I remember him as a leader for whom to lead with a firm, but fair, hand was a moral compulsion. His mind used to be very firm once it had been decided on any issue. But before taking a decision, it used to be like clay, open to impressions until the final moulding. Then the decisions would be popped into the potter's oven for glazing, never failing to emerge hard and tough, resistant and enduring.

I had the privilege of spending a great deal of time with Prof. Dhawan. He could hold the listener enthralled because of the logical and intellectual acumen he could bring to bear on his analysis of any subject. He had an unusual combination of degrees—a B.Sc. in Mathematics and Physics, an M.A. in English Literature, B.E. in Mechanical Engineering, M.S. in Aeronautical Engineering followed by a Ph.D. in Aeronautics and Mathematics from the California Institute of Technology (Caltech) in USA.

Intellectual debates with him were very stimulating and could always mentally energize me and my team members. I found him full of optimism and compassion. Although he often judged himself harshly, with no allowances or excuses, he was generous to a fault when it came to others. Prof. Dhawan used to sternly pronounce his judgements and then pardon the contrite guilty parties.

In 1975, ISRO became a government body. An ISRO council was formed consisting of directors of different work centres and senior officers in the Department of Space (DoS). This provided a symbolic link as well as a forum for participative management between the DoS, which had the Governmental powers, and the centres, which would execute the jobs. In the traditional parlance of Government departments, ISRO's centres would have been subordinate units or attached offices, but such words were never spoken either at ISRO or DoS. Participative management, which calls for active interaction between those who wield administrative powers and the executing agencies, was a novel feature of ISRO management that would go a long way in Indian R&D organizations.

The new set-up brought me in contact with TN Seshan, the Joint Secretary in the DoS. Till then, I had a latent reservation about bureaucrats, so I was not very comfortable when I first saw Seshan participating in an SLV-3 Management Board meeting. But soon, it changed to admiration for Seshan, who would meticulously go through the agenda and always come for the meetings prepared. He used to kindle the minds of scientists with his tremendous analytical capability.

The first three years of the SLV project was the period for the revelation of many fascinating mysteries of science. Being human, ignorance has always been with us, and always will be. What was new was my awareness of it, my awakening to its fathomless dimensions. I used to erroneously suppose that the function of science was to explain everything, and that unexplained phenomena were the province of people like my father and Lakshmana Sastry. However, I always refrained from discussing these matters with any of my scientist colleagues, fearing that it would threaten the hegemony of their meticulously formed views.

Gradually, I became aware of the difference between science and technology, between research and development. Science is inherently open-ended and exploratory. Development is a closed loop. Mistakes are imperative in development and are made every day, but each mistake is used for modification, upgradation or betterment. Probably, the Creator created engineers to make scientists achieve more. For each time scientists come up with a thoroughly researched and fully comprehended solution, engineers show them yet another *lumineu*, yet one more possibility. I cautioned my team against becoming scientists. Science is a passion—a never ending voyage into promises and possibilities. We had only limited time and limited funds. Our making the SLV depended upon our awareness of our own limits. I preferred existing workable solutions which would be the best options. Nothing that is new comes into time-bound projects without its own problems. In my opinion, a project leader should always work with proven technologies in most of the systems as far as possible and experiment only from multiple resources.

CHAPTER 8

The SLV-3 project had been formulated in such a way that the major technology work centres, both at VSSC and at SHAR, could handle propellant production, rocket motor testing and launch of any large diameter rocket. As participants in the SLV-3 project, we set three milestones for ourselves: development and flight qualification of all subsystems through sounding rockets by 1975; sub-orbital flights by 1976; and the final orbital flight in 1978. The work tempo had picked up now and the atmosphere was charged with excitement. Wherever I went, our teams had something interesting to show me. A large number of things were being done for the first time in the country and the ground-level technicians had had no prior exposure to this kind of work. I saw new performance dimensions growing among my team members.

Performance dimensions are factors that lead to creation. They go beyond competencies such as the skills and knowledge of the individual. Performance dimensions are broader and deeper than what a person must know and be able to do in order to function well in his or her job. They include attitudes, values and character traits. They exist at various levels of the human personality. At the behavioural level—at the outermost ring of the tree—we can observe skills and measure knowledge. Social roles and self-image dimensions are found at the intermediate level. Motives and traits exist at the innermost or core level. If we can identify those performance dimensions which are most highly correlated with job success, we can put them together to form a blueprint for outstanding performance in both thought and action.

Although SLV-3 was still in the future, its subsystems were being completed. In June 1974, we used the Centaur sounding rocket launch to test some of our critical systems. A scaled down heat shield of SLV, Rate Gyro Unit, and Vehicle Attitude Programmer were integrated into the Centaur rocket. The three systems involved wide-ranging expertise—composite materials, control engineering and software, none of them ever having been tried before in the country. The test was a complete success. Until then the Indian Space Programme had not gone beyond sounding rockets and even knowledgeable people were not ready to see and acknowledge its efforts as anything more serious than fiddling around with meteorological instruments. For the first time, we inspired the confidence of the nation. Prime Minister Indira Gandhi told Parliament on 24 July 1974, "The development and fabrication of relevant technologies, subsystems and hardware (to make India's first Satellite Launch Vehicle) are progressing satisfactorily. A number of industries are engaged in the fabrication of components. The first orbital flight by India is scheduled to take place in 1978."

Like any other act of creation, the creation of the SLV-3 also had its painful moments. One day, when my team and I were totally engrossed in the preparation of the static test of the first stage motor, the news of a death in the family reached me. My brother-in-law and mentor, Jenab Ahmed Jallaludin, was no more. For a couple of minutes, I was immobilized, I could not think, could not feel anything. When I could focus on my surroundings once more and attempted to participate in the work, I found myself talking incoherently—and then I realized that, with Jallaluddin, a part of me had passed away too. A vision of my childhood reappeared before me—evening walks around the Rameswaram temple, shining sand and dancing tides in the moonlight, stars looking down from an unlit sky on a new moon night, Jallaluddin showing me the horizon sinking into the sea, arranging money for my books, and seeing me off at Santa Cruz airport. I felt that I had been thrown into a whirlpool of time and space. My father, by now more than a hundred years old, pall-bearer for his son-in-law, who had been half his age; the bereft soul of my sister Zohara, her wounds from the loss of her four-year-old son still raw—these images came before my eyes in a blur, too terrible for me to comprehend. I leaned on the assembly jig, composed myself and left a few instructions with Dr S Srinivasan, Deputy Project Director, to carry on with the work in my absence.

Travelling overnight in a combination of district buses, I reached Rameswaram only the next day. During this time, I did my best to free myself from the very past which appeared to have come to an end with Jallaluddin. But the moment I reached my house, grief assailed me afresh. I had no words for Zohara or for my niece Mehboob, both of whom were crying uncontrollably. I had no tears to shed. We sorrowfully put Jallaluddin's body to rest.

My father held my hands for a long time. There were no tears in his eyes either. "Do you not see, Abul, how the Lord lengthens the shadows? Had it been His will, He could have made them constant. But He makes the sun their guide, little by little He shortens them. It is He who has made the night a mantle for you, and sleep a rest.

Jallaluddin has gone into a long sleep—a dreamless sleep, a complete rest of all his being within simple unconsciousness. Nothing will befall us except what Allah has ordained. He is our Guardian. In Allah, my son, put your trust." He slowly closed his wrinkled eyelids and went into a trance-like state.

Death has never frightened me. After all, everyone has to go one day. But perhaps Jallaluddin went a little too early, a little too soon. I could not bring myself to stay for long at home. I felt the whole of my inner self drowning in a sort of anxious agitation, and inner conflicts between my personal and my professional life. For many days, back in Thumba, I felt a sense of futility I had never known before—about everything I was doing.

I had long talks with Prof. Dhawan. He told me that my progress on the SLV project would bring me solace. The confusion would first lessen and would later pass away altogether. He drew my attention to the wonders of technology and its achievements.

Gradually, the hardware began emerging from the drawing boards. Sasi Kumar built a very effective network of fabrication work centres. Within days of getting a component drawing, he would embark on the fabrication with what was available. Namboodiri and Pillai were spending their days and nights at the propulsion laboratory, developing four rocket motors simultaneously. MSR Dev and Sandlas drew up meticulous plans for mechanical and electrical integration of the vehicle. Madhavan Nair and Murthy examined the systems developed by the VSSC electronics laboratories and engineered them into flight sub-systems wherever it was possible. US Singh brought up the first ground launch system, comprising of telemetry, tele-command, and radar. He also chalked out a detailed work plan with SHAR for the flight trials. Dr Sundararajan closely monitored the mission objectives and concurrently updated the systems. Dr Srinivasan, a competent launch vehicle designer, discharged all my complementary and supplementary functions as the SLV Deputy Project Director. He noticed what I had overlooked, heard the points I failed to listen to, and suggested possibilities that I had not so much as visualized.

We learned the hard way that the biggest problem of project management is to achieve a regular and efficient interfacing between the different individuals and work centres. Hard work can be set at nought in the absence of proper coordination.

I had the fortune of having YS Rajan from the ISRO headquarters as my friend in those times. Rajan was (and is) a universal friend. His friendship embraced with equal warmth turners, fitters, electricians and drivers as well as scientists, engineers, contractors and bureaucrats. Today when the press calls me a 'welder of people', I attribute this to Rajan. His close interaction with different work centres created such harmony in SLV affairs that the fine threads of individual efforts were woven into a mighty fabric of great strength.

In 1976, my father passed away. He had been in poor health for quite some time due to his advanced age. The death of Jallaluddin had also taken a toll on his health and spirit. He had lost his desire to live, as though after seeing Jallaluddin return to his divine source, he too had become eager to return to his.

Whenever I learnt about my father's indifferent health, I would visit Rameswaram with a good city doctor. Every time I did so, he would chide me for my unnecessary concern and lecture me on the expenses incurred on the doctor. "Your visit is enough for me to get well, why bring a doctor and spend money on his fees?" he would ask. This time he had gone beyond the capabilities of any doctor, care or money. My father, Jainulabdeen, who had lived on Rameswaram island for 102 years, had passed away leaving behind fifteen grandchildren and one great-grandson. He had led an exemplary life. Sitting alone, on the night after the burial, I remembered a poem written on the death of Yeats by his friend Auden, and felt as if it was written for my father:

> *Earth, receive an honoured guest;*
> *William Yeats is laid to rest:*
> *. . . . .*
> *In the prison of his days*
> *Teach the free man how to praise.*

In worldly terms, it was the death of just another old man. No public mourning was organized, no flags were lowered to halfmast, no newspaper carried an obituary for him. He was not a politician, a scholar, or a businessman. He was a plain and transparent man. My father pursued the supreme value, the Good. His life inspired the growth of all that was benign and angelic, wise and noble.

My father had always reminded me of the legendary Abou Ben Adhem who, waking one night from a deep dream of peace, saw an angel writing in a book of gold the names of those who love the Lord. Abou asked the Angel if his own name was on the list. The Angel replied in the negative. Disappointed but still cheerful, Abou said, "Write my name down as one that loves his fellowmen". The angel wrote, and vanished. The next night, it came again with a great wakening light, and showed the names of those whom the love of God had blessed. And Abou's name was the first on the list.

I sat for a long time with my mother, but could not speak. She blessed me in a choked voice when I took leave of her to return to Thumba. She knew that she was not to leave the house of her husband, of which she was the custodian, and I was not to live with her there. Both of us had to live out our own destinies. Was I too stubborn or was I excessively preoccupied with the SLV? Should I not have forgotten for a while my own affairs in order to listen to her? I regretfully realized this only when she passed away soon afterwards.

The SLV-3 Apogee rocket, developed as a common upper stage with Diamont, scheduled to be flight tested in France was mired in a series of knotty problems. I had to rush to France to sort them out. Before I could depart, late in the afternoon, I was informed that my mother had passed away. I took the first available bus to Nagarcoil. From there, I travelled to Rameswaram, spending a whole night in the train, and performed the last rites the next morning. Both the people who had formed me had left for their heavenly abode. The departed had reached the end of their journey. The rest of us had to continue walking the weary road and life had to go on. I prayed in the mosque my father had once taken me to every evening. I told Him that my mother could not have lived longer in the world without the care and love of her husband, and therefore had preferred to join him. I begged His forgiveness. "They carried out the task I designed for them with great care, dedication and honesty and came back to me. Why are you mourning their day of accomplishment? Concentrate on the assignments that lie before you, and proclaim my glory through your deeds!" Nobody had said these words, but I heard them loud and clear. An inspiring aphorism in the Qur'an on the passing away of souls filled my mind: "Your wealth and children are only a temptation whereas: Allah! with Him is an eternal award." I came out of the mosque with my mind at peace and proceeded to the railway station. I always remember that when the call for *namāz* sounded, our home would transform into a small mosque. My father and my mother leading, and their children and grandchildren following.

The next morning I was back at Thumba, physically exhausted, emotionally shattered, but determined to fulfill our ambition of flying an Indian rocket motor on foreign soil.

On my return from France, after successfully testing the SLV-3 apogee motor, Dr Brahm Prakash informed me one day about the arrival of Wernher von Braun. Everybody working in rocketry knows of von Braun, who made the lethal V-2 missiles that devastated London in the Second World War. In the final stages of the War, von Braun was captured by the Allied Forces. As a tribute to his genius, von Braun was given a top position in the rocketry programme at NASA. Working for the US Army, von Braun produced the landmark Jupiter missile, which was the first IRBM with a 3000 km range. When I was asked by Dr Brahm Prakash to receive von Braun at Madras and escort him to Thumba, I was naturally excited.

The V-2 missile (an abbreviation of the German word *Vergeltungswaffe*) was by far the greatest single achievement in the history of rockets and missiles. It was the culmination of the efforts made by von Braun and his team in the VFR (Society for Space Flight) in the 1920s. What had begun as a civilian effort soon became an official army one, and von Braun became the technical director of the German Missile Laboratory at Kummersdorf. The first V-2 missile was first tested unsuccessfully in June 1942. It toppled over on to its side and exploded. But on 16 August 1942, it became the first missile to exceed the speed of sound. Under the supervision of von Braun, more than 10,000 V-2 missiles were produced between April and October 1944 at the gigantic underground production unit near Nordhausen in Germany. That I would be travelling with this man—a scientist, a designer, a production engineer, an administrator, a technology manager all rolled into one—what more could I have asked for?

We flew in an Avro aircraft which took around ninety minutes from Madras to Trivandrum. von Braun asked me about our work and listened as if he was just another student of rocketry. I never expected the father of modern rocketry to be so humble, receptive and encouraging. He made me feel comfortable right through the flight. It was hard to imagine that I was talking to a giant of missile systems, as he was so self-effacing.

He observed that the length to diameter L/D ratio of the SLV-3, which was designed to be 22, was on the higher side and cautioned me about the aero-elastic problems which must be avoided during flight.

Having spent the major part of his working life in Germany, how did he feel in America? I asked this of von Braun who had become a cult figure in the States after creating the Saturn rocket in the Apollo mission which put man on the moon. "America is a country of great possibilities, but they look upon everything un-American with suspicion and contempt. They suffer from a deep-rooted NIH—Not Invented Here—complex and look down on alien technologies. If you want to do anything in rocketry, do it yourself," von Braun advised me. He commented, "SLV-3 is a genuine Indian design and you may be having your own troubles. But you should always remember that we don't just build on successes, we also build on failures."

On the topic of the inevitable hard work that goes with rocket development and the degree of commitment involved, he smiled and said with a glint of mischief in his eyes, "Hard work is not enough in rocketry. It is not a sport where mere hard work can fetch you honours. Here, not only do you have to have a goal but you have to have strategies to achieve it as fast as possible."

"Total commitment is not just hard work, it is total involvement. Building a rock wall is back-breaking work. There are some people who build rock walls all their lives. And when they die, there are miles of walls, mute testimonials to how hard those people had worked."

He continued, "But there are other men who while placing one rock on top of another have a vision in their minds, a goal. It may be a terrace with roses climbing over the rock walls and chairs set out for lazy summer days. Or the rock wall may enclose an apple orchard or mark a boundary. When they finish, they have more than a wall. It is the goal that makes the difference. Do not make rocketry your profession, your livelihood—make it your religion, your mission." Did I see something of Prof. Vikram Sarabhai in von Braun? It made me happy to think so.

With three deaths in the family in as many years, I needed total commitment to my work in order to keep performing. I wanted to throw all my being into the creation of the SLV. I felt as if I had discovered the path I was meant to follow, God's mission for me and my purpose on His Earth. During this period, it was as though I had pushed a hold button—no badminton in the evenings, no more weekends or holidays, no family, no relations, not even any friends outside the SLV circle.

To succeed in your mission, you must have single-minded devotion to your goal. Individuals like myself are often called 'workaholics'. I question this term because that implies a pathological condition or an illness. If I do that which I desire more than anything else in the world and which makes me happy, such work can never be an aberration. Words from the twenty-sixth Psalm come to mind while I work: "Examine me, 0 Lord, and prove me."

Total commitment is a crucial quality for those who want to reach the very top of their profession. The desire to work at optimum capacity leaves hardly any room for anything else. I have had people with me who would scoff at the 40-hours-a-week job they were being paid for. I have known others who used to work 60, 80 and even 100 hours a week because they found their work exciting and rewarding. Total commitment is the common denominator among all successful men and women. Are you able to manage the stresses you encounter in your life? The difference between an energetic and a confused person is the difference in the way their minds handle their experiences. Man needs his difficulties because they are necessary to enjoy success. All of us carry some sort of a super intelligence within us. Let it be stimulated to enable us to examine our deepest thoughts, desires, and beliefs.

Once you have done this—charged yourself, as it were, with your commitment to your work—you also need good health and boundless energy. Climbing to the top demands strength, whether to the top of Mount Everest or to the top of your career. People are born with different energy reserves and the one who tires first and burns out easily will do well to reorganize his or her life at the earliest.

In 1979, a six-member team was preparing the flight version of a complex second stage control system for static test and evaluation. The team was in countdown mode at T–15 minutes (15 minutes before the test). One of the twelve valves did not respond during checkout. Anxiety drove the members of the team to the test site to look into the problem. Suddenly the oxidizer tank, filled with red fuming nitric acid (RFNA), burst, causing severe acid burns to the team members. It was a very traumatic experience to see the suffering of the injured. Kurup and I rushed to the Trivandrum Medical College Hospital and begged to have our colleagues admitted, as six beds were not available in the hospital at that point of time.

Sivaramakrishnan Nair was one among the six persons injured. The acid had burned his body at a number of places. By the time we got a bed in the hospital, he was in severe pain. I kept vigil at his bedside. Around 3 o' clock in the morning, Sivaramakrishnan regained consciousness. His first words expressed regret over the mishap and assured me that he would make up the slippage in schedules caused by the accident. His sincerity and optimism, even in the midst of such severe pain, impressed me deeply.

Men like Sivaramakrishnan are a breed apart. They are the strivers, always reaching higher than the last time. And with their social and family life welded to their dream, they find the rewards of their drive overwhelming—the inherent joy of being in flow. This event greatly enhanced my confidence in my team; a team that would stand like a rock in success and failure.

I have used the word 'flow' at many places without really elaborating its meaning. What is this flow? And what are these joys? I could call them moments of magic. I see an analogy between these moments and the high that you experience when you play badminton or go jogging. Flow is a sensation we experience when we act with total involvement. During flow, action follows action according to an internal logic that seems to need no conscious intervention on the part of the worker. There is no hurry; there are no distracting demands on one's attention. The past and the future disappear. So does the distinction between self and the activity. We had all come under the current of the SLV flow. Although we were working very hard we were very relaxed, energetic and fresh. How did it happen? Who had created this flow?

Perhaps it was the meaningful organization of the purposes we sought to achieve. We would identify the broadest possible purpose level and then work towards developing a feasible target solution from a variety of alternatives. It was this working backwards to develop a creative change in the problem solution, that used to put us in 'flow'.

When the SLV-3 hardware started emerging, our ability to concentrate increased markedly. I felt a tremendous surge of confidence; in complete control over myself and over the SLV-3 project. Flow is a by-product of controlled creativity. The first requirement is to work as hard as you can at something that presents a challenge and is approved by your heart. It may not be an overwhelming challenge, but one that stretches you a little, something that makes you realize that you are performing a task better today than you did yesterday, or the last time you tried to do it. Another prerequisite for being in flow is the availability of a significant span of uninterrupted time. In my experience, it is difficult to switch into the flow state in less than half an hour. And it is almost impossible if you are bedevilled by interruptions.

Is it possible to switch yourself into flow by using some sort of a conditioning device in much the same way that we condition ourselves to learn effectively? The answer is yes, and the secret is to analyse previous occasions when you have been in flow, because each person has his or her unique natural frequency which responds to a particular stimulus. You alone can identify the common denominator in your case. Once you have isolated this common denominator, you can set the stage for flow.

I have experienced this state many times, almost every day of the SLV mission. There have been days in the laboratory when I have looked up to find the laboratory empty and realized that it was way past the quitting time. On other days, my team members and I have been so caught up in our work that the lunch hour slipped by without our even being conscious that we were hungry.

Analysing such occasions in retrospect, I find them similar in the sense that this flow was experienced when the project was nearing completion, or when the project had reached that phase when all the necessary data had been gathered and we were ready to start summing up the problem, outlining the demands made by conflicting criteria and the various positions presented by opposing interests and making our recommendations for action. I also realized that this tended to happen on days that were relatively quiet in the office, with no crises or meetings. Such spells increased steadily in frequency, and the SLV-3 dream was finally realized in the middle of 1979.

We had scheduled the first experimental flight trial of SLV-3 for 10 August 1979. The primary goals of the mission were to realize a fully integrated launch vehicle; to evaluate on-board systems like stage motors, guidance and control systems and electronic subsystems; and to evaluate ground systems, like checkout, tracking, telemetry and real-time data facilities in launch operations built at the Sriharikota launch complex. The 23-metre-long, four-stage SLV rocket weighing 17 tonnes finally took off elegantly at 0758 hrs and immediately started following its programmed trajectory.

Stage I performed to perfection. There was a smooth transition from this stage to the second stage. We were spellbound to see our hopes flying in the form of the SLV-3. Suddenly, the spell was broken. The second stage went out of control. The flight was terminated after 317 seconds and the vehicle's remains, including my favourite fourth stage with the payload, splashed into the sea, 560 km off Sriharikota.

The incident caused us profound disappointment. I felt a strange mix of anger and frustration. Suddenly, I felt my legs become so stiff that they ached. The problem was not with my body; something was happening in my mind.

The premature death of my hovercraft *Nandi*, the abandoning of the RATO, the abortion of the SLV-Diamond fourth stage—all came alive in a flash, like a long-buried phoenix rising from its ashes. Over the years, I had somehow learned to absorb these aborted endeavours, had come to terms with them and pursued fresh dreams. That day, I re-lived each of those setbacks in my deep despondency.

"What do you suppose could be the cause of it?" somebody asked me in the Block House. I tried to find an answer, but I was too tired to try and think it out, and gave up the effort as futile. The launch was conducted in the early morning, preceded by a full night's count-down. Moreover, I had hardly had any sleep in the past week. Completely drained—mentally as well as physically—I went straight to my room and slumped onto the bed.

A gentle touch on my shoulder woke me up. It was late in the afternoon, almost approaching evening. I saw Dr Brahm Prakash sitting by my bedside. "What about going for lunch?" he asked. I was deeply touched by his affection and concern. I found out later that Dr Brahm Prakash had come to my room twice before that but had gone away on finding me asleep. He had waited all that time for me to get up and have lunch with him. I was sad, but not alone. The company of Dr Brahm Prakash filled me with a new confidence. He made light conversation during the meal, carefully avoiding the SLV-3, but gently providing me solace.

CHAPTER 9

Dr Brahm Prakash helped me endure this difficult period. In practice, Dr Brahm Prakash employed the front-line damage control principle: "Just get the fellow home alive. He'll recover." He drew the entire SLV team close and demonstrated to me that I was not alone in my sorrow at the SLV-3's failure. "All your comrades are standing by you," he said. This gave me vital emotional support, encouragement, and guidance.

A post-flight review conducted on 11 August 1979 was attended by more than seventy scientists. A detailed technical appraisal of the failure was completed. Later, the post-flight analysis committee headed by SK Athithan pinpointed the reasons for the malfunction of the vehicle. It was established that the mishap occurred because of the failure of the second stage control system. No control force was available during the second stage flight due to which the vehicle became aerodynamically unstable, resulting in altitude and velocity loss. This caused the vehicle to fall into the sea even before the other stages could ignite.

Further in-depth analysis of the second-stage failure identified the reason as the draining of a good amount of Red Fuming Nitric Acid (RFNA) used as the oxidizer for the fuel power at that stage. Consequently, when the control force was demanded, only fuel was injected, resulting in zero force. 'A solenoid valve in the oxidizer tank remaining open due to contamination after the first command at T–8 minutes', was identified as the reason for the draining of RFNA.

The findings were presented to Prof. Dhawan at a meeting of top ISRO scientists and were accepted. Everybody was convinced by the technical cause-and-effect sequence presented and there was a general feeling of satisfaction about the whole exercise of failure-management measures taken. I was still unconvinced though and felt restless. To me, the level of responsibility is measured by one's ability to confront the decision-making process without any delay or distraction.

On the spur of the moment, I stood up and addressed Prof. Dhawan, "Sir, even though my friends have technically justified the failure, I take the responsibility for judging the RFNA leak detected during the final phase of countdown as insignificant. As a Mission Director, I should have put the launch on hold and saved the flight if possible.

In a similar situation abroad, the Mission Director would have lost his job. I therefore take responsibility for the SLV-3 failure." For quite some time there was pin-drop silence in the hall. Then Prof. Dhawan got up and said, "I am going to put Kalam in orbit!", and left the place, signalling that the meeting was over.

The pursuit of science is a combination of great elation and great despair. I went over many such episodes in my mind. Johannes Kepler, whose three orbital laws form the basis of space research, took nearly 17 years after formulating the two laws about planetary motion around the sun, to enunciate his third law which gives the relation between the size of the elliptical orbit and the length of time it takes for the planet to go around the sun. How many failures and frustrations must he have gone through? The idea that man could land on the moon, developed by the Russian mathematician Konstantin Tsiolkovsky, was realized after nearly four decades—and by the United States, at that. Prof. Chandrasekhar had to wait nearly 50 years before receiving the Nobel Prize for his discovery of the 'Chandrasekhar Limit', a discovery made while he was a graduate student at Cambridge in the 1930s. If his work had been recognized then, it could have led to the discovery of the Black Hole decades earlier. How many failures must von Braun have gone through before his Saturn launch vehicle put man on the moon? These thoughts helped to give me the ability to withstand apparently irreversible setbacks.

Early in November 1979, Dr Brahm Prakash retired. He had always been my sheet-anchor in the turbulent waters of VSSC. His belief in team spirit had inspired the management pattern for the SLV project, which later became a blueprint for all scientific projects in the country. Dr Brahm Prakash was a very wise counsellor who gave me valuable guidance whenever I deviated from my mission objectives.

Dr Brahm Prakash not only reinforced the traits which I had acquired from Prof. Sarabhai, but also helped me give them new dimensions. He always cautioned me against haste. "Big scientific projects are like mountains, which should be climbed with as little effort as possible and without urgency. The reality of your own nature should determine your speed. If you become restless, speed up. If you become tense and high-strung, slow down. You should climb the mountain in a state of equilibrium. When each task of your project is not just a means to an end but a unique event in itself, then you are doing it well," he would tell me. The echo of Dr Brahm Prakash's advice could be heard in Emerson's poem on Brahma:

*If the red slayer think he slays,
Or, if the slain think he is slain,
They know not well, the subtle ways
I keep, and pass, and turn again.*

To live only for some unknown future is superficial. It is like climbing a mountain to reach the peak without experiencing its sides. The sides of the mountain sustain life, not the peak. This is where things grow, experience is gained, and technologies are mastered. The importance of the peak lies only in the fact that it defines the sides. So I went on towards the top, but always experiencing the sides. I had a long way to go but I was in no hurry. I went in little steps—just one step after another—but each step towards the top.

At every stage, the SLV-3 team was blessed with some extraordinarily courageous people. Along with Sudhakar and Sivaramakrishnan, there was also Sivakaminathan. He was entrusted with bringing the C-Band transponder from Trivandrum to SHAR for integration with the SLV-3. The transponder is a device fitted with the rocket system to give the radar signals which are powerful enough to help it track the vehicle from the take-off site to the final impact point. The SLV-3 launch schedule was dependent on the arrival and integration of this equipment. On landing at the Madras airport, the aircraft which Sivakami was travelling in skidded and overshot the runway. Dense smoke engulfed the aircraft. Everyone jumped out of the aircraft through emergency exits, and desperately fought to save themselves all except Sivakami, who stayed in the aircraft till he removed the transponder from his baggage. He was among the last few persons, the others being mostly aircraft crew, to emerge from the smoke and he was hugging the transponder close to his chest.

Another incident from those days that I recall clearly relates to Prof. Dhawan's visit to the SLV-3 assembly building. Prof. Dhawan, Madhavan Nair and I were discussing some finer aspects of the SLV-3 integration. The vehicle was kept on the launcher in a horizontal position. When we were moving around and examining the readiness of the integrated hardware, I noticed the presence of big water-ports for extinguishing fire in case of an accident. For some reason, I felt uncomfortable at the sight of the ports facing the SLV-3 on the launcher. I suggested to Madhavan Nair that we could rotate the port so that they were apart by a full 180°. This would prevent the freak possibility of water gushing out and damaging the rocket. To our surprise, within minutes of Madhavan Nair getting the ports reversed, powerful water jets gushed out of the ports. The Vehicle Safety Officer had ensured the functioning of the fire-fighting system without realizing that it could have wrecked the entire rocket. This was a lesson in foresight. Or did we have divine protection?

On 17 July 1980, 30 hours before the launch of the second SLV-3, the newspapers were filled with all kinds of predictions. One of the newspapers reported, "The Project Director is missing and could not be contacted." Many reports preferred to trace the history of the first SLV-3 flight, and recalled how the third stage had failed to ignite because of lack of fuel and the rocket had nosedived into the ocean. Some highlighted SLV-3's possible military implications in terms of acquiring the capability for building IRBMs. Some were a general prognosis of all that ailed our country and related it to the SLV-3. I knew that the next day's launch was going to decide the future of the Indian space programme. In fact, to put it simply, the eyes of the whole nation were on us.

In the early hours of the next day, 18 July 1980—at 0803 hrs to be precise—India's first Satellite Launch Vehicle, SLV-3, lifted off from SHAR. At 600 seconds before take-off, I saw the computer displaying data about stage IV giving the required velocity to the Rohini Satellite (carried as payload) to enter its orbit. Within the next two minutes, Rohini was set into motion in a low Earth orbit. I spoke, in the midst of screeching decibels, the most important words I had ever uttered in my life, "Mission Director calling all stations. Stand by for an important announcement. All stages performed to mission requirements. The fourth stage apogee motor has given the required velocity to put Rohini Satellite into orbit". There were happy cries everywhere. When I came out of the Block House, I was lifted onto the shoulders of my jubilant colleagues and carried in a procession.

The whole nation was excited. India had made its entry into the small group of nations which possessed satellite launch capability. Newspapers carried news of the event in their headlines. Radio and television stations aired special programmes. Parliament greeted the achievement with the thumping of desks. It was both the culmination of a national dream, and the beginning of a very important phase in our nation's history. Prof. Satish Dhawan, Chairman ISRO, threw his customary guardedness to the winds and announced that it was now well within our ability to explore space. Prime Minister Indira Gandhi cabled her congratulations. But the most important reaction was that of the Indian scientific community—everybody was proud of this hundred per cent indigenous effort.

I experienced mixed feelings. I was happy to achieve the success which had been evading me for the past two decades, but I was sad because the people who had inspired me were no longer there to share my joy—my father, my brother-in-law Jallaluddin, and Prof. Sarabhai.

The credit for the successful SLV-3 flight goes, first, to the giants of the Indian space programme, Prof. Sarabhai in particular, who had preceded this effort; next to the hundreds of VSSC personnel who had through sheer will-power proved the mettle of our countrymen and also, not least, to Prof. Dhawan and Dr Brahm Prakash, who had led the project.

We had a late dinner that evening. Gradually, the din and clatter of the celebrations calmed down. I retired to my bed with almost no energy left. Through the open window, I could see the moon among the clouds. The sea breeze seemed to reflect the buoyancy of the mood on Sriharikota island that day.

Within a month of the SLV-3 success, I visited the Nehru Science Centre in Bombay for a day, in response to an invitation to share my experiences with the SLV-3. There, I received a telephone call from Prof. Dhawan in Delhi, asking me to join him the next morning. We were to meet the Prime Minister, Mrs Indira Gandhi. My hosts at the Nehru Centre were kind enough to arrange my ticket to Delhi, but I had a small problem. It had to do with my clothes. I was dressed casually as is my wont and wearing slippers—not, by any standards of etiquette, suitable attire in which to meet the Prime Minister! When I told Prof. Dhawan about this problem, he told me not to worry about my dress. "You are beautifully clothed in your success," he quipped.

Prof. Dhawan and I arrived at the Parliament House Annexe the next morning. A meeting of the Parliamentary Panel on Science & Technology chaired by the Prime Minister was scheduled. There were about 30 Members of the Lok Sabha and Rajya Sabha in the room, which was lit by a majestic chandelier. Prof. MGK Menon and Dr Nag Chaudhuri were also present. Shrimati Gandhi spoke to the Members about the success of the SLV-3 and lauded our achievement. Prof. Dhawan thanked the gathering for the encouragement given by them to space research in the country and expressed the gratitude of the ISRO scientists and engineers. Suddenly, I saw Shrimati Gandhi smiling at me as she said, "Kalam! We would like to hear you speak."

I was surprised by the request as Prof. Dhawan had already addressed the gathering.

Hesitantly, I rose and responded, "I am indeed honoured to be in this great gathering of nation-builders. I only know how to build a rocket system in our country, which would inject a satellite, built in our country, by imparting to it a velocity of 25,000 km per hour." There was thunderous applause. I thanked the members for giving us an opportunity to work on a project like the SLV-3 and prove the scientific strength of our country. The entire room was irradiated with happiness.

Now that Project SLV-3 had been successfully completed, VSSC had to reorganize its resources and redefine its goals. I wanted to be relieved of the project activities, and consequently Ved Prakash Sandlas from my team was made the Project Director for the SLV-3 Continuation Project, which aimed at making operational satellite launch vehicles of a similar class. With a view to upgrade the SLV-3 by means of certain technological innovations, the development of Augmented Satellite Launch Vehicles (ASLVs) had been on the cards for some time. The aim was to enhance the SLV-3 payload capability from 40 kg to 150 kg. MSR Dev from my team was appointed Project Director ASLV. Then, to reach the sun-synchronous orbit (900 km), a PSLV was to be made. The Geo Satellite Launch Vehicle (GSLV) was also envisaged, though as a distant dream. I took up the position of Director, Aerospace Dynamics and Design Group, so that I could configure the forthcoming launch vehicles and technology development.

The existing VSSC infrastructure was inadequate to handle the size and weight of the future launch vehicle systems and the implementation of all these projects was going to require highly specialized facilities. New sites were identified for the expanded activities of VSSC, at Vattiyoorkavu and Valiamala. Dr Srinivasan drew up a detailed plan of the facilities. Meanwhile, I carried out an analysis of the application of SLV-3 and its variants with Sivathanu Pillai, and compared the existing launch vehicles of the world for missile applications. We established that the SLV-3 solid rocket systems would meet the national requirements of payload delivery vehicles for short and intermediate ranges (4000 km). We contended that the development of one additional solid booster of 1.8 m diameter with 36 tonnes of propellant along with SLV-3 subsystems would meet the ICBM requirement (above 5000 km for a 1000-kg payload). This proposal was, however, never considered. It nevertheless paved the way for the formulation of the Re-entry Experiment (REX) which, much later on, became *Agni*.

The next SLV-3 flight, SLV3-D1, took off on 31 May 1981. I witnessed this flight from the visitors' gallery. This was the first time I witnessed a launch from outside the Control Centre. The unpalatable truth I had to face was that by becoming the focus of media attention, I had aroused envy among some of my senior colleagues, all of whom had equally contributed to the success of SLV-3. Was I hurt at the coldness of the new environment? Perhaps yes, but I was willing to accept what I couldn't change.

I have never lived off the profits of others' minds. My life, in keeping with my nature, has never been that of a ruthless achiever. The SLV-3 was made not by force and manipulation, but through consistent collective effort. Then why this sense of bitterness? Was it peculiar to the VSSC top level or a universal reality? As a scientist, I was trained to reason out reality. In science, reality is that which exists. And because this bitterness was real, I had to reason it out. But can these things be reasoned out?

Were my post-SLV experiences leading me into a critical situation? Yes and no. Yes, because the glory of SLV-3 had not gone to everyone who deserved it—but hardly anything could have been done about that. No, because a situation can be considered critical for a person only when realization of the internal necessity becomes impossible. And that certainly was not the case. In fact, the concept of conflict is built upon this basic idea. In retrospect, I can only say that I was fully aware of a great need for actualization and renewal.

In January 1981, I was invited by Dr Bhagiratha Rao of the High Altitude Laboratory (now the Defence Electronics Applications Laboratory (DEAL)), Dehradun, to give a lecture on the SLV-3. The renowned nuclear scientist, Prof. Raja Ramanna, whom I had always admired, and who was then the Scientific Adviser to the Defence Minister, presided over the gathering. He spoke on India's efforts in generating nuclear energy and the challenge in conducting the first nuclear test for peaceful purposes. As I had been so closely involved with SLV-3, it was natural that I was soon in full spate about it. Later, Prof. Raja Ramanna invited me for a private meeting over tea.

The first thing that struck me when I met Prof. Ramanna was his genuine pleasure at meeting me. There was an eagerness in his talk, an immediate, sympathetic friendliness, accompanied by quick, graceful movements. The evening brought back memories of my first meeting with Prof. Sarabhai—as if it was yesterday. The world of Prof. Sarabhai was internally simple and externally easy. Each of us working with him was driven by a single-minded need to create, and lived under conditions which made the object of that need directly accessible. Sarabhai's world was tailor-made to our dreams. It had neither too much nor too little of anything needed by any one of us. We could divide it by our requirements without a remainder.

My world, by now, had no simplicity left in it. It had become an internally complex and externally difficult world. My efforts in rocketry and in achieving the goal of making indigenous rockets were impeded by external obstacles and complicated by internal wavering. I was aware that it required a special effort of the will to sustain my trajectory. The coordination of my present with my past had already been jeopardised. The coordination of my present with my future was uppermost in my mind when I went to have tea with Prof. Ramanna.

He did not take long to come to the point. The *Devil* Missile programme had been shelved in spite of tremendous achievements made by Narayanan and his team at DRDL. The entire programme of military rockets was reeling under a persistent apathy. The DRDO needed somebody to take command of their missile programmes which had been stuck at the drawing board and static test bed stages for quite a while. Prof. Ramanna asked me if I would like to join DRDL and shoulder the responsibility of shaping their Guided Missile Development Programme (GMDP). Prof. Ramanna's proposal evoked a mixture of emotions in me.

When again would I have such an opportunity to consolidate all our knowledge of rocketry and apply it?

I felt honoured by the esteem in which Prof. Ramanna held me. He had been the guiding spirit behind the Pokharan nuclear test, and I was thrilled by the impact he had helped create on the outside world about India's technical competence. I knew I would not be able to refuse him. Prof. Ramanna advised me to talk to Prof. Dhawan on this issue so that he could work out the modalities of my transfer from ISRO to DRDL.

I met Prof. Dhawan on 14 January 1981. He gave me a patient hearing, with his typical penchant for weighing everything carefully to make sure he didn't miss a point. A markedly pleasant expression came to his face. He said, "I am pleased with their appraisal of my man's work". He then smiled. I have never met anyone with a smile quite like Prof. Dhawan's—a soft white cloud—you could picture it in any shape you wanted to.

I wondered how I should proceed. "Should I formally apply for the post so that DRDL could send the appointment order?" I enquired of Prof. Dhawan. "No. Don't pressurise them. Let me talk to the top-level management during my next visit to New Delhi," Prof. Dhawan said. "I know you have always had one foot in DRDO, now your whole centre of gravity seems to have shifted towards them." Perhaps what Prof. Dhawan was telling me had an element of truth in it, but my heart had always been at ISRO. Was he really unaware of that?

Republic Day, 1981, brought with it a pleasant surprise. On the evening of 25 January, Mahadevan, Secretary to Prof. UR Rao, rang up from Delhi to inform me about the Home Ministry announcement about the conferment of the Padma Bhushan award on me. The next important call was from Prof. Dhawan to congratulate me. I felt blissfully elated as it was from my guru. I rejoiced with Prof. Dhawan at his receiving the Padma Vibhushan and I congratulated him wholeheartedly. I then rang up Dr Brahm Prakash and thanked him. Dr Brahm Prakash chided me for the formality and said, "I feel as if my son has got the award." I was so deeply touched by Dr Brahm Prakash's affection that I could no longer keep my emotions in check.

I filled my room with the music of Bismillah Khan's shehnai. The music took me to another time, another place. I visited Rameswaram and hugged my mother. My father ran his caring fingers through my hair. My mentor, Jallaluddin, announced the news to the crowd gathered on Mosque Street. My sister, Zohara, prepared special sweets for me. Pakshi Lakshmana Sastry put a tilak on my forehead. Fr. Solomon blessed me holding the holy cross. I saw Prof. Sarabhai smiling with a sense of achievement—the sapling which he had planted twenty years ago had finally grown into a tree whose fruits were being appreciated by the people of India.

My Padma Bhushan evoked mixed reactions at VSSC. While there were some who shared my happiness, there were others who felt I was being unduly singled out for recognition. Some of my close associates turned envious. Why do some people fail to see the great values of life because of sadly twisted thought processes? Happiness, satisfaction, and success in life depend on making the right choices, the winning choices. There are forces in life working for you and against you. One must distinguish the beneficial forces from the malevolent ones and choose correctly between them.

An inner voice told me that the time had come for a long felt, but ignored, need for renewal. Let me clean my slate and write new 'sums'. Were the earlier sums done correctly? Evaluating one's own progress in life is not an easy task. Here the student has to set his own questions, seek his own answers and evaluate them to his own satisfaction. Judgement aside, eighteen years at ISRO was too long a stay to leave without pain. As for my afflicted friends, the lines by Lewis Carroll seemed very appropriate:

You may charge me with murder —
Or want of sense
(We are all of us weak at times):
But the slightest approach to a false pretence
Was never among my crimes!

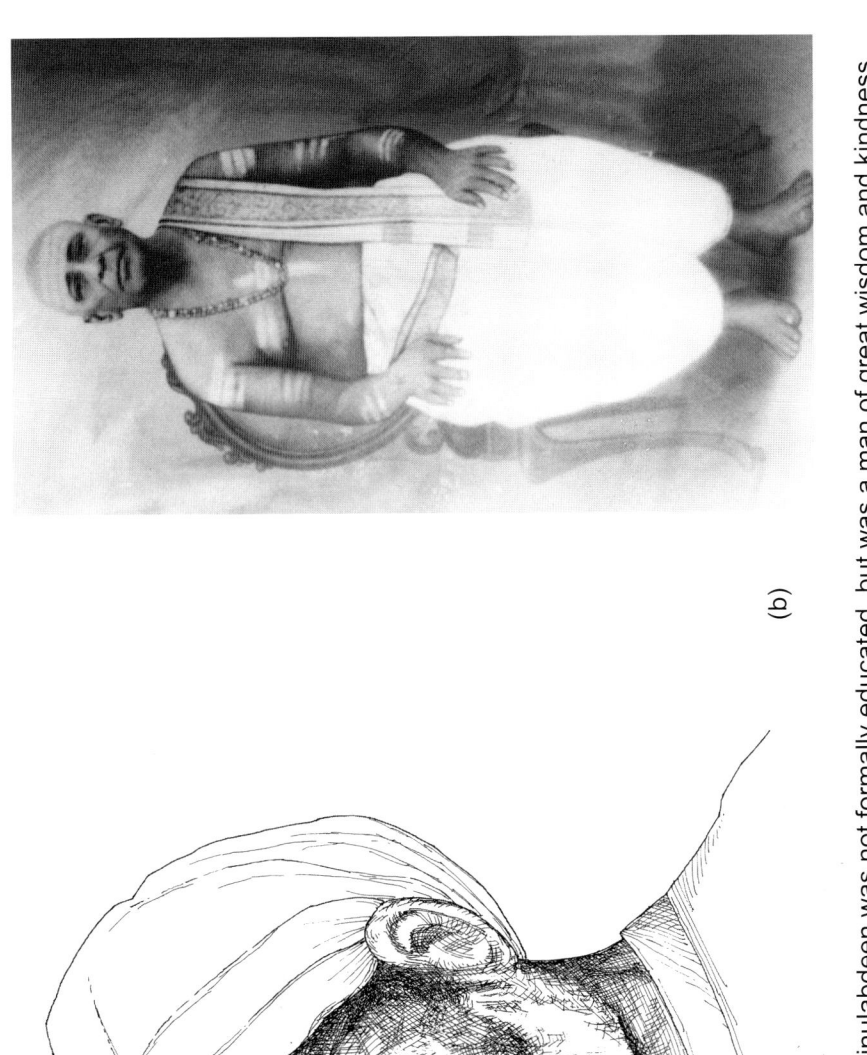

Plate 1 (a) My father Jainulabdeen was not formally educated, but was a man of great wisdom and kindness. (b) Pakshi Lakshmana Sastry, a close friend of my father and the head priest of the Rameswaram Temple.

Plate 2 The locality in which I grew up – (a) My house on Mosque Street; (b) Thousands of pilgrims from great distances descend on the ancient temple of Lord Shiva. I often assisted my brother Kasim Mohammed in his shop selling artifacts on this street.

Plate 3 STR Manickam (inset), friend of my brother Mustafa Kamal, had a large collection of books in his house, from where I would borrow books while at Rameswaram.

Plate 4 The old mosque in our locality where my father would take me and my brothers every evening to offer prayers.

Plate 5 My brother pointing at the T-square I used while studying engineering.

Plate 6 A family get-together.

Plate 7 The simple surroundings of Schwartz High School, Ramanathapuram. The words on the plaque read "Let not thy winged days be spent in vain. When once gone, no gold can buy them back again."

Plate 8 A group photograph of Kalam (bottom left) and other students and teachers of Schwartz High School. (Source: Harry Sheridon, Private Secretary to President Kalam) – *New to this edition*

Plate 9 My teachers at Schwartz High School – Iyadurai Solomon (standing, left) and Ramakrishna Iyer (sitting, right). They are the best examples of small-town Indian teachers committed to nurturing talent and inspiring young minds.

St. JOSEPH'S COLLEGE, TIRUCHIRAPALLI
B.Sc. (PHYSICS) 1952-54

Sitting: (L to R.) M.V Narasimhan (Monitor), Rev. Fr C Cyriac S.J, Mr. P. John, Mr. N. Sivaraman, Mr M V Kuriyan, Mr. C.D. Joseph M A, Mr M. I. Francis Raj M A, Mr. N. Ananthakrishnan B.A. (Hons), Mr. P.R. Subramaniam M A (Hons), Rev. Fr. T.N. Sequeira S.J., Rev Fr X. Erhart S.J (Principal) Rev Fr C. Fernandes S.J. (Rector), Rev. Fr. J.B. Rajam S.J., D.Sc., Rev. Fr. B.J Coyle S.J., Mr. P. Savarimuthu M A, Mr. S. Bhanumoorthy B A (Hons), Mr. L.K. Krishnamurthy B.Sc. (Hons), Mr. S.L. Chinnadurai BSc. (Hons), K. Rengasamy Iyer, Mr. K. Parthasarathi, Mr. P.N. Babusundaram, Mr. C K Ramakrishnan M A, Mr. S. Sundaram B Sc (Hons).

Standing 1st Row Chinnappan (Attender), C.G. Vaitheeswaran, A.M.X. Kanthraj, S. Thiagarajan, B.V. Krishnamurthi, A. Ramachandran, M.D. Santhanam, S. Ramanujam, N. Seshasayee, N. Sivaramakrishnan, A.K. Arunachalam, S.R. Ramamurthy, V.A. Chacko, Baby James, P.T. Paul, R.S Prabakaran, K. Krishnan, G. Rengarajan, K.P. Rathinam, B. Ramadurai. N. Chakravarthi, S. Mahadevan, S. Venkatesan, Arputham, (Lab Asst).

Standing 2nd Row D. Peter, S.V. Rajagopal, A. Stephen, A. Bakyam (Attender), D. Krishnamurthy, S. Rengarajan, P. Sivasankaran, R. Nagarajan, T.N. Venkataraman, P.M. Abdul Kadhar, J. Abdul Kalam, G. Sivaramakrishnan, M.S. Sedhumadhavan, S. Nagarajan, S.J Bright, M.K. Vaidyanathan, N.S. Narayanan, A. Sabapathi, V.P.Srinivasan, C.S. Krishnamurthy, Y. Sundaram.

Standing 3rd Row N. Janakiraman, V.N. Viswanathan, R. Nanjayyan, N. Ramamurthy, S. Rangarajan, R. Govindarajan (Secretary), P.R. Venkataraj, S. Seshadri, Bosco Savarinathan, M.K. George, P.T. George, V.T. Zacharius, T. George, Ceril Raj Fernando, R. Jason, B.S. Santhanam.

Plate 10 (*In spite of the poor quality of the photograph, it has been included for its archival value*). BSc. Physics, Class of 1954, St. Joseph's College, Trichy. (Kalam is in the middle of the second row from the top). (Source: APJMJ Sheik Saleem) – *New to this edition*

Plate 11 The twin-engine indigenous hovercraft prototype *Nandi* developed at ADE, Bangalore. As inventor and pilot, I took my rightful place at the controls.

Plate 12 With colleagues. From left: (standing) Ayyappan Nair and HSR Iyengar; (sitting) DR Dhanaseelan, S Krishnaswamy, Kalam and VG Uppin. (Source: APJMJ Sheik Saleem) – *New to this edition*

Plate 13 The Christian community in Thumba very graciously gave up this beautiful Church to house the first unit of the Space Research Centre.

Plate 14 At NASA. (From left) R Aravamudan, Kalam, HGS Murthy, B Ramakrishna Rao and D Easwaradas.
(Source: *Ever Upwards: ISRO in Images*, Universities Press, 2019)
– New to this edition

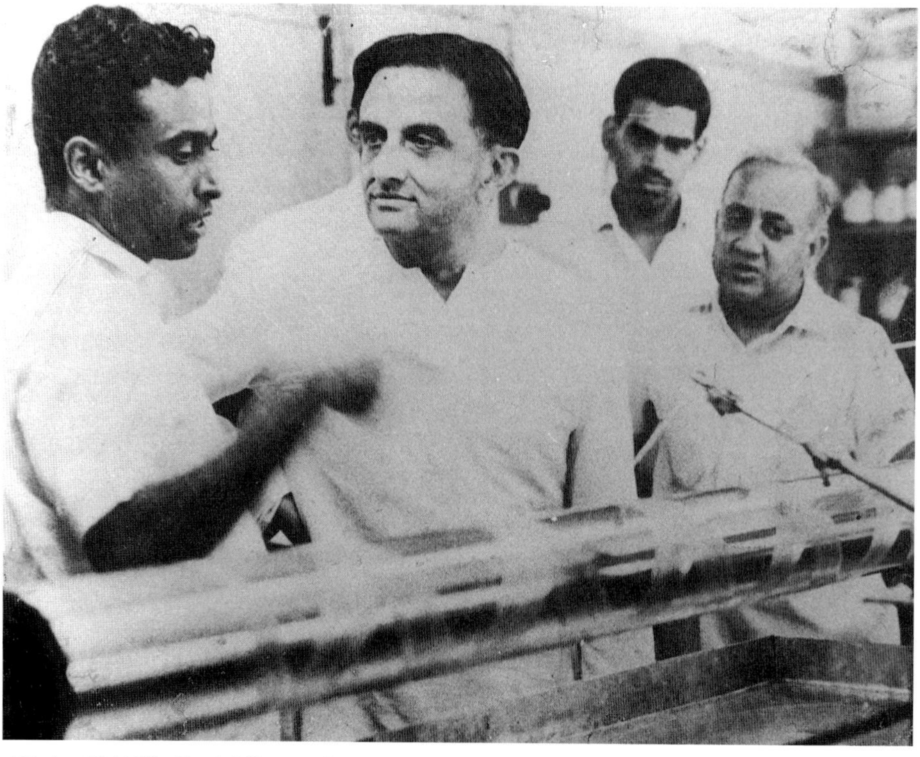

Plate 15 With Prof. Vikram Sarabhai, a great visionary and the master planner behind India's Missile Development Programme, at Thumba.

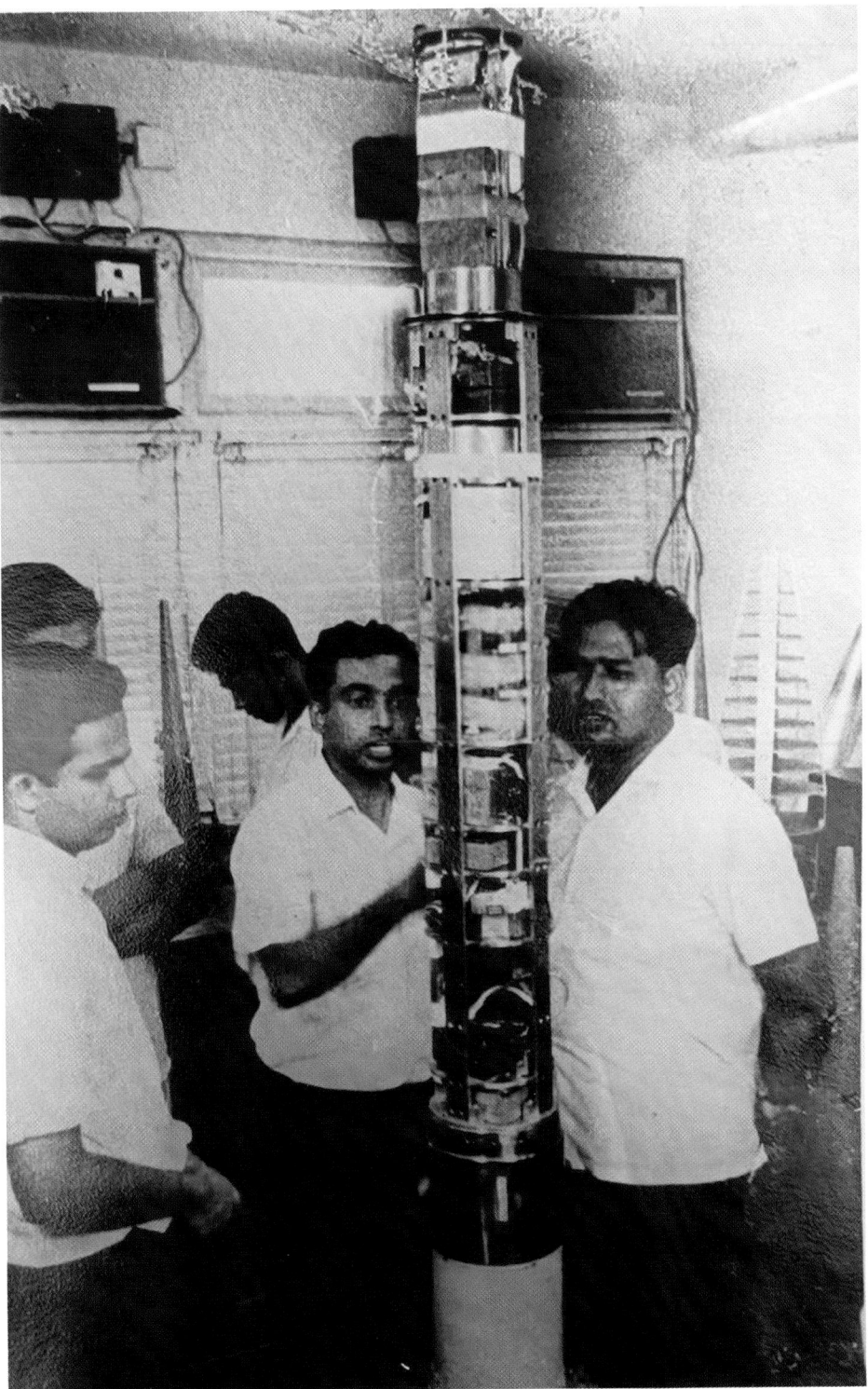

Plate 16 With the Nike-Apache sounding rocket. Kalam was responsible for rocket integration and safety.
(Source: Harry Sheridon, Private Secretary to President Kalam)
– *New to this edition*

Plate 17 (*In spite of the poor quality of the photograph, it has been included for its archival value*). With R Aravamudan (in vest), working on a sounding rocket payload. (Source: APJMJ Sheik Saleem) – *New to this edition*

Plate 18 (*In spite of the poor quality of the photograph, it has been included for its archival value*). RATO (Rocket Assisted Take Off) motor at the test stand at TERLS. (From left) JV Nair, MR Kurup, Thomas, MK Abdul Majeed, Kalam and Gp. Capt. Narayanan. (Source: *Ever Upwards: ISRO in Images*, Universities Press, 2019) – *New to this edition*

Plate 19 (*In spite of the poor quality of the photograph, it has been included for its archival value*). Sharing a happy moment with colleagues. (Source: APJMJ Sheik Saleem) – *New to this edition*

Plate 20 Two gurus of Indian Space Research who mentored and gently guided the young scientists – Prof. Satish Dhawan and Dr Brahm Prakash — at one of the SLV-3 review meetings.

Plate 21 *(In spite of the poor quality of the photograph, it has been included for its archival value).* In the old Composite Area of VSSC with Satish Dhawan and Yash Pal. (Source: APJMJ Sheik Saleem) – *New to this edition*

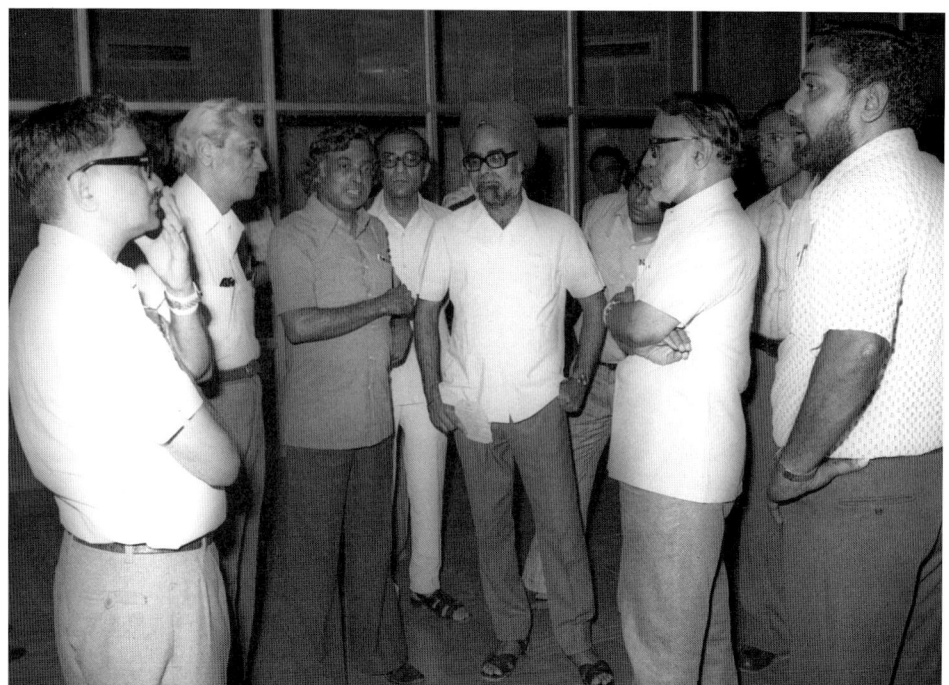

Plate 22 Briefing the Space Commission members in SHAR (8 August 1978). From left: Col N Pant, Satish Dhawan, Kalam, Manmohan Singh, MGK Menon, K Narayana and R Jayamani.
(Source: *Ever Upwards: ISRO in Images*, Universities Press, 2019)
– New to this edition

Plate 23 A presentation by a member of my SLV-3 team. In an unusual move, I made each of them present their portion of the work. My idea of participative project management.

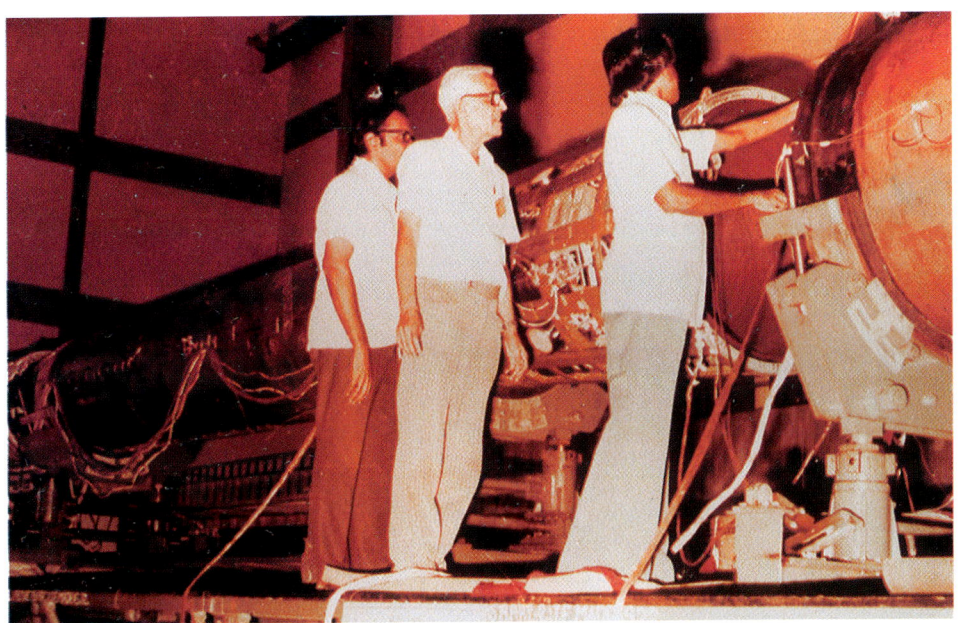

Plate 24 Prof. Brahm Prakash inspecting SLV-3 in its final phase of integration. He helped me deal with subsequent frustrations in its launching and consoled me when I was at my lowest ebb.

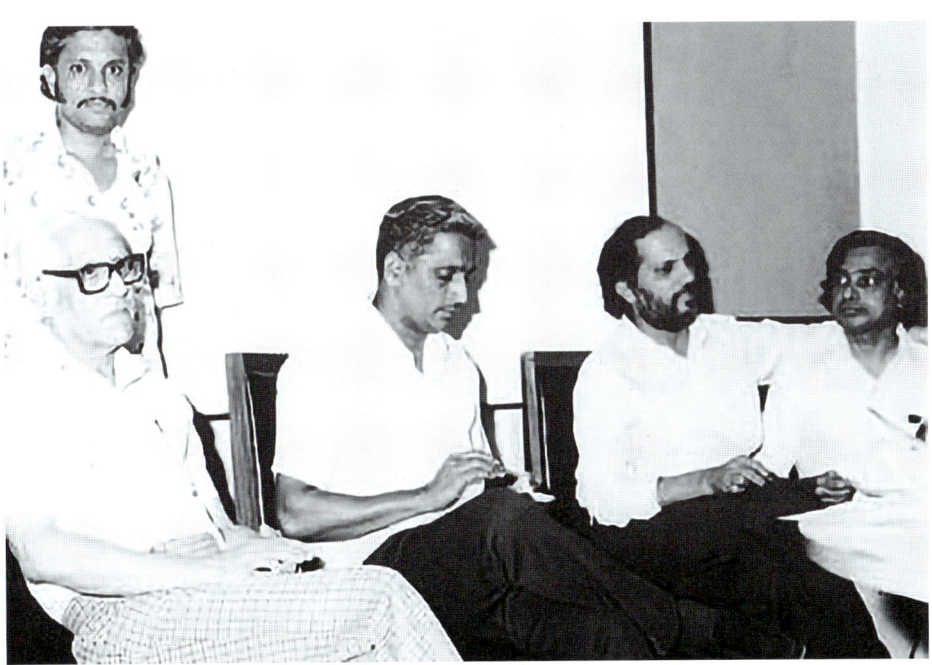

Plate 25 With Brahm Prakash, his PA, Vijayan (standing) and V R Gowariker. (Source: APJMJ Sheik Saleem) – *New to this edition*

Plate 26 A group photograph taken at VSSC during SLV-3 times. Sitting (from left): AE Muthunayagam, SC Gupta, VR Gowariker, Kalam, Satish Dhawan, Brahm Prakash, MR Kurup, D Easwaradas and R Aravamudan. Middle row (from left): TS Ram, Anantharam, N Vedachalam, V Sudhakar, BK Sarkar, K Sudhakara Rao, MK Abdul Majeed, EVS Namboodiri, G Madhavan Nair, VP Kulkarni, DS Rane and S Ramanath. Last row (from left): BC Pillai, T Pillai, CR Sathya, A Sivathanu Pillai, Sridharan Das, US Singh, MSR Dev, VP Sandlas, D Sasikumar, S Srinivasan, Sundararajan, MC Mathur, R Rajaram Nagappa, RS Bhute and Supramaniane. (Source: *Ever Upwards: ISRO in Images*, Universities Press, 2019) – *New to this edition*

Plate 27 Sharing a lighter moment with Satish Dhawan.
(Source: APJMJ Sheik Saleem) – *New to this edition*

Plate 28 During integration of the SLV-3 in Sriharikota.
Satish Dhawan flanked by S Srinivasan (left).
(Source: *Ever Upwards: ISRO in Images*, Universities Press, 2019)
– *New to this edition*

Plate 29 SLV-3 on the launch pad. This gave us many anxious moments!

Plate 30
Prof. Satish Dhawan and I explaining SLV-3 results to Prime Minister Indira Gandhi.

Plate 31
With Dr Raja Ramanna, the Chairman of the Atomic Energy Commission. (Source: APJMJ Sheik Saleem) – *New to this edition*

Plate 32
With Satish Dhawan in 1982. (Source: APJMJ Sheik Saleem) – *New to this edition*

Plate 33 Fully integrated ASLV on the launch pad.
(Source: *Ever Upwards: ISRO in Images*, Universities Press, 2019)
– *New to this edition*

Plate 34 With the fully assembled PSLV on it, the mobile launch pedestal leaves the Vehicle Assembly Building. Typical vehicle specification – Height: 44 m, Lift-off mass: 320 tonnes, Payload: 1750 kg in sun-synchronous polar orbit. (Source: *Ever Upwards: ISRO in Images*, Universities Press, 2019)
– New to this edition

Plate 35 Receiving the Padma Bhushan from President Neelam Sanjeeva Reddy in 1981.

Plate 36 The successful launch of *Prithvi*, the surface-to-surface missile system.

Plate 37 *Agni* on the launch pad, my long-cherished dream.

You said it
By LAXMAN

Plate 38 One of the cartoons in the media after the failure of the first two *Agni* launches.

Plate 39 Many a slip between the cup and the lip....

Plate 40 Being carried by a jubilant crowd after the successful launch of *Agni*.

Plate 41 With Prime Minister Rajiv Gandhi.
(Source: APJMJ Sheik Saleem) – *New to this edition*

III

PROPITIATION
[1981–1989]

Let craft, ambition, spite,
Be quenched in Reason's night,
Till weakness turn to might,
Till what is dark be light,
Till what is wrong be right!

Lewis Carroll

CHAPTER 10

A minor tussle over my services occurred at this time, between ISRO, which was a little hesitant to relieve me, and DRDO, which wanted to take me in. Many months went by, and many letters were exchanged between ISRO and DRDO; and meetings were held in the secretariats of the Defence R&D establishment and the Department of Space to precipitate a mutually convenient course of action. Meanwhile, Prof. Ramanna retired from the office of the Scientific Adviser to Defence Minister. Dr VS Arunachalam, till then Director of the Defence Metallurgical Research Laboratory (DMRL) in Hyderabad, succeeded Prof. Ramanna. Dr Arunachalam was known for his confidence, and he cared little for the intricacies and nuances of the scientific bureaucracy. Meanwhile, I understand that the Defence Minister at that time, R Venkataraman, discussed the matter of my taking over the missile laboratory with Prof. Dhawan. Prof. Dhawan also seemed to be waiting for a decisive step at the highest level in the Defence Ministry. Overcoming the niggling doubts that had caused delays over the past year, the decision to appoint me Director, DRDL was finally taken in February 1982.

Prof. Dhawan used to visit my room in the ISRO headquarters and spend many hours in evolving space launch vehicle projects. It was a great privilege to work with such a great scientist. Before I left ISRO, Prof. Dhawan asked me to give a talk on the Space Programme Profile in India by the year 2000. Almost the entire ISRO management and staff attended my talk, which was by way of a farewell meeting.

I had met Dr VS Arunachalam in 1976, when I visited DMRL in connection with the aluminium alloy investment casting for the SLV inertial guidance platform. Taking it as a personal challenge, Dr Arunachalam had the investment casting, the first of its kind in the country, made in the incredibly short time of two months. His youthful energy and enthusiasm never failed to amaze me. This young metallurgist had within a short span of time lifted the science of metal-making to the technology of metal-forming and then to the art of alloy development. With a tall and elegant figure, Dr Arunachalam was like an electrically charged dynamo himself. I found him an unusually friendly person with a forceful manner, as well as an excellent working partner.

I visited DRDL in April 1982 to acquaint myself with my potential work site. The Director of DRDL then, SL Bansal, took me around and introduced me to the senior scientists in the laboratory. DRDL was working on five staff projects and sixteen competence build-up projects. They were also involved in several technology-oriented activities with a view to gain lead time for the development of indigenous missile systems in future. I was particularly impressed by their efforts on the twin 30 tonne Liquid Propellant Rocket Engine.

Meanwhile, Anna University, Madras, conferred the honorary degree of Doctor of Science on me. It had been nearly twenty years since I had acquired my degree in aeronautical engineering. I was happy that Anna University had recognized my efforts in the field of rocketry, but what pleased me most was the recognition of the value of our work in academic circles. To my delight, the honorary doctorate degree was awarded at a convocation presided over by Prof. Raja Ramanna.

I joined DRDL on 1 June 1982. Very soon, I realized that this laboratory was still haunted by the winding up of the *Devil* missile project. Many excellent professionals had not yet recovered from the disappointment. People outside the scientific world may find it difficult to comprehend how a scientist feels when the umbilical cord to his work is suddenly snapped, for reasons totally alien to his understanding and interests. The general mood and work tempo at DRDL reminded me of Samuel Taylor Coleridge's poem, *The Rime of the Ancient Mariner*:

> *Day after day, day after day,*
> *We stuck, nor breath, nor motion;*
> *As idle as a painted ship*
> *Upon a painted ocean.*

I found almost all my senior colleagues living with the pain of dashed hopes. There was a widespread feeling that the scientists of this laboratory had been cheated by the senior officials in the Ministry of Defence. It was clear to me that the burial of the Devil was essential for the rise of hope and vision.

When about a month later, Admiral OS Dawson, then the Chief of Naval Staff, visited DRDL, I used it as an opportunity to make a point with my team. The Tactical Core Vehicle (TCV) project had been hanging fire for quite some time. It was conceived as a single core vehicle with certain common subsystems to meet the requirements of the services for a quick reaction Surface-to-Air Missile, and an anti-radiation Air-to-Surface Missile which could be launched from helicopters or fixed wing aircraft. I emphasized the sea-skimming role of the core vehicle to Admiral Dawson. I focussed not on its technical intricacies, but on its battlefield capabilities; and I highlighted the production plans. The message was loud and clear to my new associates—do not make anything which you cannot sell later and do not spend your life on making one thing only. Missile development is a multi-dimensional business—if you remain in any one dimension for a long time, you will get stuck.

My initial few months at DRDL were largely interactive. I had read at St. Joseph's that an electron may appear as a particle or wave depending on how you look at it. If you ask a particle question, it will give you a particle answer; if you ask a wave question, it will give you a wave answer. I not only described and explained our goals, but also made them an interplay between our work and ourselves. I still recall quoting Ronald Fischer at one of the meetings, "The sweetness we taste in a piece of sugar is neither a property of the sugar nor a property of ourselves. We are producing the experience of sweetness in the process of interacting with the sugar."

Very good work on a Surface-to-Surface missile with a vertical rise-turn straight line climb-ballistic path had been done by that time. I was astonished to see the determination of the DRDL workforce, who, in spite of the premature winding up of their earlier projects, were eager to go ahead. I arranged reviews for its various subsystems, to arrive at precise specifications. To the horror of many old-timers in DRDO, I started inviting people from the Indian Institute of Science, Indian Institutes of Technology, Council for Scientific and Industrial Research, Tata Institute of Fundamental Research, and many other educational institutions where related experts could be found. I felt that the stuffy work centres of DRDL needed a breath of fresh air. Once we opened the windows wide, the light of scientific talent began to pour in. Once more, Coleridge's *Ancient Mariner* came to mind: "*Swiftly, swiftly flew the ship, Riding gently the oncoming tide.*"

Sometime in the beginning of 1983, Prof. Dhawan visited DRDL. I reminded him of his own advice to me almost a decade ago: "You have to dream before your dreams can come true. Some people stride towards whatever it is that they want in life; others shuffle their feet and never get started because they do not know what they want—and do not know how to find it either." ISRO was lucky to have had Prof. Sarabhai and Prof. Dhawan at the helm—leaders who elucidated their goals, made their missions larger than their lives, and could then inspire their entire workforce. DRDL had not been so lucky. This excellent laboratory played a truncated role that did not reflect its existing or potential capabilities or even fulfill the expectations in South Block. I told Prof. Dhawan about the highly professional, but slightly bewildered team I had. Prof. Dhawan responded with his characteristic broad smile which could be interpreted in any way one chose.

In order to accelerate the pace of R&D activities at DRDL, it was imperative that decisions on vital scientific, technical and technological problems be taken quickly. Throughout my career I had zealously pursued openness in scientific matters. I had seen from very close quarters the decay and disintegration that go with management through closed-door consultations and secret manipulations. I always despised and resisted such efforts. So the first major decision which we took was to create a forum of senior scientists where important matters could be discussed and debated as a collective endeavour. Thus, a high-level body called the Missile Technology Committee was formed within DRDL. The concept of management by participation was evoked and earnest efforts were made to involve middle-level scientists and engineers in the management activities of the laboratory.

Days of debate and weeks of thinking finally culminated in the long-term 'Guided Missile Development Programme'. I had read somewhere, "Know where you are going. The great thing in the world is not knowing so much where we stand, as in what direction we are moving." So what if we did not have the technological might of the Western countries? We knew we had to attain that might, and this determination was our driving force. To draw up a clear and well-defined missile development programme for the production of indigenous missiles, a committee was constituted under my chairmanship. The members were ZP Marshall, then the Chief of Bharat Dynamics Limited, Hyderabad, NR Iyer, AK Kapoor and KS Venkataraman. We drafted a paper for the perusal of the Cabinet Committee for Political Affairs (CCPA). The paper was given its final shape after consulting the representatives of the three Defence Services. We estimated an expenditure of about Rs 390 crores, spread over a period of twelve years.

Development programmes often get stuck by the time they reach the production stage, mainly because of lack of funding. We wanted to get funds to develop and produce two missiles—a low-level quick reaction Tactical Core Vehicle and a medium-range Surface-to-Surface Weapon

System. We planned to make a surface-to-air medium-range weapon system with multi-target handling capability during the second phase. DRDL had been known for its pioneering work in the field of anti-tank missiles. We proposed to develop a third generation anti-tank guided missile having 'fire-and-forget' capabilities. All my colleagues were pleased with the proposal. They saw an opportunity to pursue afresh activities initiated long ago. But I was not entirely satisfied. I longed to revive my buried dream of a Re-entry Experiment Launch Vehicle (REX). I persuaded my colleagues to take up a technology development project to generate data for use in the design of heat shields. These shields were required for building up capability to make long-range missiles in the future.

I made a presentation in South Block. The presentation was presided over by the Defence Minister of the time, R Venkataraman, and attended by the three Service Chiefs: General Krishna Rao, Air Chief Marshal Dilbagh Singh and Admiral Dawson. The Cabinet Secretary, Krishna Rao Sahib, Defence Secretary, SM Ghosh, and Secretary, Expenditure, R Ganapathy, were present. Everyone seemed to have all sorts of doubts—about our capabilities, about the feasibility and availability of required technological infrastructure, about the viability; the schedule and cost. Dr Arunachalam stood by me like a rock throughout the entire question-answer session. Members were skeptical and apprehensive of drift—which they felt was common among scientists. Although some questioned our ambitious proposal, everyone, even the doubting Thomases, were very excited about the idea of India having her own missile systems. In the end, we were asked by Defence Minister Venkataraman to meet him in the evening, about three hours later.

We spent the intervening time working on permutations and combinations. If they sanctioned only Rs 100 crores, how would we allocate it? Suppose they gave us Rs 200 crores, then what would we do? When we met the Defence Minister in the evening, I had a hunch we were going to get some funds at any rate. But when he suggested that we launch an integrated guided missile development programme, instead of making missiles in phases, we could not believe our ears.

We were quite dumbfounded by the Defence Minister's suggestion. After a long pause, Dr Arunachalam replied, "We beg for time to rethink and return, sir!" "You come back tomorrow morning, please," the Defence Minister replied. It was reminiscent of Prof. Sarabhai's zeal and vision. That night, Dr Arunachalam and I laboured together on reworking our plan.

We worked out some very important extensions and improvements in our proposal, taking all the variables, such as design, fabrication, system integration, qualification, experimental flights, evaluation, updating, user trials, producibility, quality, reliability, and financial viability into account. We then integrated them into a single function of total accountability, in order to meet the needs of the country's armed forces with an indigenous endeavour. We worked out the concepts of design, development, production concurrency and proposed the participation of user and inspection agencies right from the drawing-board stage. We also suggested a methodology to achieve state-of-the-art systems after all the years of developmental activities. We wanted to deliver contemporary missiles to our Services and not some outdated inventory of weapons. It was a very exciting challenge that had been thrown to us.

By the time we finished our work, it was already morning. Suddenly, at the breakfast table, I remembered that I was to attend my niece Zameela's wedding at Rameswaram that evening. I thought it was already too late to do anything. Even if I could catch the Madras flight later in the day, how would I reach Rameswaram from there? There was no air link between Madras and Madurai from where I could board the evening train to Rameswaram. A pang of guilt dampened my spirits. Was it fair, I asked myself, to forget my family commitments and obligations? Zameela was more like a daughter to me. The thought of missing her wedding because of professional preoccupations at Delhi was very distressing. I finished breakfast and left for the meeting.

When we met Defence Minister Venkataraman and showed him our revised proposal, he was visibly pleased. The proposal of the missile development project had been turned overnight into the blueprint of an integrated programme with far-reaching consequences. It would have wide-ranging technological spin-offs, and was exactly what the Defence Minister had had in mind the previous evening. Notwithstanding the great respect I had for the Defence Minister, I was not really sure if he would clear our entire proposal. But he did. I was absolutely delighted!

The Defence Minister stood up, signalling that the meeting was over. Turning to me, he said, "Since I brought you here, I was expecting you to come up with something like this. I am happy to see your work." In a split second, the mystery surrounding the clearance of my appointment as Director, DRDL in 1982 was cleared. So it was Defence Minister Venkataraman who had brought me in! Bowing in thanks, I turned towards the door when I heard Dr Arunachalam telling the Minister about Zameela's wedding being scheduled for that evening at

Rameswaram. It amazed me that Dr Arunachalam should bring up this matter before the Minister. Why would a person of his stature, sitting in the all-powerful South Block, be concerned about a wedding which was to take place on a far-flung island in a small house on Mosque Street?

I have always had a high regard for Dr Arunachalam. He has, together with a command over language, as he displayed on this occasion, an uncanny presence of mind. I was overwhelmed when the Defence Minister located an Air Force helicopter doing sorties between Madras and Madurai later in the day to take me to Madurai as soon as I disembarked at Madras from the regular Indian Airlines flight, which was leaving Delhi in an hour's time. Dr Arunachalam told me, "You have earned this for your hard work of the last six months."

Flying towards Madras, I scribbled on the back of my boarding pass:

Who never climbed the weary league —
Can such a foot explore
The purple territories
On Rameswaram's shore?

The Air Force helicopter landed close to the Indian Airlines aircraft as soon as it arrived from Delhi. Within the next few minutes I was on my way to Madurai. The Air Force commandant there was kind enough to take me to the railway station, where the train to Rameswaram was just about to roll out of the platform. I was in Rameswaram well in time for Zameela's wedding. I blessed my brother's daughter with a father's love.

The Defence Minister put up our proposal before the Cabinet and saw it through. His recommendations on our proposal were accepted and an unprecedented amount of Rs 388 crores was sanctioned for this purpose. Thus was born India's prestigious Integrated Guided Missile Development Programme, later abbreviated to IGMDP.

When I presented the government sanction letter before the Missile Technology Committee at DRDL, they were enthused with fire and action. The proposed projects were christened in accordance with the spirit of India's self-reliance. Thus, the Surface-to-Surface weapon system became *Prithvi* ("the Earth") and the Tactical Core Vehicle was called *Trishul* (the trident of Lord Shiva). The Surface-to-Air area defence system was named *Akash* ("sky") and the anti-tank missile project *Nag* ("Cobra"). I gave the name *Agni* ("Fire") to my long cherished dream of REX. Dr Arunachalam came to DRDL and formally launched the

IGMDP on 27 July 1983. It was a great event in which every single employee of DRDL participated. Everybody who was somebody in Indian Aerospace Research was invited. A large number of scientists from other laboratories and organizations, professors from academic institutions, representatives of the armed forces, production centres, and inspection authorities, who were our business partners now, were present on this occasion. A closed-circuit TV network had to be pressed into operation to ensure proper communication between the participants for we had no single place to accommodate all the invitees. This was the second most significant day in my career, next only to 18 July 1980, when the SLV-3 had launched Rohini into the Earth's orbit.

CHAPTER 11

The launch of the IGMDP was like a bright flash on the Indian scientific firmament. Missile Technology had been considered the domain of a few selected nations in the world. People were curious to see how, with what India had at that point of time, we were going to achieve all that was promised. The magnitude of the IGMDP was really unprecedented in the country and the schedules projected were quite quixotic by the norms and standards prevailing in Indian R&D establishments. I was fully aware that obtaining sanction for the programme could at best be seen as only ten per cent of the work done. To get it going would be quite a different matter altogether. The more you have, the more there is to maintain. Now that we had been given all the necessary money and freedom to proceed, I had to take my team forward and fulfill the promises I had made.

What would be needed to realize this missile programme, from the design to the deployment stages? Excellent manpower was available; money had been sanctioned; and some infrastructure also existed. What was lacking then? What else does a project need to succeed apart from these three vital inputs? From my SLV-3 experience, I thought I knew the answer. The crux was going to be our mastery over missile technology. I expected nothing from abroad. Technology is a group activity and we would need leaders who could not only put their heart and soul into the missile programme, but also carry along with them hundreds of other engineers and scientists. We knew we had to be prepared to encounter numerous contradictions and procedural absurdities that were prevalent in the participating laboratories. We would have to counteract the existing attitudes of our public sector units, which believed that their performance would never be tested. The whole system—its people, procedures, infrastructure—would have to learn to extend itself. We decided to achieve something that was way beyond our collective national capability and I, for one, had no illusions about the fact that unless our teams worked on the basis of proportion or probability, nothing would be achieved.

The most remarkable thing about DRDL was its large pool of highly talented people, many of whom were, unfortunately, full of egotism and rebelliousness. Unfortunately, they had not even accumulated enough experience to make them confident about their own judgement. On the whole, they would discuss matters very enthusiastically, but would finally accept what a select few said. They would unquestioningly believe in outside specialists.

A particularly interesting person I met in DRDL was AV Ranga Rao. He was very articulate and had an impressive personality. His usual garb consisted of a red neck-tie with a checked coat and loose trousers. He would wear this in the hot climate of Hyderabad, where even a long-sleeved shirt and shoes are considered an avoidable inconvenience. With his thick white beard and a pipe clamped between his teeth, there was a certain aura around this extremely gifted, but rather egocentric individual.

I consulted Ranga Rao on revamping the existing management system to achieve an optimum utilization of human resources. Ranga Rao had a series of meetings with the scientists sharing our vision of developing indigenous missile technology and explaining the different aspects of the IGMDP. After prolonged discussions, we decided to reorganize the laboratory into a technology-oriented structure. We needed to accommodate a matrix type of structure for the execution of various activities needed for the projects. In less than four months, four hundred scientists began to work on the missile programme.

During this period, the most important task before me was the selection of the Project Directors to lead individual missile projects. We had a very large pool of talent. In fact, it was a market of plenty. The question was whom to pick—a go-getter, a planner, a maverick, a dictator or a team man? I had to get the right type of leader who could clearly visualize the goal, and channelize the energies of his team members who would be working at different work centres in pursuit of their own individual goals.

It was a difficult game, some rules of which I had learnt while working on ISRO's high priority projects for two decades. The wrong choice would jeopardize the entire future of the programme. I had a detailed discussion with a large number of prospective scientists and engineers. I wanted these five Project Directors to train another twenty-five project directors and team leaders of tomorrow.

Many of my senior colleagues—naming them would be unfair, because it could be only my imagination—tried to befriend me during this period. I respected their concern for a lonely man, but avoided any close contacts. Through loyalty to a friend one can be easily led into doing something that is not in the best interests of the organization.

Perhaps the main motive behind my isolation was my desire to escape from the demands of relationships, which I consider very difficult in comparison to making rockets. All I desired was to be true to my way of life, to uphold the science of rocketry in my country and to retire with a clean conscience. I took quite some time and did a lot of hard thinking to decide who should lead the five projects. I examined the working styles of many scientists before making my decision. I think some of my observations may interest you.

A basic aspect of a person's working style is how he plans and organizes tasks. At one extreme is the cautious planner, who carefully spells out each step before making any move. With a sharp eye for what can possibly go wrong, he tries to cover all contingencies. At the other end is the fast mover, who weaves and dodges without a plan. Inspired by an idea, the fast mover is always ready for action.

Another aspect of a person's working style is control—the energy and attention devoted to ensuring that things happen in a certain way. At one extreme is the tight controller, a strict administrator with frequent checkpoints. Rules and policies are to be followed with religious fervour. At the opposite end are those who move with freedom and flexibility. They have little patience for bureaucracy. They delegate easily and give their subordinates wide latitude for movement. I wanted leaders who tread the middle path, those who could control without stifling dissent or being rigid.

I wanted men who had the capability to grow with possibilities, with the patience to explore all possible alternatives, with the wisdom to apply old principles to new situations; people with the skill to negotiate their way forward. I wanted them to be accommodating, to be willing to share their power with others and work in teams, delegating good jobs, assimilating fresh opinions, respecting intelligent people, and listening to wise counsel. They would have to be able to sort out things amicably, and take responsibility for slip-ups. Above all, they should be able to take failure in their stride and share in both success and failure.

My search for someone to lead the *Prithvi* project ended with Col VJ Sundaram who belonged to the EME Corps of the Indian Army. With a post-graduate degree in Aeronautical Engineering and expertise in mechanical vibrations, Sundaram was head of the Structures Group at DRDL. I found in him a readiness to experiment with new ways of resolving conflicting points of view. He was an experimenter and innovator in team work. He had an extraordinary capability for evaluating alternative ways of operating. He would suggest moving forward into new terrains that could lead to a solution which had not been perceived earlier. Though a particular goal might be clear to a project leader, and he may be capable of giving adequate directions for accomplishing it, there can be resistance from subordinates if the goal makes no sense to them. Therein lies the importance of a leader who provides effective work directions. I thought the Project Director of *Prithvi* would be the first to make decisions with production agencies and the armed forces, and Sundaram would be the ideal choice to see that sound decisions were taken.

For *Trishul*, I was looking for a man who not only had a sound knowledge of electronics and missile warfare, but who could also communicate the complexities to his team in order to promote understanding and to earn his team's support. I found in Cmde SR Mohan, who sailed into Defence R&D from the Indian Navy, a talent for detail and an almost magical power of persuasion.

For *Agni*, my dream project, I needed somebody who would tolerate my occasional meddling in the running of this project. In RN Agarwal I found the right person. He was an alumnus of MIT with a brilliant academic record and had been managing the Aeronautical Test Facilities at DRDL with keen professional acumen.

Due to technological complexities, *Akash* and *Nag* were then considered missiles of the future; their activities were expected to peak about half a decade later. Therefore, I selected the relatively young Prahlada and NR Iyer for *Akash* and *Nag*. Two other young men, VK Saraswat and AK Kapoor, were made deputies to Sundaram and Mohan, respectively.

In those days, there was no forum in DRDL where issues of general importance could be openly discussed and decisions debated. Scientists, it must be remembered, are basically emotional people. Once they stumble, it is difficult for them to pull themselves together. Setbacks and disappointments have always been and always will be an inherent part of any career, even one in science. However, I did not want any of my scientists to face disappointments alone. I also wanted to ensure that none of them set their goals when they were at a low ebb. To avoid such eventualities a Science Council was created—a sort of *panchayat* where the community would sit together and take common decisions. Every three months, all scientists—juniors and seniors, veterans and freshers—would sit together and let off steam.

The very first meeting of the Council was eventful. After a spell of half-hearted enquiries and expressions of doubt, one senior scientist, MN Rao, shot a straight question: "On what basis did you select these five Pandavas (he meant the Project Directors)?" I was, in fact, expecting this question. I wanted to tell him that I found all these five

Pandavas married to the Draupadi of positive thinking. Instead, I told Rao to wait and see. I had chosen them to take charge of a long-term programme where new storms would arise every day.

Every tomorrow, I told Rao, will give opportunities to these enthusiastic people—the Agarwals, Prahladas, Iyers, and Saraswats—to gain a fresh perspective on their goals and a strong hold on their commitments.

What makes a productive leader? In my opinion, a productive leader must be very competent in staffing. He should continually introduce new blood into the organization. He must be adept at dealing with problems and new concepts. The problems encountered by an R&D organization typically involve trade-offs among a wide variety of known and unknown parameters. Skill in handling these complex entities is important in achieving high productivity. The leader must be capable of instilling enthusiasm in his team. He should give appropriate credit where it is due; praise publicly, but criticize privately.

One of the most difficult questions came from a young scientist: "How are you going to stop these projects from going the *Devil* way?" I explained to him the philosophy behind IGMDP—it begins with design and ends in deployment. The participation of the production centres and user agencies right from the design stage had been ensured and there was no question of going back till the missile systems had been successfully deployed in the battlefield.

While the process of forming teams and organizing work was going on, I found that the space available at DRDL was grossly inadequate to meet the enhanced requirements of IGMDP. Some of the facilities would have to be located at a nearby site. The missile integration and checkout facility built during the *Devil* phase consisted only of a 120 sq. metre shed thickly populated with pigeons. Where was the space and the facility to integrate the five missiles which would arrive here shortly? The Environmental Test Facility and the Avionics Laboratory were equally cramped and ill-equipped.

I visited the nearby Imarat Kancha area. It used to be the test range for anti-tank missiles developed by DRDL decades ago. The terrain was barren—there were hardly any trees—and dotted with large boulders typical of the Deccan plateau. I felt as if there was some tremendous energy trapped in these stones. I decided to locate the integration and checkout facilities needed for the missile projects here. For the next three years, this became my mission.

We drew up a proposal to establish a model high-technology research centre with very advanced technical facilities like an inertial instrumentation laboratory, full-scale environmental and electronic warfare (EMI/EMC) test facilities, a composites production centre, high enthalpy facility, and a state-of-the-art missile integration and checkout centre. By any standards, this was a gigantic task. An altogether different brand of expertise, grit and determination were required to realize this project. Goals and objectives had already been decided upon. Now they had to be shared with a large number of people from various agencies, through the problem-solving and communication processes that the leader of the team must build and maintain. Who would be the most suitable person to do so? I saw almost all the required leadership qualities in MV Suryakantha Rao. Then, as a large number of agencies would participate in the creation of Research Centre Imarat (RCI), someone had to protect hierarchical sensitivities. I selected Krishna Mohan, who was in his mid-thirties, to complement Suryakantha Rao, who was in his late fifties at that time. Krishna Mohan would encourage involvement rather than relying on obedience and monitoring people at their workplaces.

According to the established procedure, we approached the Military Engineering Services (MES) for the RCI construction work. They said it would take five years to complete the task. The matter was discussed in depth at the highest level in the Ministry of Defence and a landmark decision to entrust the responsibility of building defence structures to an outside construction company was taken. We liaised with the Survey of India and the National Remote Sensing Agency for the inspection of the contour maps and for obtaining aerial photographs of the Imarat Kancha to prepare a layout for the approach roads and the location of the facilities. The Central Ground Water Board identified twenty locations amid the rocks to tap water. Infrastructure to provide 40 MVA power and 5 million litres of water per day was planned.

It was also at this time that Col SK Salwan, a mechanical engineer with boundless energy, joined us. In the final phase of construction, Salwan discovered an ancient place of worship among the boulders. It seemed to me that this place was blessed.

Now that we had started working on the design of the missile systems and development had already commenced for their integration and checkout, the next logical step was to look for a suitable site for the missile flight trials. With SHAR also in Andhra Pradesh, the search for a suitable site spread towards the eastern coastline and finally ended at Balasore in Orissa. A site along the north-eastern coast was identified for a National Test Range. Unfortunately the entire project ran into rough weather because of the political issues raised around the evacuation of people living in that area. We decided therefore to create an interim infrastructure adjacent to the Proof Experimental Establishment (PXE) at Chandipur in Balasore district of Orissa. A funding of Rs 30 crores had been given to construct the range, called the Interim Test Range (ITR). Dr HS Rama Rao and his team did an excellent job of working out innovative and cost-effective specifications for electro-optical tracking instruments, a tracking telescope system and an instrumentation tracking radar. Lt Gen RS Deswal and Maj Gen KN Singh took charge of creating the launch pad and range infrastructure. There was a beautiful bird sanctuary in Chandipur. I asked the engineers to design the test range without disturbing it.

Creating the RCI was perhaps the most satisfying experience of my life. Developing this centre of excellence of missile technology was akin to the joy of a potter shaping artifacts of lasting beauty from the mundane clay.

Defence Minister R Venkataraman visited DRDL in September 1983 to appraise himself of the activities of IGMDP. He advised us to list all the resources we needed to achieve our goals, overlooking nothing, and then include in the list our own positive imagination and faith. "What you imagine is what will transpire. What you believe is what you will achieve," he said. Both Dr Arunachalam and I saw in the horizon endless possibilities stretching out before IGMDP; and our enthusiasm proved infectious. We were excited and encouraged to see the best professionals in the country gravitating towards IGMDP. Who would not want to associate with a winner? The word had evidently got around that the IGMDP was a born winner.

CHAPTER 12

We were at a meeting laying down the targets for 1984, when news came of Dr Brahm Prakash's death on the evening of 3 January at Bombay. It was a great emotional loss for me, for I had had the privilege of working under him during the most challenging period of my career. His compassion and humility were exemplary. His healing touch on the day of the failed SLV-E1 flight surfaced in my memory, serving to deepen my sorrow.

If Prof. Sarabhai was the creator of VSSC, Dr Brahm Prakash was the executor. He had nurtured the institution when it most needed nourishment. Dr Brahm Prakash played a very important role in shaping my leadership skills. In fact my association with him was a turning point in my life. His humility mellowed me and helped me discard my aggressive approach. His humility did not consist merely in being modest about his talents or virtues, but in respecting the dignity of all those who worked under him and in recognizing the fact that no one is infallible, not even the leader. He was an intellectual giant with a frail constitution; he had a childlike innocence and I always considered him a saint among scientists.

During this period of renaissance at DRDL, an altitude control system and an on-board computer developed by P Banerjee, KV Ramana Sai and their team was almost ready. The success of this effort was very vital for any indigenous missile development programme. All the same, we had to have a missile to test this important system.

After many brainstorming sessions, we decided to improvise a *Devil* missile to test the system. A *Devil* missile was disassembled, many modifications made, extensive subsystem testing was done and the missile checkout system was reconfigured. After installing a makeshift launcher, the modified and extended-range *Devil* missile was fired on 26 June 1984 to flight test the first indigenous Strap-down Inertial Guidance system. The system met all the requirements. This was the first and very significant step in the history of Indian missile development, which had so far been restricted to reverse engineering, towards designing our own systems. A long-denied opportunity was at last utilized by missile scientists at DRDL. The message was loud and clear. We could do it!

It did not take long for the message to reach Delhi. Prime Minister Indira Gandhi expressed her desire to personally apprise herself of the progress of the IGMDP. The entire organization was filled with an aura of excitement. On 19 July 1984, Shrimati Gandhi visited DRDL.

Prime Minister Indira Gandhi was a person with a tremendous sense of pride—in herself, in her work and in her country. I deemed it an honour to receive her at DRDL as she had instilled some of her own pride into my otherwise modest frame of mind. She was immensely conscious that she was the leader of eight hundred million people. Every step, every gesture, every movement of her hands was optimized. The esteem in which she held our work in the field of guided missiles boosted our morale immensely.

During the one hour that she spent at DRDL, she covered wide-ranging aspects of the IGMDP, from flight system plans to multiple development laboratories. In the end, she addressed the 2000-strong DRDL community. She asked for the schedules of the flight system that we were working on. "When are you going to flight test *Prithvi?*" Shrimati Gandhi asked. I said, "June 1987." She immediately responded, "Let me know what is needed to accelerate the flight schedule." She wanted scientific and technological results fast. "Your fast pace of work is the hope of the entire nation," she said. She also told me that the emphasis of the IGMDP should be not only on schedule but also on the pursuance of excellence. "No matter what you achieve, you should never be completely satisfied and should always be searching for ways to prove yourself," she added. Within a month, she demonstrated her interest and support by sending the newly appointed Defence Minister, SB Chavan, to review our projects. Shrimati Gandhi's follow-up approach was not only impressive, it was effective too. Today, everyone associated with aerospace research in our country knows that excellence is synonymous with the IGMDP.

We had our home-grown, but effective, management techniques. One such technique was concerned with follow-up of project activities. It basically consisted of analysing the technical as well as procedural applicability of a possible solution, testing it with the work centres, discussing it with the general body of associates and implementing it after enlisting everybody's support. A large number of original ideas sprung up from the grass root level of participating work centres. If you were to ask me to indicate the single most important managerial tactic in this successful programme, I would point to the pro-active follow-up. Through follow-up on the work done at different laboratories on design, planning, supporting services, and by the inspection agencies and academic institutions, rapid progress has been achieved in the most harmonious manner. In fact, the work code in the Guided Missile Programme Office was: if you need to write a letter to a work centre, send a fax; if you need to send a telex or fax, telephone; and if the need arises for telephonic discussions, visit the place personally.

The power of this approach came to light when Dr Arunachalam conducted a comprehensive status review of IGMDP on 27 September 1984. Experts from DRDO Laboratories, ISRO, academic institutions, and production agencies gathered to critically review the progress made and problems faced in the first year of implementation. Major decisions like the creation of facilities at Imarat Kancha and the establishment of a test facility were crystallized during the review. The future infrastructure at the Imarat Kancha was given the name of Research Centre Imarat (RCI), retaining the original identity of the place.

It was a pleasure to find an old acquaintance, TN Seshan, on the review board. Between SLV-3 and now, we had developed a mutual affection. However, this time as the Defence Secretary, Seshan's queries about the schedules and viability of financial propositions presented were much more pointed. Seshan is a person who enjoys verbally bringing adversaries to their knees. Using his sharp-edged humour, Seshan would make his opponents look ridiculous. Although he is prone to be loud and can turn argumentative on occasion, in the end he would always ensure maximization of all available resources towards a solution that was within implementation. At a personal level, Seshan is a very kind-hearted and considerate person. My team was particularly pleased to answer his questions about the advanced technology employed in the IGMDP. I still remember his uncanny curiosity about the indigenous development of carbon-carbon composites. And to let you into a small secret—Seshan is perhaps the only person in the world who enjoys calling me by my full name which contains 31 letters and five words—Avul Pakir Jainulabdeen Abdul Kalam.

The missile programme had been pursued concurrently and had partners in design, development and production from 12 academic institutions and 30 laboratories from DRDO, the Council of Scientific and Industrial Research (CSIR), ISRO and industry. In fact, more than 50 professors and 100 research scholars worked on missile-related problems in the laboratories of their respective institutes. The quality of work achieved through this partnership in that one year had given me tremendous confidence that any development task could be undertaken within the country so long as we have our focussed schedules. Four months before this review, I think it was during April–June 1984, six of us in the missile programme visited academic campuses and enlisted promising young graduates. We presented an outline of the missile programme before the professors and the aspiring students, about 350 of them, and requested them to participate. I informed the reviewers that we were expecting around 300 young engineers to join our laboratories.

Roddam Narasimha, then Director of the National Aeronautical Laboratory, used the occasion of this review to put up a strong case for technology initiative. He cited the experiences of the Green Revolution, which had demonstrated beyond doubt that if the goals were clear, there was enough talent available in the country to tackle major technological challenges.

When India carried out its first nuclear explosion for peaceful purposes, we declared ourselves the sixth country in the world to explode a nuclear device. When we launched SLV-3 we were the fifth country to achieve satellite launch capability. When were we going to be the first or second country in the world to achieve a technological feat?

I listened carefully to the review members as they aired their opinions and doubts, and I learned from their collective wisdom. It was indeed a great education for me. Ironically, all through school, we were taught to read, write and speak, but never to listen, and the situation remains much the same today. Traditionally, Indian scientists have been very good speakers, but have inadequately developed listening skills. We made a resolution to be attentive listeners. Are engineering structures not built on the foundation of functional utility? Does technical know-how not form its bricks? And, are these bricks not put together with the mortar of constructive criticism? The foundation had been laid, the bricks baked, and now the mortar to cement our act together was being mixed.

We were working on the action plan that had emerged from the earlier month's review, when the news of Shrimati Gandhi's assassination broke. This was followed by the news of widespread violence and riots. A curfew had been imposed in Hyderabad city. We rolled up the PERT charts and a city map was spread out over the table to organize transport and safe passage for all employees. In less than an hour, the laboratory wore a deserted look. I was left sitting alone in my office. The circumstances of Shrimati Gandhi's death were very ominous. The memories of her visit barely three months ago further deepened my pain. Why should great people meet with such horrific ends? I recollected my father telling someone in a similar context: "Good and bad people live together under the sun as the black thread and the white are woven together in a cloth. When either one of the black or white thread breaks, the weaver shall look into the whole cloth, and he shall examine the loom also." When I drove out of the laboratory there was not a single soul on the road. I kept thinking about the loom of the broken thread.

Shrimati Gandhi's death was a tremendous loss to the scientific community. She had given impetus to scientific research in the country. But India is a very resilient nation. It gradually absorbed the shock of Shrimati Gandhi's assassination, although at the cost of thousands of lives and a colossal loss of property. Her son, Rajiv Gandhi, took over as the new Prime Minister of India. He went to the polls and obtained a mandate from the people to carry forward the policies of Mrs. Gandhi, the Integrated Guided Missile Development Programme being a part of them.

By the summer of 1985, all the groundwork had been completed for building the Missile Technology Research Centre at Imarat Kancha. Prime Minister Rajiv Gandhi laid the foundation stone of the RCI on 3 August 1985. He appeared very pleased with the progress made. There was a childlike curiosity in him which was very engaging. The grit and determination displayed by his mother when she visited us a year ago was also present in him, although with a small difference. Shrimati Gandhi was a taskmaster, whereas Prime Minister Rajiv Gandhi used his charisma to achieve his ends. He told the DRDL family that he realized the hardships faced by Indian scientists and expressed his gratitude towards those who preferred to stay back and work in their motherland rather than go abroad for comfortable careers. He said that nobody could concentrate on work of this type unless he was free from the trivialities of daily life, and assured us that whatever was necessary would be done to make scientists' lives more comfortable.

Within a week of his visit, I left for the USA with Dr Arunachalam on an invitation from the United States Air Force. Roddam Narasimha of National Aeronautical Laboratory and KK Ganapathy of HAL accompanied us. After finishing our work at the Pentagon in Washington, we landed in San Francisco on our way to Los Angeles to visit Northrop Corporation. I utilized this opportunity to visit the Crystal Cathedral built by my favourite author, Robert Schuller. I was amazed by the sheer beauty of this all-glass, four-pointed, star-shaped structure that is more than 400 feet from one point to another.

The glass roof which is 100 feet longer than a football field seemed to float in space. This Cathedral has been built at the cost of several million dollars through donations organized by Schuller. "God can do tremendous things through the person who doesn't care about who gets the credit. The ego involvement must go," writes Schuller. "Before God trusts you with success, you have to prove yourself humble enough to handle the big prize." I prayed to God in Schuller's church to help me build a Research Centre at Imarat Kancha—that would be my Crystal Cathedral.

CHAPTER 13

The young engineers, 280 to be precise, changed the dynamics of DRDL. It was a valuable experience for all of us. We were now in a position to develop, through these young teams, a re-entry technology and structure, a millimetric wave radar, a phased array radar, rocket systems and other such equipment. When we first assigned these tasks to the young scientists, they did not fully grasp the importance of their work. Once they did, they felt uneasy under the burden of the tremendous faith placed in them. I still remember one young man telling me, "There is no big shot in our team, how will we be able to break through?" I told him, "A big shot is a little shot who keeps on shooting, so keep trying." It was astonishing to see how in the young scientific environment, negative attitudes changed to positive and things that were previously thought impractical began happening. Many older scientists were rejuvenated simply by being part of a young team.

It has been my personal experience that the true flavour, the real fun, the continuous excitement of work lies in the process of doing it rather than in having it over and done with. To return to the four basic factors that I am convinced are involved in successful outcomes: goal-setting, positive thinking, visualizing, and believing.

By now, we had gone through an elaborate exercise of goal-setting and enthused the young scientists about these goals. At the review meetings, I would insist that the youngest scientists present their team's work. That would help them in visualizing the whole system. Gradually, an atmosphere of confidence grew. Young scientists started questioning senior colleagues on solid technical issues. Nothing daunted them, because they feared nothing. If there were doubts, they rose above them. They soon became persons of power. A person with belief never grovels before anyone, whining and whimpering that it's all too much, that he lacks support, that he is being treated unfairly. Instead, such a person tackles problems head on and then affirms, 'As a child of God, I am greater than anything that can happen to me'. I tried to keep the work environment lively with a good blend of the experience of the older scientists mixed with the skills of their younger colleagues. This positive dependence between youth and experience had created a very productive work culture at DRDL.

The first launch of the Missile Programme was conducted on 16 September 1985, when *Trishul* took off from the test range at Sriharikota (SHAR). It was a ballistic flight meant for testing the in-flight performance of the solid propellant rocket motor. Two C-Band radars and Kalidieo-theodolite (KTLs) were used to track the missile from the ground. The test was successful. The launcher, rocket motor and telemetry systems functioned as planned. The aerodynamic drag, however, was higher than the estimates predicted on the basis of wind tunnel testing. In terms of technology breakthrough or experience enrichment, this test was of little value but the real achievement of this test was to remind my DRDL friends that they could fly missiles without being driven by the brute demands of compliance or reverse engineering. In a swift stroke, the psyche of the DRDL scientists experienced a multi-dimensional expansion.

This was followed by the successful test flight of the Pilotless Target Aircraft (PTA). Our engineers had developed the rocket motor for the PTA designed by the Bangalore-based Aeronautical Development Establishment (ADE). The motor had been type-approved by DTD&P(Air). This was a small but significant step towards developing missile hardware that is not only functional but also acceptable to the user agencies. A private sector firm was engaged to produce a reliable, airworthy, high thrust-to-weight-ratio rocket motor with technology input from DRDL. We were slowly graduating from single laboratory projects to multi-laboratory programmes to laboratory-industry exercises. The development of PTA symbolized a great confluence of four different organizations. I felt as if I was standing at a meeting point and looking at the roads coming from ADE, DTD&P(Air) and ISRO. The fourth road was the DRDL, a highway to national self-reliance in missile technology.

Taking our partnership with the academic institutions of the country a step further, Joint Advanced Technology Programmes were started at the Indian Institute of Science (IISc), and Jadavpur University. I have always had a deep regard for academic institutions and reverence for excellent academicians. I value the inputs that academicians can make to development. Formal requests had been placed with these institutions and arrangements arrived at under which expertise from their faculties would be extended to DRDL in pursuance of its projects.

Let me highlight a few contributions of academic institutions to the various missile systems. *Prithvi* had been designed as an inertially guided missile. To reach the target accurately, the trajectory parameters have to be loaded into its brain—an on-board computer. A team of young engineering graduates at Jadavpur University under the guidance of Prof. Ghoshal developed the required robust guidance algorithm. At the IISc, postgraduate students under the leadership of Prof. IG Sharma developed air defence software for multi-target acquisition by *Akash*. The re-entry vehicle system design methodology for Agni was developed by a young team at IIT Madras and DRDO scientists. Osmania University's Navigational Electronics Research and Training Unit had developed state-of-the-art signal processing algorithms for *Nag*. I have only given a few examples of collaborative endeavour. In fact, it would have been very difficult to achieve our advanced technological goals without the active partnership of our academic institutions.

Let us consider the example of the *Agni* payload breakthrough. *Agni* is a two-stage rocket system and employs re-entry technology developed in the country for the first time. It is boosted by a first-stage solid rocket motor derived from SLV-3 and further accelerated at the second stage with the liquid rocket engines of *Prithvi*. For the *Agni*, the payload is delivered at hypersonic speeds, which calls for the design and development of a re-entry vehicle structure. The payload with guidance electronics is housed in the re-entry vehicle structure, which is meant to protect the payload by keeping the inside temperature within the limit of 40°C, when the outside skin temperature is greater than 2500°C. An inertial guidance system with an on-board computer guides the payload to the required target. For any re-entry missile system, three-dimensional preforms are core material for making the carbon-carbon nose tip that will remain strong even at such high temperatures. Four laboratories of DRDO and the CSIR achieved this in a short span of 18 months—something other countries could do only after a decade of research and development!

Another challenge involved in the *Agni* payload design was related to the tremendous speed with which it would re-enter the atmosphere. In fact, *Agni* would re-enter the atmosphere at twelve times the speed of sound (12 Mach, as we call it in science). At this tremendous speed, we had no experience of how to keep the vehicle under control. To carry out a test, we had no wind tunnel to generate that kind of speed. If we sought American help, we would have been seen as aspiring to something they considered their exclusive privilege. Even if they consented to co-operate, they would be certain to quote a price for their wind tunnel greater than our entire project budget. Now, the question was how to beat the system. Prof. SM Deshpande of the IISc found four young, bright scientists working in the field of fluid dynamics and, within six months, developed the software for Computational

Fluid Dynamics for Hypersonic Regimes, which is one of its kind in the world.

Another achievement was the development of a missile trajectory simulation software, ANUKALPANA, by Prof. IG Sharma of IISc to evaluate multi-target acquisition capabilities of an *Akash*-type weapon system. No country would have given us this kind of software, but we developed it indigenously.

In yet another example of creating a synergy of scientific talent, Prof. Bharati Bhatt of IIT Delhi, working with the Solid Physics Laboratory (SPL) and Central Electronics Limited (CEL), broke the monopoly of the western countries by developing ferrite phase shifters for use in the multi-function, multi-tasking 3-D Phased Army Radar for surveillance, tracking and guidance of *Akash*. Prof. Saraf of IIT Kharagpur, working with BK Mukhopadhyay, my colleague at RCI, made a millimetric wave (MMW) antenna for the *Nag* Seeker Head in two years, a record even by international standards. The Central Electrical and Electronics Research Institute (CEERI), Pilani, developed an Impatt Diode in consortium with the SPL and RCI to overcome technological foreign dependence in creating these components, which are the heart of any MMW device.

As work on the project spread horizontally, performance appraisal became more and more difficult. DRDO has an assessment-linked policy. Leading nearly 500 scientists, I had to finalize their performance appraisals in the form of Annual Confidential Reports (ACRs). These reports would be forwarded to an assessment board comprised of outside specialists for recommendations. Many people viewed this part of my job uncharitably. Missing a promotion was conveniently translated as a dislike I had towards them. Promotions of other colleagues were seen as subjective favours granted by me. Entrusted with the task of performance evaluation, I had to be a fair judge.

To truly understand a judge, you must understand the riddle of the scales; one side heaped high with hope, the other side holding apprehension. When the scales dip, bright optimism turns into silent panic.

When a person looks at himself, he is likely to misjudge what he finds. He sees only his intentions. Most people have good intentions and hence conclude that whatever they are doing is good. It is difficult for an individual to objectively judge his actions, which may be, and often are, contradictory to his good intentions. Most people come to work with the intention of doing it. Many of them do their work in a manner they find convenient and leave for home in the evening with a sense of satisfaction. They do not evaluate their performance, only their intentions. It is assumed that because an individual has worked with the intention of finishing his work in time, if delays occurred, they were due to reasons beyond his control. He had no intention of causing the delay. But if his action or inaction caused that delay, was it not intentional?

Looking back on my days as a young scientist, I am aware that one of the most constant and powerful urges I experienced was my desire to be more than what I was at that moment. I desired to feel more, learn more, express more. I desired to grow, improve, purify, expand. I never used any outside influence to advance my career. All I had was the inner urge to seek more within myself. The key to my motivation has always been to look at how far I had still to go rather than how far I had come. After all, what is life but a mixture of unsolved problems, ambiguous victories, and amorphous defeats?

The trouble is that we often merely analyse life instead of dealing with it. People dissect their failures for causes and effects, but seldom deal with them and gain experience to master them and thereby avoid their recurrence. This is my belief: that through difficulties and problems, God gives us the opportunity to grow. So when your hopes and dreams and goals are dashed, search among the wreckage, you may find a golden opportunity hidden in the ruins.

To motivate people to enhance their performance and deal with depression is always a challenge for a leader. I have observed an analogy between a force field equilibrium and resistance to change in organizations. Let us imagine change to be a coiled spring in a field of opposing forces, such that some forces support change and others resist it. By increasing the supportive forces such as supervisory pressure, prospects of career growth and monetary benefits or decreasing the resisting forces such as group norms, social rewards, and work avoidance, the situation can be directed towards the desired result—but for a short time only, and that too only to a certain extent. After a while the resisting forces push back with greater force as they are compressed even more tightly. Therefore, a better approach would be to decrease the resisting force in such a manner that there is no concomittant increase in the supporting forces. In this way, less energy will be needed to bring about and maintain change.

The result of the forces I mentioned above is motive. It is a force which is internal to the individual and forms the basis of his behaviour in the work environment. In my experience, most people possess a strong inner drive for growth, competence, and self-actualization. The problem, however, has been the lack of a work environment that stimulates and permits them to give full expression to this drive. Leaders can create a high productivity level by providing the appropriate organizational structure and job design, and by acknowledging and appreciating hard work.

I first attempted to build such a supportive environment in 1983, while launching IGMDP. The projects were in the design phase at that time. The reorganization resulted in at least forty per cent to fifty per cent increase in the level of activity. Now that the multiple projects were entering into the development and flight-testing stage, the major and minor milestones reached gave the programme visibility and continuous commitment. With the absorption of a young team of scientists, the average age had been brought down from 42 to 33 years. I felt it was time for a second reorganization. But how should I go about it? I took stock of the motivational inventory available at that time—let me explain to you what I mean by this term. The motivational inventory of a leader is made up of three types of understanding: an understanding of the needs that people expect to satisfy in their jobs, an understanding of the effect that job design has on motivation, and an understanding of the power of positive reinforcement in influencing people's behaviour.

The 1983 reorganization was done with the objective of renewal: it was indeed a very complex exercise handled deftly by AV Ranga Rao and Col R Swaminathan. We created a team of newly-joined young scientists with just one experienced person and gave them the challenge of building the strap-down inertial guidance system, an on-board computer and a ram rocket in propulsion system. These exercises were being attempted for the first time in the country, and the technology involved was comparable with world-class systems. The guidance technology is centred around the gyro and accelerometer package, and electronics, to process the sensor output. The on-board computer carries the mission computations and flight sequencing. A ram rocket system breathes air to sustain its high velocity for long durations after it is put through a booster rocket. The young teams not only designed these systems but also developed them into operational equipment. Later *Prithvi* and then *Agni* used similar guidance systems, with excellent results. The effort of these young teams made the country self-reliant in the area of protected technologies. It was a good demonstration of the 'renewal factor'. Our intellectual capacity was renewed through contact with enthusiastic young minds and had achieved these outstanding results.

Now, besides the renewal of manpower, emphasis had to be laid on augmenting the strength of project groups. Often people seek to satisfy their social, egoistic and self-actualization needs at their workplaces. A good leader must identify two different sets of environmental features. One which satisfies a person's needs, and the other which creates dissatisfaction with his work. We have already observed that people look for those characteristics in their work that relate to the values and goals which they consider important as giving meaning to their lives. If a job meets the employees' need for achievement, recognition, responsibility, growth and advancement, they will work hard to achieve goals.

Once the work is satisfying, a person then looks at the environment and circumstances in the workplace. He observes the policies of the administration, qualities of his leader, security, status and working conditions. Then, he correlates these factors to the inter-personal relations he has with his peers and examines his personal life in the light of these factors. It is the agglomerate of all these aspects that decides the degree and quality of a person's effort and performance.

The matrix organization evolved in 1983 proved excellent in meeting all these requirements. So, while retaining this structure of the laboratory, we undertook a task-design exercise. The scientists working in technology directorates were made system managers to interact exclusively with one project. An external fabrication wing was formed under PK Biswas, a developmental fabrication technologist of long standing, to deal with the public sector undertakings (PSUs) and private sector firms associated with the development of the missile hardware. This reduced pressure on the in-house fabrication facilities and enabled them to concentrate on jobs which could not be undertaken outside, which in fact occupied all the three shifts.

Work on *Prithvi* was nearing completion when we entered 1988. For the first time in the country, clustered Liquid Propellant (LP) rocket engines with programmable total impulse were going to be used in a missile system to attain flexibility in payload range combination. Now, besides the scope and quality of the policy decisions Sundaram and I were providing to the *Prithvi* team, the project's success depended on creative ideas being converted into workable products and the quality and thoroughness of the team members' contribution. Saraswat, with Y Gyaneshwar and P Venugopalan, did a commendable job in this regard. They instilled in their team a sense of pride and achievement. The importance of these rocket engines was not restricted to the *Prithvi* project—it was a national achievement. Under their collective leadership, a large number of engineers and technicians understood and committed themselves to the team goals, as well as the specific goals which each one of them was committed to accomplish personally. Their entire team worked under a self-evident sort of direction. Working together with the Ordnance Factory, Kirkee, they also completely eliminated the import content in the propellant for these engines.

Leaving the vehicle development in the safe and efficient hands of Sundaram and Saraswat, I started looking at the mission's vulnerable areas. Meticulous planning had gone into the development of the launch release mechanism (LRM) for the smooth lift-off of the missile. The joint development of explosive bolts to hold the LRM prior to the launch by DRDL and Explosive Research and Development Laboratory (ERDL) was an excellent example of multi–work-centre coordination.

While flying, drifting into spells of contemplation and looking down at the landscape below has always been my favourite preoccupation. It is so beautiful, so harmonious, so peaceful from a distance that I wonder where all those boundaries are which separate district from district, state from state, and country from country. Maybe such a sense of distance and detachment is required in dealing with all the activities of our life.

Since the Interim Test Range at Balasore was still at least a year away from completion, we had set up special facilities at SHAR for the launch of *Prithvi*. These included a launch pad, block house, control consoles and mobile telemetry stations. I had a happy reunion with my old friend, MR Kurup, who was the Director, SHAR Centre, by then. Working with Kurup on the *Prithvi* launch campaign gave me great satisfaction. Kurup worked for *Prithvi* as a team member, ignoring the boundary lines that divide DRDO and ISRO, DRDL and SHAR. Kurup used to spend a lot of time with us at the launch pad. He complemented us with his experience in range testing and range safety and worked with great enthusiasm in propellant filling, making the maiden *Prithvi* launch campaign a memorable experience.

Prithvi was launched at 11:23 hrs on 25 February 1988. It was an epoch-making event in the history of rocketry in the country. *Prithvi* was not merely a surface-to-surface missile with the capability of delivering a 1000 kg conventional warhead to a distance of 150 km with an accuracy of 50 meter CEP; it was in fact the basic module for all future guided missiles in the country. It already had the provision for modification from a long-range surface to an air missile system, and could also be deployed on a ship.

The accuracy of a missile is expressed in terms of its Circular Error Probable (CEP). This measures the radius of a circle within which 50 per cent of the missiles fired will impact. In other words, if a missile has a CEP of 1 km (such as the Iraqi Scud missiles fired in the Gulf War), this means that half of them should impact within 1 km of their target. A missile with a conventional high-explosive warhead and a CEP of 1 km would not normally be expected to destroy or disable fixed military targets, such as a Command and Control Facility or an Air Base. It would, however, be effective against an undefined target such as a city.

The German V-2 missiles fired at London between September 1944 and March 1945 had a conventional high-explosive warhead and a very large CEP of some 17 km. Yet the 500 V-2s which hit London succeeded in causing more than 21,000 casualties and destroying about 200,000 homes.

When the West were crying themselves hoarse over the NPT, we stressed upon building competence in core guidance and control technologies to achieve a CEP as precise as 50 m. With the success of the *Prithvi* trials, the cold reality of a possible strategic strike even without a nuclear warhead had silenced the critics to whispers about a possible technology-conspiracy theory.

The launch of *Prithvi* sent shock waves across the unfriendly neighbouring countries. The response of the Western bloc was initially one of shock and then of anger. A seven-nation technology embargo was clamped, making it impossible for India to buy anything even remotely connected with the development of guided missiles. The emergence of India as a self-reliant country in the field of guided missiles upset all the developed nations of the world.

CHAPTER 14

Indian core competence in rocketry has been firmly established again, beyond any doubt. The robust civilian space industry and viable missile-based defences has brought India into the select club of nations that call themselves superpowers. Always encouraged to follow Buddha's or Gandhi's teachings, how and why did India become a missile power is a question that needs to be answered for future generations.

Two centuries of subjugation, oppression and denial have failed to kill the creativity and capability of the Indian people. Within just a decade of gaining independence and achieving sovereignty, Indian Space and Atomic Energy Programmes were launched with a perfect orientation towards peaceful applications. There were neither funds for investing in missile development nor any established requirement from the Armed Forces. The bitter experiences of 1962 forced us to take the basic first steps towards missile development.

Would a *Prithvi* suffice? Would the indigenous development of four or five missile systems make us sufficiently strong? Or would having nuclear weapons make us stronger? Missiles and atomic weapons are merely parts of a greater whole. As I saw it, the development of *Prithvi* represented the self-reliance of our country in the field of advanced technology. High technology is synonymous with huge amounts of money and massive infrastructure. Neither of these was available, unfortunately, in adequate measure. So what could we do? Perhaps the *Agni* missile being developed as a technology demonstrator project, pooling all the resources available in the country, could provide an answer?

I was very sure, even when we discussed REX in ISRO about a decade ago, that Indian scientists and technologists working together had the capability to achieve this technological break-through. India can most certainly achieve state-of-the-art technology through a combined effort of the scientific laboratories and the academic institutions. If one can liberate Indian industry from the self-created image of being mere fabricating factories, they can implement indigenously developed technology and attain excellent results. To do this, we adopted a three-fold strategy—multi-institutional participation, the consortium approach, and the empowering technology. These were the stones rubbed together to create *Agni*.

The *Agni* team was comprised of more than 500 scientists. Many organizations were networked to undertake this huge effort of launching *Agni*. The *Agni* mission had two basic orientations—work and workers. Each member was dependent on the others in his team to accomplish his target. Contradiction and confusion are the two things most likely to occur in such situations. Different leaders accommodate concern for workers while getting work done, in their own personal ways. Some shed all concern for workers in order to get results. They use people merely as instruments to reach goals. Some give less importance to the work, and make an effort to gain the warmth and approval of people working with them. But what this team achieved was the highest possible integration in terms of both the quality of work and human relationships.

Involvement, participation and commitment were the key words to functioning. Each of the team members appeared to be performing by choice. The launching of *Agni* was the common stake not only for our scientists, but for their families too. VR Nagaraj was the leader of the electrical integration team. Dedicated technologist that he is, Nagaraj would forget basic requirements like food and sleep while on the integration gig. His brother-in-law passed away while he was at ITR. His family kept this information from Nagaraj so that there would be no interruption in his work towards the launching of *Agni*.

The *Agni* launch had been scheduled for 20 April 1989. This was going to be an unprecedented exercise. Unlike space launch vehicles, a missile launch involves wide-ranging safety hazards. Two radars, three telemetry stations, one telecommand station and four electro-optical tracking instruments to monitor the missile trajectory had been deployed. In addition, the telemetry station at Car Nicobar (ISTRAC) and the SHAR radars were also commissioned to track the vehicle. Dynamic surveillance was employed to cover the electrical power that flows from the missile batteries within the vehicle and to control system pressures. Should any deviation be noticed either in voltage or in pressure, the specially designed automatic checkout system would signal *"Hold"*. The flight operations would then be sequenced only if the defect was rectified. The countdown for the launch started at T–36 hours. The countdown from T–7.5 minutes was to be computer controlled.

All activities preparatory to the launch went according to schedule. We had decided to move the people living in nearby villages to safety at the time of the launch. This attracted media attention, and led to much controversy. By the time 20 April 1989 arrived, the whole nation was watching us. Foreign pressure was exerted through diplomatic channels to abort the flight trial, but the Indian Government stood behind us like a rock and staved off any distraction to our work. We were at T–14 seconds when the computer signalled "*Hold*", indicating that one of the instruments was functioning erratically. This was immediately rectified. Meanwhile, the down-range station asked for a "*Hold*". In another few seconds, multiple *Holds* were necessitated, resulting in irreversible internal power consumption. We had to abort the launch. The missile had to be opened up to replace the on-board power supplies. A weeping Nagaraj, by now informed about the tragedy in his family, met me and promised that he would be back within three days. The profiles of these courageous people will never be written about in any history book, but it is such silent people on whose hard work generations thrive and nations progress. Sending Nagaraj off, I met my team members who were in a state of shock and sorrow. I shared my SLV-3 experience with them. "I lost my launch vehicle in the sea but recovered successfully. Your missile is in front of you. In fact you have lost nothing but a few weeks of rework." This shook them out of their immobility and the entire team went back to retrieve the subsystems and re-charge them.

The press was up in arms, and fielded various interpretations of the postponement of the flight to suit the fancies of their readership. Cartoonist Sudhir Dar sketched a shopkeeper returning a product to the salesman saying that like *Agni* it would not take off. Another cartoonist showed one *Agni* scientist explaining that the launch was postponed because the press button did not make contact. The *Hindustan Times* showed a leader consoling press reporters, "There's no need for any alarm ... it's a purely peaceful, non-violent missile".

After a detailed analysis conducted virtually round the clock for the next ten days, our scientists had the missile ready for launch on 1 May 1989. But, again, during the automatic computer checkout period at T–10 seconds, a *Hold* signal was indicated. A closer inspection showed that one of the control components, S1–TVC was not working according to the mission requirements. The launch had to be postponed yet again. Now, such things are very common in rocketry and quite often happen in other countries too. But the expectant nation was in no mood to appreciate our difficulties. *The Hindu* carried a cartoon by Keshav showing a villager counting some currency notes and commenting to another, "Yes, it's the compensation for moving away from my hut near the test site—a few more postponements and I can build a house of my own...". Another cartoonist designated *Agni* as "IDBM—Intermittently

Delayed Ballistic Missile." Amul's cartoon suggested that what *Agni* needed to do was use their butter as fuel!

I took some time off, leaving my team at ITR to talk to the DRDL-RCI community. The entire DRDL-RCI community assembled after working hours on 8 May 1989. I addressed the gathering of more than 2000 persons, "Very rarely is a laboratory or an R&D establishment given an opportunity to be the first in the country to develop a system such as *Agni*. A great opportunity has been given to us. Naturally major opportunities are accompanied by equally major challenges. We should not give up and we should not allow the problem to defeat us. The country doesn't deserve anything less than success from us. Let us aim for success". I had almost completed my address, when I found myself telling my people, "I promise you, we will be back after successfully launching *Agni* before the end of this month."

Detailed analysis of the component failure during the second attempt led to the refurbishment of the control system. This task was entrusted to a DRDO-ISRO team. The team carried out the rectification of the first stage control system at the Liquid Propellant System Complex (LPSC) of ISRO and completed the task in record time with tremendous concentration and will-power. It was nothing short of amazing how hundreds of scientists and staff worked continuously and completed the system readiness with acceptance tests in just 10 days. The aircraft took off from Trivandrum with the rectified control systems and landed close to ITR on the eleventh day. But now it was the turn of hostile weather conditions to impede us. A cyclone threat was looming large. All the work centres were connected through satellite communication and HF links. Meteorological data started flowing in at ten-minute intervals.

Finally, the launch was scheduled for 22 May 1989. The previous night, Dr Arunachalam, Gen KN Singh and I were walking together with the Defence Minister KC Pant, who had come to ITR to witness the launch. It was a full moon night, it was high tide and the waves crashed and roared, as if singing of His glory and power. Would we succeed with the *Agni* launch tomorrow? This question was foremost in all our minds, but none of us was willing to break the spell cast by the beautiful moonlit night. Breaking a long silence, the Defence Minister finally asked me, "Kalam! What would you like me to do to celebrate the *Agni* success tomorrow?" It was a simple question, to which I could not think of an answer immediately. What did I want? What was it that I did not have? What could make me happier? And then I found the answer. "We need 100,000 saplings to plant at RCI," I said. His face lit up with a friendly glow. "You are buying the blessings of Mother Earth for *Agni*," Defence Minister KC Pant quipped. "We will succeed tomorrow," he predicted.

The next day *Agni* took off at 0710 hrs. It was a perfect launch. The missile followed a textbook trajectory. All flight parameters were met. It was like waking up to a beautiful morning from a nightmarish sleep. We had reached the launch pad after five years of continuous work at multiple work centres. We had lived through the ordeal of a series of snags in the last five weeks. We had survived pressure from everywhere to stop the whole thing. But we did it at last! It was one of the greatest moments of my life. A mere 600 seconds of elegant flight washed off our entire fatigue in an instant. What a wonderful culmination of our years of labour. I wrote in my diary that night:

> *Do not look at Agni*
> *as an entity directed upward*
> *to deter the ominous*
> *or exhibit your might.*
> *It is fire*
> *in the heart of an Indian.*
> *Do not even give it*
> *the form of a missile*
> *as it clings to the*
> *burning pride of this nation*
> *and thus is bright.*

Prime Minister Rajiv Gandhi called the Agni launch "a major achievement in our continuing efforts to safeguard our independence and security by self-reliant means. The technology demonstration through Agni is a reflection of our commitment to the indigenous development of advanced technologies for the nation's defence." "The country is proud of your efforts," he told me. President Venkataraman saw in the Agni success the fulfilment of his dream. He cabled from Simla, "It is a tribute to your dedication, hard work and talent."

A great deal of misinformation and disinformation had been spread by vested interests about this technology mission. *Agni* had never been intended only as a nuclear weapon system. What it did was to afford us the option of developing the ability to deliver non-nuclear weapons with high precision at long ranges. That it provided us with a viable non-nuclear option was of the greatest relevance to contemporary strategic doctrines.

Great ire was raised by the test firing of *Agni*, according to a well-known American defence journal, especially in the United States, where Congressmen threatened to put a stop to all dual-use and missile-related technologies, along with all multinational aid.

Gary Milhollin, a so-called specialist in missiles and warhead technologies, had made a claim in *The Wall Street Journal* that India had made *Agni* with the help of West Germany. I had a hearty laugh reading that the German Aerospace Research Establishment (DLR) had developed *Agni*'s guidance system, the first-stage rocket, and a composite nose cone, and that the aerodynamic model of *Agni* was tested in the DLR wind tunnel. An immediate denial came from the DLR, who in turn speculated that France had supplied the *Agni* guidance electronics. American Senator Jeff Bingaman even went to the extent of suggesting that I picked up everything needed for *Agni* during my four-month stay at Wallop's Island in 1962. The fact that I had been in Wallop's Island more than 25 years ago and that at that time the technology used in *Agni* did not exist even in the United States was not mentioned.

In today's world, technological backwardness leads to subjugation. Can we allow our freedom to be compromised on this account? It is our duty to guarantee the security and integrity of our nation against this threat. Should we not uphold the mandate bequeathed to us by our forefathers who fought for the liberation of our country from imperialism? Only when we are technologically self-reliant will we able to fulfill their dream.

Till the *Agni* launch, the Indian Armed Forces had been structured for a strictly defensive role to safeguard our nation, to shield our democratic processes from the turbulence in the countries around us and to raise the cost of any external intervention to an unacceptable level for countries which may entertain such notions. With *Agni*, India had reached the stage where she had the option of preventing wars involving her.

Agni marked the completion of five years of IGMDP. Now that it had demonstrated our competence in the crucial area of re-entry technology and with tactical missiles like *Prithvi* and *Trishul* already test-fired, the launches of *Nag* and *Akash* would take us into areas of competence where there is little or no international competition. These two missile systems contained within themselves the stuff of major technological breakthroughs. There was a need to focus our efforts more intensively on them.

In September 1989, I was invited by the Maharashtra Academy of Sciences in Bombay to deliver the Jawaharlal Nehru Memorial Lecture. I used this opportunity to share with the budding scientists my plans of making an indigenous Air-to-Air missile, *Astra*. It would dovetail with the development of the Indian Light Combat Aircraft (LCA). I told them that our work in Imaging Infra Red (IIR) and Millimetric Wave (MMW) radar technology for the *Nag* missile system had placed us in the vanguard of international R&D efforts in missile technology. I also drew their attention to the crucial role that carbon-carbon and other advanced composite materials play in mastering the re-entry technology. *Agni* was the conclusion of a technological effort that was given its start by Prime Minister Indira Gandhi when the country decided to break free from the paralysing fetters of technological backwardness and slough off the dead skin of subordination to industrialized nations.

The second flight of *Prithvi* at the end of September 1988 was again a great success. *Prithvi* has proved to be the best surface-to-surface missile in the world today. It can carry 1000 kg of warhead to a distance of 250 km and deliver it within a radius of 50 metres. Through computer-controlled operations, numerous warhead weight and delivery distance combinations can be achieved in a very short time and in battlefield conditions. It is a hundred per cent indigenous in all respects—design, operations, deployment. It can be produced in large numbers as the production facilities at BDL were concurrently developed during the development phase itself. The Army was quick to recognize the potential of this commendable effort and approached the CCPA for placing orders for *Prithvi* and *Trishul* missile systems, something that had never happened before.

IV

CONTEMPLATION

[1990–1991]

We create and destroy
And again recreate
In forms of which no one knows

Al-Waquiah
Qu'ran 56:61

CHAPTER 15

On Republic Day 1990, the nation celebrated the success of its missile programme. I was conferred the Padma Vibhushan along with Dr Arunachalam. Two of my other colleagues—JC Bhattacharya and RN Agarwal—were also decorated with the Padma Shree awards. It was the first time in the history of free India that so many scientists affiliated to the same organization found their names on the awards list. Memories of the Padma Bhushan awarded a decade ago came alive. I still lived more or less as I had lived then—in a room ten feet wide and twelve feet long, furnished mainly with books, papers and a few pieces of hired furniture. The only difference was at that time, my room was in Trivandrum and now it was in Hyderabad. The mess bearer brought me my breakfast of idlis and buttermilk and smiled in silent congratulation for the award. I was touched by the recognition bestowed on me by my countrymen. A large number of scientists and engineers leave this country at their first opportunity to earn more money abroad. It is true that they definitely get greater monetary benefits, but could anything compensate for this love and respect from one's own countrymen?

I sat alone for a while in silent contemplation. The sand and shells of Rameswaram, the care of Iyadurai Solomon in Ramanathapuram, the guidance of Rev. Father Sequeira in Trichi and Prof. Pandalai in Madras, the encouragement of Dr Mediratta in Bangalore, the hovercraft ride with Prof. Menon, the pre-dawn visit to the Tilpat Range with Prof. Sarabhai, the healing touch of Dr Brahm Prakash on the day of the SLV-3 failure, the national jubilation on the SLV-3 launch, Madam Gandhi's appreciative smile, the post–SLV-3 simmering at VSSC, Dr Ramanna's faith in inviting me to DRDO, the IGMDP, the creation of RCI, *Prithvi*, *Agni*...a flood of memories swept over me. Where were all these men now? My father, Prof. Sarabhai, Dr Brahm Prakash? I wished I could meet them and share my joy with them. I felt the paternal forces of heaven and the maternal and cosmic forces of nature embrace me as parents would hug their long-lost child. I scribbled in my diary:

> *Away! fond thoughts, and vex my soul no more!*
> *Work claimed my wakeful nights, my busy days*
> *Albeit brought memories of Rameswaram shore*
> *Yet haunt my dreaming gaze!*

A fortnight later, Iyer and his team celebrated the awards for the missile programme with the maiden flight of *Nag*. They repeated the feat again on the very next day, thus testing twice over the first Indian all-composite airframe and the propulsion system. These tests also proved the worth of the indigenous thermal batteries.

India had achieved the status of having a third-generation anti-tank missile system with 'fire-and-forget' capability—on par with any state-of-the-art technology in the world. Indigenous composite technology had achieved a major milestone. The success of *Nag* also confirmed the efficacy of the consortium approach, which had led to the successful development of *Agni*.

Nag uses two key technologies—an Imaging Infra Red (IIR) system and a Millimetric Wave (MMW) seeker radar as its guiding eye. No single laboratory in the country possessed the capability of developing these highly advanced systems. But the urge to succeed existed, which resulted in a very effective joint effort. The Semi Conductor Complex at Chandigarh developed the Charge Coupled Devices (CCD) array. The Solid Physics Laboratory, Delhi, made the matching Mercury Cadmium Telluride (MCT) detectors. The Defence Science Centre (DSC), Delhi, put together an indigenous cooling system based on the Joules Thomson effect. The transmitter receiver front end was devised at the Defence Electronics Application Laboratory (DEAL), Dehradun.

The special gallium arsenide gun, Schottky barrier mixer diodes, compact comparator for antenna system—India was banned from buying any one of these high-technology devices, but innovation cannot be suppressed by international restrictions.

I went to Madurai Kamaraj University the same month to deliver their convocation address. When I reached Madurai, I asked after my high-school teacher, Iyadurai Solomon, who was by now a Reverend and eighty years old. I was told that he lived in a suburb of Madurai, so I took a taxi and looked for his house. Rev. Solomon knew that I was going to give the convocation address that day. However, he had no way of getting there. There was a touching reunion between teacher and pupil. Dr PC Alexander, the Governor of Tamil Nadu, who was presiding over the function, was deeply moved on seeing the elderly teacher who had not forgotten his pupil of long ago, and requested him to share the dais.

"Every convocation day of every University is like opening the floodgates of energy which, once harnessed by institutions, organizations and industry, aids in nation-building," I told the young graduates. Somehow I felt I was echoing Rev. Solomon's words, spoken about half a century ago. After my lecture, I bowed down before my teacher. "Great dreams of great dreamers are always transcended," I told Rev. Solomon. "You have not only reached my goals, Kalam! You have eclipsed them," he told me in a voice choked with emotion.

The next month, I happened to be in Trichi and used that opportunity to visit St. Joseph's College. I did not find Rev. Father Sequeira, Rev. Father Erhart, Prof. Subramanyam, Prof. Iyyamperumal Konar, or Prof. Thothathri Iyengar there, but it seemed to me that the stones of the St. Joseph's building still carried the imprint of the wisdom of those great people. I shared with the young students my memories of St. Joseph's and paid tribute to the teachers who had moulded me.

We celebrated the nation's forty-fourth Independence Day with the test firing of *Akash*. Prahlada and his team evaluated a new solid propellant booster system based on a composite modified double base propellant. This propellant with its unprecedented high-energy properties was crucial in assuring the long-range surface-to-air missiles. The country had taken an important step in ground-based air defence of vulnerable areas.

Towards the end of 1990, Jadavpur University conferred on me the honour of Doctor of Science at a special convocation. I was a little embarrassed at finding my name mentioned along with that of the legendary Nelson Mandela, who was also honoured at the same convocation. What could I possibly have in common with a legend like Mandela? Perhaps it was our persistence in our missions. My mission of advancing rocketry in my country was perhaps nothing when compared with Mandela's mission of achieving dignity for a great mass of humanity; but there was no difference in the intensity of our passions. "Be more dedicated to making solid achievements than in running after swift but synthetic happiness," was my advice to the young audience.

The Missile Council declared 1991 the Year of Initiative for DRDL and RCI. When we chose the route of concurrent engineering in IGMDP, we selected a rough track. With the completion of developmental trials on *Prithvi* and *Trishul*, our choice was on test now. I exhorted my colleagues to commence user trials within the year. I knew that it was going to be a tough task, but that was not going to discourage us.

Rear Admiral Mohan retired and his deputy, Kapoor, was to take over *Trishul*. I had always admired Mohan's understanding of missile command guidance. This sailor-teacher-scientist could outwit any other expert in the country in this field. I will always remember his candid exposition of various aspects of the Command Line of Sight (CLOS) guidance system during the *Trishul* meetings. Once, he showed me a verse that he had composed to highlight the woes of an IGMDP Project Director. It was a good way of letting off steam:

> *Impossible timeframes,*
> *PERT charts to boot*
> *Are driving me almost crazy as a coot;*
> *Presentations to MC add to one's woes,*
> *If they solve anything, Heaven only knows.*
> *Meetings on holidays, even at night,*
> *The family is fed up,*
> *And all ready to fight.*
> *My hands are itching*
> *to tear my hair —*
> *But alas! I haven't any more to tear ...*

I told him, "I have handed over all my problems to my best teams in DRDL, RCI, and other participating labs. That has given me a full head of hair."

The year 1991 began on a very ominous note. On the night of 15 January 1991, the Gulf War broke out between Iraq and the Allied Forces led by the USA. In one stroke, thanks to satellite television invading Indian skies by that time, rockets and missiles captured the imagination of the entire nation. People started discussing Scuds and Patriots in coffee houses and tea shops. Children began flying paper kites shaped like missiles, and playing war games along the lines of what they saw on American television networks. The successful test firing of *Prithvi* and *Trishul* during the course of the Gulf War was enough to make an anxious nation relax. The newspaper reports of the programmable trajectory capability of the *Prithvi* and *Trishul* guidance system, using microwave frequencies in virtually unjammable bands, created widespread awareness. The nation was quick to draw parallels between the missiles operational in the Gulf War and our own warhead carriers. A common query I encountered was whether *Prithvi* was superior to a Scud, whether *Akash* could perform like a Patriot, and so on. Hearing a "Yes" or a "Why not?" from me, people's faces would light up with pride and satisfaction.

The Allied Forces had a marked technological edge, as they were fielding systems built using the technologies of the eighties and nineties. Iraq was fighting with the by-and-large vintage weapon systems of the sixties and seventies.

Now, this is where the key to the modern world order lies—superiority through technology. Deprive the opponent of the latest technology and then dictate your terms in an unequal contest. When the Chinese war philosopher, Sun Tzu, ruminated over 2000 years ago that what matters in war is not decimating the enemy army physically but breaking his will so as to make him concede defeat in the mind, he seems to have visualized the domination of technology in the twentieth century theatres of war. The missile force coupled with the electronic warfare used in the Gulf War was a feast for military strategic experts. It acted as a curtain-raiser for the twenty-first century war scenario, with missiles and electronic and information warfare playing the lead roles.

In India, even today, the term technology, for most people, conjures up images of smoky steel mills or clanking machines. This is a rather inadequate conception of what technology denotes. The invention of the horse collar in the Middle Ages led to major changes in agricultural methods, and was as much a technological advance as the invention of the Bessemer furnace centuries later. Moreover, technology includes techniques as well as the machines that may or may not be necessary to apply them. It includes ways to make chemical reactions occur, ways to breed fish, eradicate weeds, light theatres, treat patients, teach history, fight wars, or even prevent them.

Today, most advanced technological processes are carried out far from assembly lines or open hearths. Indeed, in electronics, in space technology, in most of the new industries, relative silence and clean surroundings are characteristic, even essential. The assembly line, with the organization of armies of men, to carry out simple, routine functions is an anachronism. Our symbols of technology must change before we can keep pace with changes in technology itself. We should never forget that technology feeds on itself. Technology makes more technology possible. In fact, technological innovation consists of three stages linked together in a self-reinforcing cycle. First, there is the creative stage, with the blueprint of a feasible idea. This is made real by its practical application, and this finally ends in its diffusion through society. The process is then complete; the loop is closed when the diffusion of technology embodying the new idea in its turn helps generate new creative ideas. Today, all over the developed world, the time gap between each of the steps in this cycle has been shortened. In India, we are just progressing towards that stage—closing the loop.

After the Gulf War concluded with the victory of the technologically superior Allied Forces, over 500 scientists of DRDL and RCI gathered to discuss issues that had emerged. I posed a question before the assembly: was technology or weapon symmetry with other nations feasible, and if so, should it be attempted? The discussion led to many more serious questions, such as, how to establish effective electronic warfare support? How to make missile development proceed apace with the development of equally necessary systems like the LCA; and what were the key areas where a push would bring progress?

At the end of a lively discussion spread over three hours, the consensus emerged that there was no way to redress asymmetry in military capability except to have the same capability in specific areas as your potential opponent. The scientists vowed to achieve a reduced CEP in the accuracy of *Prithvi*'s delivery, perfecting the Ka band guidance system for *Trishul* and realising all carbon-carbon re-entry control surfaces for *Agni* by the end of the year. The vow was later fulfilled. The year also saw tube-launched *Nag* flights, and the manoeuvre of *Trishul* at seven metres above sea level, at speeds which exceeded three times the speed of sound. The latter was a breakthrough in the development of an indigenous ship-launched anti–sea-skimmer missile.

The same year, I received an honorary degree of Doctor of Science from the IIT Bombay. In the citation read by Prof. B Nag on the occasion, I was described as "an inspiration behind the creation of a solid technological base from which India's future aerospace programmes can be launched to meet the challenges of the twenty-first century". Well, perhaps Prof. Nag was only being polite, but I do believe that India will enter the next century with its own satellite in geostationary orbit 36,000 km away in space, positioned by its own launch vehicle. India will also become a missile power. Ours is a country with tremendous vitality. Even though the world may not see its full potential or feel its full power, no one dare ignore it any more.

On 15 October, I turned sixty. I looked forward to retirement and planned to open a school for less privileged children. My friend, Prof. P Rama Rao, who was heading the Department of Science and Technology in the Government of India, even struck up a partnership with me to establish what he called the Rao-Kalam school. We were unanimous in our opinion that carrying out certain missions and reaching certain milestones, however important they may be or however impressive they might appear to be, is not all there is to life. But we had to postpone our plan as neither of us was relieved from our post by the Government of India.

It was during this period that I decided to write my memoirs and express my observations and opinions on certain issues.

The biggest problem Indian youth faced, I felt, was a lack of clarity of vision, a lack of direction. It was then that I decided to write about the circumstances and people who made me what I am today; the idea was not merely to pay tribute to some individuals or highlight certain aspects of my life. What I wanted to say was that no one, however poor, underprivileged or small, need feel disheartened about life. Problems are a part of life. Suffering is the essence of success. As someone said:

> *God has not promised*
> *Skies always blue,*
> *Flower-strewn pathways*
> *All our life through;*
> *God has not promised*
> *Sun without rain,*
> *Joy without sorrow,*
> *Peace without pain.*

I will not be presumptuous enough to say that my life can be a role model for anybody; but some poor child living in an obscure place, in an underprivileged social setting may find a little solace in the way my destiny has been shaped. It could perhaps help such children liberate themselves from the bondage of their illusory backwardness and hopelessness. Irrespective of where they are right now, they should be aware that God is with them and when He is with them, who can be against them?

> *But God has promised*
> *Strength for the day,*
> *Rest for the labour*
> *Light for the way.*

It has been my observation that most Indians suffer unnecessary misery all their lives because they do not know how to manage their emotions. They are paralysed by some sort of a psychological inertia. Phrases like 'the next best alternative', 'the only feasible option or solution', and 'till things take a turn for the better' are commonplace in our business conversations. Why not write about the deep-rooted character traits which manifest themselves in such widespread, self-defeatist thought patterns and negative behaviour? I have worked with many people and organizations and have had to deal with people who were so full of their own limitations that they had no other way to prove their self-worth than by intimidating me. Why not write about the victimization which is a hallmark of the tragedy of Indian science and technology? And about the pathways to organizational success? Let the latent fire in the heart of every Indian acquire wings, and the glory of this great country light up the sky.

CHAPTER 16

Technology, unlike science, is a group activity. It is not based on individual intelligence, but on the interaction of many people. I think the biggest success of IGMDP is not the fact that in record time the country acquired the capability of making five state-of-the-art missile systems but that through it, some superb teams of scientists and engineers have been created. If someone asks me about my personal achievements in Indian rocketry, I would put it down to having created a challenging environment for teams of young people to work in.

In their formative stages, teams are much like children in spirit. They are as excitable, as full of vitality, enthusiasm, curiosity and the desire to please and excel. As with children, however, these positive attributes can be destroyed by the behaviour of misguided parents. For teams to be successful, the environment must offer scope for innovation. I confronted many such challenges during the course of my work at DTD&P(Air), ISRO, DRDO and elsewhere, but always ensured for my teams an environment which allowed innovation and risk-taking.

When we first began creating project teams during the SLV-3 project and later in IGMDP, people working in these teams found themselves in the frontline of their organizations' ambitions. Since a great deal of psychological investment had been made in these teams, they became both highly visible and highly vulnerable. They were personally expected to make a disproportionate contribution to win collective glory.

I was aware that any failure in the organizational support system would negate the investment in team strategies. The teams would be relegated to the league of average working groups and might fail even there, unable to meet the high expectations set for them. On several occasions, the organization was on the verge of losing its nerve and imposing restraints. The high level of uncertainty and complexity associated with team activity very often proves to be a trap for the unwary.

In the early years of the SLV-3 project, I often had to counter nervousness of the top people because progress was not tangibly or immediately visible. Many felt that the organization had lost control over SLV-3, that the team would run on unchecked, and cause chaos and confusion. But on all occasions, these fears were proved imaginary. There were many people in powerful positions in organizations, for example at VSSC, who underestimated our responsibility and commitment to organizational objectives. Dealing with such people was a crucial part of the whole operation, and this was performed dexterously by Dr Brahm Prakash.

When you work as a project team, you need to develop a complex view of the success criteria. There are always multiple and often conflicting sets of expectations that exist about a team's performance. Then, quite often, the project teams are virtually torn apart in their attempt to accommodate the needs and constraints of sub-contractors outside the organization and specialist departments within the organization. Good project teams are able to quickly identify the key person or people with whom negotiations must take place. A crucial aspect of the team leader's role is to negotiate with these key people for their requirements, and to ensure that the dialogue continues on a regular basis as the situation develops or changes. If there is one thing outsiders dislike, it is unpleasant surprises. Good teams ensure that there are none.

The SLV-3 team developed their own internal success criteria. We articulated our standards, expectations and objectives. We summarized what was needed to happen for us to be successful and how we would measure success. For instance, how we were going to accomplish our tasks, who would do what and according to what standards, what were the time limits and how would the team conduct itself with reference to others in the organization.

The process of arriving at the success criteria within a team is an intricate and skilled one because there are a lot of things going on below the surface. On the surface, the team is simply working to achieve the project's goals. But I have repeatedly seen how people are poor at articulating what they want—until they see a work centre doing something they don't want them to do. A project team member must in fact act like a detective. He should probe for clues as to how the project is proceeding, and then piece together different bits of evidence to build up a clear, comprehensive and deep understanding of the project's requirements.

At another level, the relationship between the project teams and the work centres should be encouraged and developed by the project leader. Both parties must be very clear in their minds about their mutual interdependence and the fact that both of them have a stake in the project. At yet another level, each side should assess the other's capabilities and identify areas of strength and weakness in order to plan what needs doing and how it should be done. In fact, the whole game can be seen as a process of contracting. It is about exploring and arriving at an agreement on what each party expects of the other; about realistically understanding the constraints of the other party; and about communicating the success criteria while defining some simple rules about how the relationship is to work; but above all, it's the best means of developing clarity in the relationship, both at the technical and personal levels, in order to avoid any nasty surprises in the future. In IGMDP, Sivathanu Pillai and his team did some remarkable work in this area through their home-grown technique, PACE, which stands for Programme Analysis, Control and Evaluation. Each day between 12 noon and 1 p.m., they would sit with a project team and a particular work centre that was on the critical path and assess the level of success among themselves. The excitement of planning ways to succeed and the vision of future success provide an irresistible form of motivation which, I have found, always makes things happen.

The concept of Technology Management has its roots in the Developmental Management models which originated in the early Sixties out of a conflict between harmony-seeking and output-oriented management structures. There are basically two types of management orientations: *primal*, which values an economic employee, and *rational*, which values an organizational employee. My concept of management is woven around an employee who is a technology person. While the primal management school recognizes people for their independence, and rational management acknowledges them for their dependability, I value them for their interdependence. Whereas the primal manager champions independent enterprise and the rational manager serves cooperation, I moot interdependent joint ventures, getting the forces together, networking people, resources, time schedules, costs, and so on.

Abraham Maslow was the first person to suggest the new psychology of self-actualization at a conceptual level. In Europe, Rudolf Steiner and Reg Revans developed this concept into the system of individual learning and organizational renewal. The Anglo-German management philosopher, Fritz Schumacher, introduced Buddhist economics and authored the concept of "Small is Beautiful". In the Indian subcontinent, Mahatma Gandhi emphasized grass root level technology and put the customer at the centre of the entire business activity. JRD Tata brought in progress-driven infrastructure. Dr Homi Jehangir Bhabha and Prof. Vikram Sarabhai launched the high, technology-based atomic energy and space programmes with a clear-cut emphasis on the natural laws of totality and flow. Advancing the developmental philosophy of Dr Bhabha and Prof. Sarabhai, Dr MS Swaminathan ushered the Green Revolution into India working on another natural principle of integrity. Dr Verghese Kurien brought in a powerful cooperative movement through a revolution in the dairy industry. Prof. Satish Dhawan developed mission management concepts in space research. These are but a few examples of individuals who have not only articulated but also implemented their ideas, thus changing forever the face of research and business organizations all over the world.

In the IGMDP, I attempted to integrate the vision of Prof. Sarabhai and the mission of Prof. Dhawan by adapting the high-technology setting of Dr Brahm Prakash's space research. I attempted to add the natural law of latency in founding the Indian Guided Missile Programme in order to create a completely indigenous variety of technology management. Let me use a metaphor to illuminate this.

The tree of technology management takes root only if there is the self-actualization of needs, renewal, interdependence, and natural flow. The growth patterns are characteristic of the evolution process, which means that things move in a combination of slow change and sudden transformation; each transformation causes either a leap into a new, more complex level or a devastating crash to some earlier level; dominant models reach a certain peak of success when they turn troublesome; and the rate of change always accelerates.

The stem of the tree is the molecular structure in which all actions are formative, all policies are normative, and all decisions are integrative. The branches of this tree are resources, assets, operations, and products which are nourished by the stem through a continuous performance evaluation and corrective update.

This tree of technology management, if carefully tended, bears the fruits of an adaptive infrastructure: technological empowerment of the institutions, the generation of technical skills among people, and finally self-reliance of the nation and improvement in the quality of life of its citizenry.

When IGMDP was sanctioned in 1983, we did not have an adequate technology base. A few pockets of expertise were available, but we lacked the authority to utilize that expert technology. The multi-project environment of the programme provided a challenge, for five advanced missile systems had to be simultaneously developed. This demanded judicious sharing of resources, establishing priorities, and ongoing induction of manpower. Eventually, the IGMDP had 78 partners, including 36 technology centres and 41 production centres spread over public sector undertakings, ordnance factories, private industries, and professional societies, hand-in-hand with a well-knit bureaucratic structure in the Government. In the management of the Programme, as much as in the technological inputs, we attempted to develop a model that was appropriate, even tailor-made, for our very specific needs and capabilities. We borrowed ideas that had been developed else-where, but adapted them in the light of what we knew were our strengths and what we recognized as the constraints we would be compelled to work under. All in all, the combination of appropriate management and our cooperative endeavours helped to unearth the talent and potential that lay unused in our research laboratories, government institutions and private industries.

The Technology Management philosophy of IGMDP is not exclusive to missile development. It represents the national urge to succeed and an awareness that the world will never again be directed by muscle or money power. In fact, both these powers will depend on technological excellence. Technology respects only technology. And, as I said in the beginning, technology, unlike science, is a group activity. It does not grow only through individual intelligence, but by intelligences interacting and ceaselessly influencing one another. And that is what I tried to make IGMDP: a 78-strong Indian family which also makes missile systems.

There has been much speculation and philosophizing about the life and times of our scientists, but not enough exploration in determining where they wanted to go and how they reached there. In sharing with you the story of my struggle to become a person, I have perhaps given you some insight into this journey. I hope it will help at least a few young people to stand up to the authoritarianism in our society. A characteristic feature of this social authoritarianism is its insidious ability to addict people to the endless pursuit of external rewards, wealth, prestige, position, promotion, approval of one's lifestyle by others, ceremonial honours, and status symbols of all kinds.

To successfully pursue these goals, they have to learn elaborate rules of etiquette and familiarize themselves with customs, traditions, protocols and so on. The youth of today must unlearn this self-defeating way of life. The culture of working only for material possessions and rewards must be discarded. When I see wealthy, powerful and learned people struggling to be at peace with themselves, I remember people like Ahmed Jallaluddin and Iyadurai Solomon. How happy they were with virtually no possessions!

> *On the coast of Coromandel*
> *Where the earthy shells blow,*
> *In the middle of the sands*
> *Lived some really rich souls.*
> *One cotton lungi and half a candle –*
> *One old jug without a handle*
> *These were all the worldly possessions*
> *Of these kings in the middle of the sands.*

How did they feel so secure without anything to fall back upon? I believe they drew sustenance from within. They relied more on the inner signals and less on the external cues that I have mentioned above. Are you aware of your inner signals? Do you trust them? Have you taken control over your life into your own hands? Take this from me, the more decisions you can make avoiding external pressures, which will constantly try to manipulate you, the better your life will be, the better your society will become. In fact the entire nation will benefit by having strong, inward-looking people as their leaders. A citizenry that thinks for itself, a country of people who trust themselves as individuals, would be virtually immune to manipulation by any unscrupulous authority or vested interest.

Your willingness to use your own inner resources to invest in your life, especially your imagination, will bring you success. When you address a task from your own uniquely individual standpoint, you become a whole person.

Everyone on this planet is sent forth by Him to cultivate all the creative potential within us and live at peace with our own choices. We differ in the way we make our choices and evolve our destiny. Life is a difficult game. You can win only by retaining your birthright to be a person. And to retain this right, you will have to be willing to take the social or external risks involved in ignoring pressures to do things the way others say they should be done. What will you call Sivasubramania Iyer inviting me to have lunch in his kitchen? Zohara, my sister, mortgaging her gold bangles and chains to get me into engineering college? Prof. Sponder insisting that I should sit with him in the front row for the group photograph? Making a hovercraft in a motor-garage setup? Sudhakar's courage? Dr Brahm Prakash's support? Narayanan's management? Venkataraman's vision? Arunachalam's drive? Each is an example of a strong inner strength and initiative. As Pythagoras had said twenty-five centuries ago, "Above all things, reverence yourself."

I am not a philosopher. I am only a man of technology. I spent all mylife learning rocketry. But as I have worked with a very large cross-section of people in different organizations, I had an opportunity to understand the phenomenon of professional life in its bewildering complexity. When I look back upon what I have narrated so far, my own observations and conclusions appear as dogmatic utterances. My colleagues, associates, leaders; the complex science of rocketry; the important issues of technology management; all seem to have been dealt with in a perfunctory manner. The despair and happiness, the achievements and the failures—differing markedly in context, time and space—all appear grouped together.

When you look down from an aircraft, people, houses, rocks, fields, trees, all appear as one homogeneous landscape; it is very difficult to distinguish one from another. What you have just read is a similar bird's-eye view of my life seen, as it were, from afar.

> *My worthiness is all my doubt –*
> *His merit – all my fear –*
> *Contrasting which my quality*
> *Does however – appear.*

This is the story of the period ending with the first *Agni* launch—life will go on. This great country will make enormous strides in all fields if we think like a united nation of 900 million people. My story—the story of the son of Jainulabdeen, who lived for over a hundred years on Mosque Street in Rameswaram island and died there; the story of a lad who sold newspapers to help his brother; the story of a pupil reared by Sivasubramania Iyer and Iyadurai Solomon; the story of a student taught by teachers like Pandalai; the story of an engineer spotted by MGK Menon and groomed by the legendary Prof. Sarabhai; the story of a scientist tested by failures and setbacks; the story of a leader supported by a large team of brilliant and dedicated professionals. This story will end with me, for I have no belongings in the worldly sense. I have acquired nothing, built nothing, possess nothing—no family, sons, daughters.

I am a well in this great land
Looking at its millions of boys and girls
To draw from me
The inexhaustible divinity
And spread His grace everywhere
As does the water drawn from a well.

I do not wish to set myself up as an example to others, but I believe that a few readers may draw inspiration and come to experience that ultimate satisfaction which can only be found in the life of the spirit. God's providence is your inheritance. The bloodline of my great-grandfather Avul, my grandfather Pakir, and my father Jainulabdeen, may end with Abdul Kalam, but His grace will never cease, for it is Eternal.

This book is interwoven with my deep involvement with India's first Satellite Launch Vehicle SLV-3 and Agni Programmes, an involvement which eventually led to my participation in the recent important national event related to the nuclear tests in May 1998. I have had the great opportunity and honour of working with three scientific establishments—Space, Defence Research and Atomic Energy. I found, while working in these establishments, that the best of human beings and the best of innovative minds were available in plenty. One feature common to all three establishments is that the scientists and technologists were never afraid of failures during their missions. Failures contain within themselves the seeds of further learning which can lead to better technology, and eventually, to a high level of success. These people were also great dreamers and their dreams finally culminated in spectacular achievements. I feel that if we consider the combined technological strength of all these scientific institutions, it would certainly be comparable to the best found anywhere in the world. Above all, I have had the opportunity of working with the great visionaries of the nation, namely Prof. Vikram Sarabhai, Prof. Satish Dhawan and Dr Brahm Prakash, each of whom have greatly enriched my life.

A nation needs both economic prosperity and strong security for growth and development. Our Self Reliance Mission in Defence System 1995–2005 will provide the Armed Forces with a state-of-the-art competitive weapons system. The Technology Vision–2020 plan will put into place certain schemes and plans for the economic growth and prosperity of the nation. These two plans have evolved out of the nation's dreams. I earnestly hope and pray that the development resulting from these two plans—Self Reliance Mission and Technology Vision–2020—will eventually make our country strong and prosperous and take our rightful place among the ranks of the "developed" nations.

Plate 42 Receiving the Padma Vibhushan award from President R Venkataraman in 1990. (Source: APJMJ Sheik Saleem) – *New to this edition*

Plate 43 With President Venkataraman. (Source: APJMJ Sheik Saleem) – *New to this edition*

Plate 44 With Prime Minister PV Narasimha Rao, RN Agarwal and A Sivathanu Pillai.
(Source: APJMJ Sheik Saleem) – *New to this edition*

Plate 45 With PV Narasimha Rao at DRDL, Hyderabad.
(Source: APJMJ Sheik Saleem) – *New to this edition*

Plate 46 With the three Service Chiefs. To my left is Admiral VS Shekhawat, on my right are General BC Joshi and Air Chief Marshal SK Kaul.

Plate 47 Receiving the Bharat Ratna from President KR Narayanan.

Plate 48 With MS Subbulakshmi at the Bharat Ratna ceremony in 1998. The other awardees for 1997–98 were Gulzarilal Nanda (posthumous), Aruna Asaf Ali (posthumous) and Chidambaram Subramaniam. Satyajit Ray's son was also present to collect the award (conferred 1992) on behalf of his father.
(Source: Harry Sheridon, Private Secretary to President Kalam) – *New to this edition*

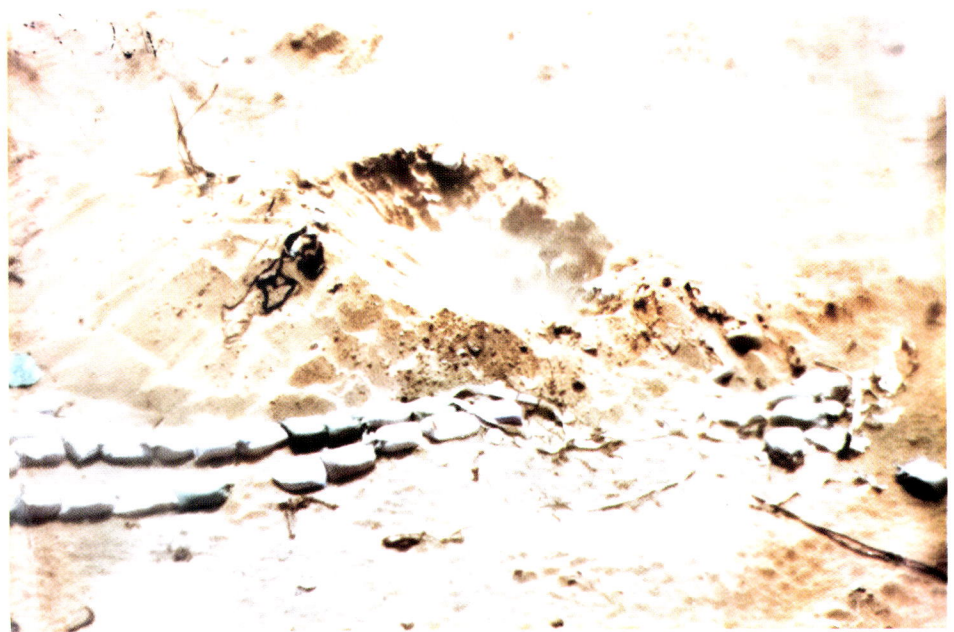

Plate 49 Pokhran-II aerial image of one of the subsidence craters at the site of the nuclear tests on 11 May 1998.
(Source: Harry Sheridon, Private Secretary to President Kalam) – *New to this edition*

Plate 50 With Rajagopala Chidambaram at a press conference following the Pokhran tests. (Source: *Wings of Fire: An Autobiography (Abridged, Special Student Edition with Exercises)*, Universities Press, 2004) – *New to this edition*

Plates 51 and 52 With Prime Minister Atal Bihari Vajpayee at the Pokhran test site. Vajpayee was instrumental in India becoming a nuclear power.
(Source: Harry Sheridon, Private Secretary to President Kalam) – *New to this edition*

Plate 53 Being sworn in as the eleventh President of India. (Source: Photo Cell, President's Secretariat, Rashtrapati Bhavan)
– *New to this edition*

Plate 54 Bidding farewell to Dr K R Narayanan, the tenth President of India. (Source: Photo Cell, President's Secretariat, Rashtrapati Bhavan) – *New to this edition*

Plate 55 At the Sabarmati Ashram on his visit to Ahmedabad, Gujarat.
(Source: Harry Sheridon, Private Secretary to President Kalam) – *New to this edition*

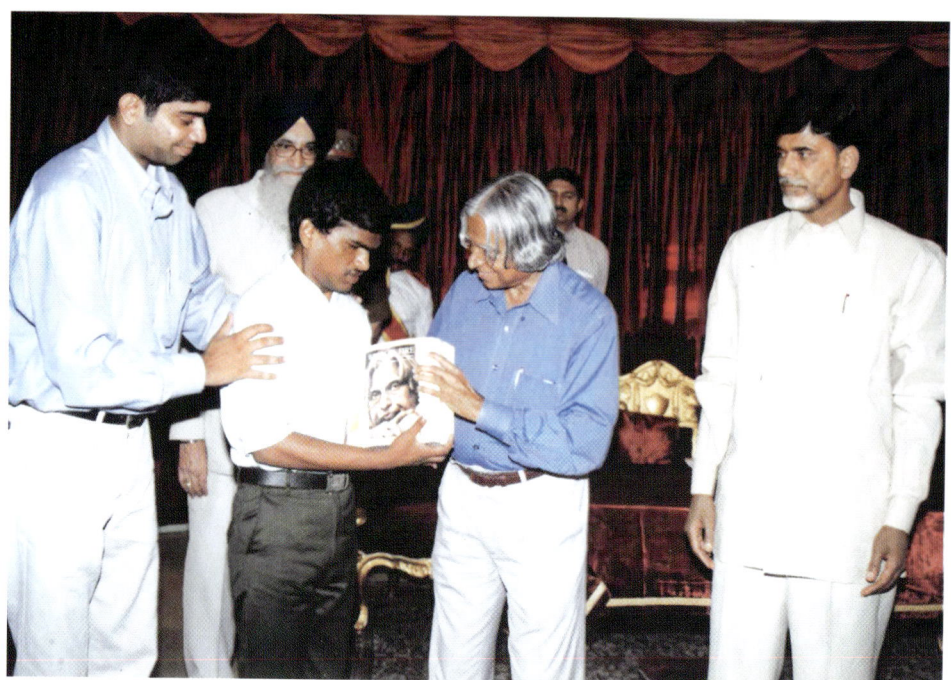

Plates 56 and 57 Gifting copies of the Braille edition of *Wings of Fire* to two visually impaired children, Govind (above) and Swathi (below), during the book's release on 7 June 2003 in Raj Bhavan, Hyderabad. Also seen are N Chandrababu Naidu and Surjit Singh Barnala, Chief Minister and Governor of Andhra Pradesh, respectively.
– New to this edition

Plate 58 During an interaction with school students in Assam. Left: Lt Gen SK Sinha, PVSM, ADC (Retd), Governor of Assam; Middle: Harry Sheridon, Private Secretary to President Kalam; Right: Shri Tarun Gogoi, Chief Minister of Assam.
(Source: Harry Sheridon, Private Secretary to President Kalam) – *New to this edition*

Plate 59 With Bishop Joan, Abbot of the Rila Monastery, and Harry Sheridon during Dr Kalam's state visit to Bulgaria in 2003.
(Source: Harry Sheridon, Private Secretary to President Kalam) – *New to this edition*

Plate 60 With the Jawans at Siachen Base Camp. (Source: Photo Cell, President's Secretariat, Rashtrapati Bhavan) – *New to this edition*

Plate 61 Picture taken at VSSC on the occasion of the unveiling of the bust of Prof. Sarabhai in front of the main building. Standing (from left): AC Bahl, DS Rane, BC Pillai, Abdul Majeed, (not identified), Sreedharan Das, EVS Namboothiri, BN Suresh, V Sundara Ramaiah, K Narayana, (not identified), RV Perumal, PS Goel, N Vedachalam, Sudhakar Rao, Yash Pal, (not identified), (not identified), PS Veeraraghavan, D Narayana Moorthi, S Ramakrishnan, RAD Pillai, KK Athithan, (not identified), YS Rajan, Prabhakaran and Karthikeya Sarabhai. Sitting (from left): MK Mukarjee, SC Gupta, AE Muthunayagam, K Kasturirangan, Mrs Menon, MGK Menon, Mrinalini Sarabhai, Kalam, EV Chitnis, G Madhavan Nair, TN Seshan and Mallika Sarabhai.

(Source: *Ever Upwards: ISRO in Images*, Universities Press, 2019) – *New to this edition*

Plate 62 With former ISRO colleagues. From left: GK Kuruvila, V Gnanagandhi, MYS Prasad (partly seen), G Madhavan Nair, G Ravindranath, V Adimurthy, Balakrishnan, N Narayana Moorthy, Seshagiri Rao and G Viswanathan.
(Source: *Ever Upwards: ISRO in Images*, Universities Press, 2019) – *New to this edition*

Plate 63 With Nelson Mandela in South Africa. (Source: Press Information Bureau)
– *New to this edition*

Plate 64 With Parvez Musharraf, President of Pakistan.
(Source: Photo Cell, President's Secretariat, Rashtrapati Bhavan)
– *New to this edition*

Plate 65 On a visit to Visakhapatnam, boarding the submarine *INS Sindhurakshak*.
(Source: Photo Cell, President's Secretariat, Rashtrapati Bhavan)
– *New to this edition*

Plate 66 At the banquet in honour of President George W Bush of the USA.
(Source: Photo Cell, President's Secretariat, Rashtrapati Bhavan)
– *New to this edition*

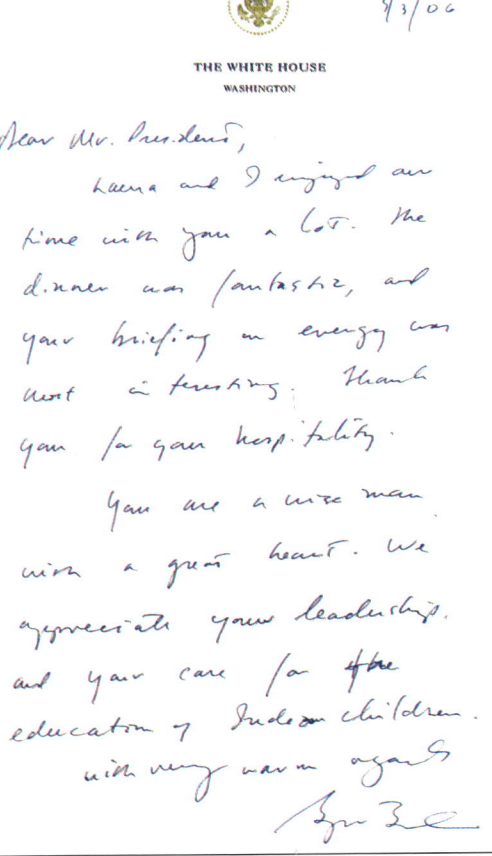

Plate 67 President Bush's letter to President Kalam, thanking him for his kind hospitality during his visit to India.
(Source: Harry Sheridon, Private Secretary to President Kalam).
– *New to this edition*

Plate 68 At the shehnai recital by Ustad Bismillah Khan.

(Source: Photo Cell, President's Secretariat, Rashtrapati Bhavan) – *New to this edition*

Plate 69 In the Sukhoi sortie, at the Lohegaon Air Force Base in Pune.
(Source: Photo Cell, President's Secretariat, Rashtrapati Bhavan)
– *New to this edition*

Plate 70 Addressing the audience after the flight on the Sukhoi Su-30MKI.
(Source: Photo Cell, President's Secretariat, Rashtrapati Bhavan)
– *New to this edition*

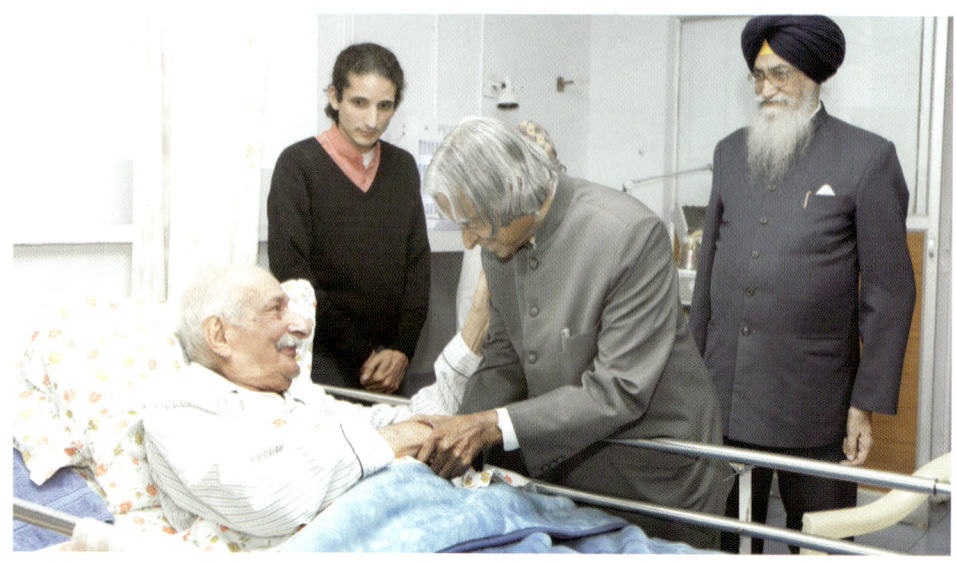

Plate 71 Visiting Field Marshal Sam Manekshaw at the Military Hospital in Wellington. (Source: Photo Cell, President's Secretariat, Rashtrapati Bhavan)
– *New to this edition*

Plates 72 and 73 (above) Addressing the European Parliament (below) before an appreciative audience.
(Source: Photo Cell, President's Secretariat, Rashtrapati Bhavan) – *New to this edition*

Plate 74 Receiving New Year greetings from his many admirers.
(Source: Photo Cell, President's Secretariat, Rashtrapati Bhavan)
– *New to this edition*

Plate 75 Meeting guests in the forecourt at his farewell on 25 July 2007.
Seen here are Prime Minister Manmohan Singh and his wife, and Sonia Gandhi.
(Source: Photo Cell, President's Secretariat, Rashtrapati Bhavan) – *New to this edition*

Plate 76 Taking the Farewell Guard of Honour.
(Source: Photo Cell, President's Secretariat, Rashtrapati Bhavan) – *New to this edition*

Plate 77 Meeting the incoming President, Smt. Pratibha Patil.
(Source: Photo Cell, President's Secretariat, Rashtrapati Bhavan)
– *New to this edition*

Plate 78 At Mission Operation Complex, Peenya, Bangalore. Celebrating the Moon impact probe landing on the Moon's surface. Also seen are S Ramakrishnan, UR Rao, G Madhavan Nair, SK Shivakumar, TK Alex, K Radhakrishnan and Kishore Nath. (Source: *Ever Upwards: ISRO in Images*, Universities Press, 2019)
– *New to this edition*

President APJ Abdul Kalam about to begin his talk on the topic **"How to make our planet more livable?"** on 27 July, 2015 in the IIM Shillong Auditorium.

Plate 79 This was to be his last speech. Dr Kalam collapsed soon after he began speaking and was rushed to the hospital, where he passed away.
(Source: IIM Shillong) – *New to this edition*

V

DISPERSION
[1991–2002]

Parts V and VI present the personal reminiscences of Prof. Arun Tiwari and are based on the conversations he had with Dr Kalam. These are, therefore, a collection of personal stories and memories and are a reflection of his perspective on Dr Kalam.

CHAPTER 17

GIVING BACK

The guest house at the Defence Research and Development Organisation (DRDO) in Hyderabad had been Dr Kalam's place of residence for 10 years. In 1991, Prof. P Rama Rao visited the Powder Metallurgy Plant in Hyderabad, at a walking distance from the DRDO.

Prof. Rama Rao met Dr Kalam at the guest house over tea. Dr Kalam reminded him about the Rao–Kalam school and expressed his resolve to set up this school soon. Prof. Rama Rao replied, rather philosophically, that he wished people were in control of their lives. He told Dr Kalam that he had finalized the acquisition of 95 acres in Hyderabad, on the eastern side of DRDL, where DST would be setting up the International Advanced Research Centre for Powder Metallurgy and New Materials (ARCI).

Dr Kalam asked him why it should be called "international." Prof. Rama Rao replied that science and technology are global enterprises; to be self-reliant, India should work with other advanced countries and not try to reinvent the wheel. After a pause, he said that if India missed the bus now, as it had in the case of electronic hardware, it would forever need to buy products for the technologies used in nanomaterials, fuel cells, solar and automotive energy materials.

He also told Dr Kalam that his mission should not end with the missile programme. He even suggested that he should come to Delhi.

Soon Dr Kalam realized it was not just Prof. Rama Rao's personal wish . . . there were others who wanted him to be in Delhi too. On 29 August 1991, Dr VS Arunachalam called him. It was Onam and, after exchanging a few words about *Chingam* and how Lord Vishnu visited Emperor Mahabali as Vamana, he said he would be retiring next year. Dr Kalam must take the baton of leading DRDO from him, he said. Dr Kalam responded that he was not an academic scientist; rather, he was an engineer who had somehow accomplished some scientific feats. He personally felt heading the DRDO was too much to expect from him. Dr Arunachalam laughed and reminded Dr Kalam of his hesitation when he became the Director of DRDL. He closed the discussion by suggesting that Dr Kalam let Dr Arunachalam decide this time as well.

In the winter of 1991, Dr Arunachalam took Dr Kalam to meet Sharad Pawar, then Defence Minister of India, to whom he reported. The minister had a robust personality and was warm in his manner. He held Dr Kalam's hand and asked him if rocket fuel could be made from sugarcane molasses. This was an unexpected question for Dr Kalam, who was ready to talk about missiles. He responded that, yes, indeed, sugarcane molasses, which produces ethanol, can be used as rocket fuel. The session ended there.

Thereafter, Dr Arunachalam started involving Dr Kalam in high-level committees and tasked him with self-reliance in critical technologies. Prof. Rama Rao was a member of most of these committees. Dr Kalam became a regular visitor to Delhi.

Dr Arunachalam informed Dr Kalam that he would be working in the Prime Minister's Office (PMO) soon; Dr Kalam was to succeed him as the Scientific Adviser to the Defence Minister and Director General of DRDO.

On 10 July 1992, Dr Kalam handed over control of DRDL to Lt Gen. Dr VJ Sundaram. They spent two weeks in discussions and DRDL soon began limited series production of the *Prithvi* and *Agni* missiles. The armed forces' dedication to these two missile systems was earned when the missiles fulfilled their field needs on deployment and operability. Lt Gen. Sundaram was DRDL's face with the three services and he commanded a lot of respect. DRDL had also completed the development of a naval derivative of the *Prithvi* and *Agni* missiles, in short- and long-range configurations.

Dr Kalam now had an office in the iconic South Block in New Delhi. He opted to live in a portion of the DRDO guest house in the Asiad Village, in the Siri Fort area, near Hauz Khas in South Delhi. Dr Kalam could see the Asiad Tower from his window. A well-laid jogging track surrounded another park in the complex, and he developed a habit of taking a morning walk there.

The Government of India had set up a committee of members from the three services and military manufacturing organizations; this Self-Reliance Committee largely dealt with classified work. Prime Minister PV Narasimha Rao was convinced that an open market and new technology would bring the nation to a position of greater economic strength. Dr Kalam was asked to head the Self-Reliance Committee and tasked with creating a roadmap for developing critical key technology indigenously. "Why me?" Dr Kalam introspected. But he believed there was a hidden hand that picked people for different roles. He felt he must rise to the occasion.

Prof. Rama Rao also invited Dr Kalam to preside over the Technology Information, Forecasting, and Assessment Council (TIFAC), an autonomous body established in 1988 under the Department of Science and Technology. YS Rajan, Executive Director of TIFAC, had served as scientific secretary to Prof. Satish Dhawan at the ISRO headquarters; he was known to Dr Kalam. TIFAC gave Dr Kalam a broad view and he learned how to evaluate the trajectories of the technologies—what the country needed to acquire, what to collaborate on, and what it could do alone.

In 1994, Dr Kalam received an invitation to address the Indian Science Congress in Jaipur. He reflected for a few days before accepting. He told himself it was time for scientific organizations, academic institutions, the private sector and social streams to converge and deliver what would be valuable for the Indian people. Indian science must have a human face. Technology must serve people, make their lives better, and enrich their livelihoods. He decided to use this platform to call for the development of technology spin-offs. When he said in his lecture, "Let my brain remove your pain," spontaneous applause broke out. It was the headlines in some newspapers the next day.

He used the Self-Reliance Committee to help organizations introspect—a sort of *atma bodha* (self-knowledge). Nine Defence Public Sector Undertakings (DPSUs) have been the backbone of Indian technology. They covered the high-end technology spectrum—aviation, electronics and warships. Hindustan Aeronautics Limited (HAL) was the largest, almost half of the combined valuation of the DPSUs. Bharat Electronics Ltd. (BEL) had nine production facilities and thirty-one manufacturing divisions across seven states. Bharat Earth Movers Limited (BEML) met the basic needs of defence forces—bulldozers, cranes, heavy-duty trucks and railway wagons. Bharat Dynamics Ltd. (BDL) build tactical missiles. MIDHANI's special steels, super alloys and titanium alloys satisfied core requirements for atomic energy projects, space and defence production. Mazagon Dock Shipbuilders Ltd. (MDL), Bombay; Garden Reach Shipbuilders and Engineers (GRSE), Calcutta; Goa Shipyard Ltd. (GSL), Goa; and Hindustan Shipyard Ltd. (HSL), Visakhapatnam, were all involved in shipbuilding and other naval engineering services.

Dr Kalam articulated the goal of reversing, in 10 years, the status of 30 per cent indigenous and 70 per cent imported to 70 per cent indigenous and 30 per cent imported. The critical technologies they decided upon were gallium arsenide devices, fibre optics, creative weapons subsystems, heavy particle beams, focal plane array and hypersonic propulsion. "Core" and "mother" technologies were required for constructing state-of-the-art defence systems; a Defence Technology Fund of Rs 100 crore was created. This would help develop the Light Combat Aircraft (LCA), which would need carbon fibres, multimode radars and stealth capability. Dr Kota Harinarayana, Chief Designer in the HAL Nasik Division, was already heading the LCA team.

When Sharad Pawar became the Chief Minister of Maharashtra in March 1993, Prime Minister Rao took additional charge of the Defence Ministry. Dr Kalam now had direct access to the Prime Minister. It was during this time that a decision to develop a nuclear weapon was taken. Dr Kalam was entrusted with overseeing the development of the nuclear weapon without disturbing the atomic power stations that operated with international help.

After the dissolution of the Soviet Union in 1991, India had no "superpower" friends. With hostile neighbours on either side, there was no option but to become a nuclear-armed country. Dr R Chidambaram, Director of BARC, and Dr Kalam became buddies. Dr Kalam had no experience of working with the Department of Atomic Energy; he had worked primarily with the Space and Defence sectors. The chemistry between them was a great blessing for the nuclear programme as it evolved.

In 1996, the Navy urgently required a quick-reaction air defence system to shield its warships at sea from anti-ship missiles and aircraft. This was in response to the Pakistan Navy obtaining Harpoon missiles from the US and Exocet sea-skimming missiles from France; these missiles could approach Indian ships at near-sonic speed and cause catastrophic damage regardless of weather conditions and daylight. The development of *Trishul*, the missile intended for this purpose, had been delayed.

When the Prime Minister inquired what could be done, Dr Kalam replied that the services needed to be served. Showing courage, he accepted there had been a delay in developing a sea-skimming missile, and this cleared the way for the purchase of another missile.

The Israeli Barak missile was the best option. But how was it to be procured? Many in the Indian establishment viewed Israel with suspicion; Israel returned the sentiment. Indian passport holders had been banned from entering Israel until 1992. In fact, it had been PV Narasimha Rao who had helped Israel establish an embassy in New Delhi in 1992; he had developed a relationship with Israel during his tenure as Minister of External Affairs from 1980 to 1984 and then from 1988 to 1989. This smoothed the purchase of the Barak missile and this later developed into a 350-million-dollar collaborative effort between the Israeli military technology sector and the DRDO.

In the 1991 Gulf War, American Tomahawk cruise missiles demonstrated their utility by devastating Iraq's command and communication centres and exposing Iraqi military forces to unhindered air strikes. It seemed unbelievable that a few hundred cruise missiles could isolate the 1.2-million-strong Iraqi military in the span of a few hours. Dr Kalam articulated that India had to be armed with a cruise missile system.

The Prime Minister stated that there were no funds for this. He asked Dr Kalam to utilize his goodwill within the Russian scientific community. This was a new challenge for a technologist; Dr Kalam now had to don the hat of a diplomat and an international negotiator.

Dr Kalam explained to his Russian counterparts why it was time for India and Russia to develop a "missile system" by pooling their resources. The idea gained traction after the dissolution of the Soviet Union. NPO Mashinostroyeniya, a Russian firm based near Moscow, had been developing missile systems for the Russian military since World War II and was in an advanced stage of developing a supersonic cruise missile. India would not pay to "buy" the missiles, but "work together" to "test" and "refine" the missile system.

The Russians were wary of entering a public sector system and were pushing for a private sector company to partner with. Dr Kalam negotiated a 50.5–49.5 per cent partnership to avoid the joint venture becoming a public sector company while remaining a government enterprise. His long-time friend and trusted colleague from ISRO, Sivathanu Pillai, became the CEO of the new company, which was headquartered in a newly constructed campus in the Delhi Cantonment area. The company was named BrahMos, an acronym for the Brahmaputra and Moscow Rivers. Once again, Dr Kalam proved his truism of "strength respects strength."

If IGMDP was a tree that Dr Kalam helped grow in the DRDO, BrahMos was his own brainchild. He was keen to make it a future weapon—a missile that would be precise and swift enough to evade detection. He was a visionary who could see how future wars would be fought and how assaults would be made and countered. Increased attack speed immediately lowers the enemy's reaction time. "BrahMos must be faster than the Tomahawk, the best long-range American cruise missile of that time; this is the 'specification' from my side," he had said. No wonder BrahMos was made a supersonic missile that would fly at almost three times the speed of sound.

In 1996, the general elections brought in a series of changes in government. After a fortnight's stint by Atal Bihari Vajpayee, HD Deve Gowda took over as the Prime Minister. Former Chief Minister of Uttar Pradesh, Mulayam Singh Yadav, was named Defence Minister. He liked Dr Kalam and praised him in public forums.

In April 1997, IK Gujral became the Prime Minister. He reappointed every single minister from Prime Minister Gowda's cabinet. When Prime Minister Gujral met Dr Kalam, he told him, "Doctor Sahib, I see you as a symbol of India's scientific strength."

Having one's Prime Minister and Defence Minister as one's admirers would be a surreal feeling for any human being. Dr Kalam wondered if he deserved this. But these leaders had no such doubts. In November 1997, the Cabinet approved conferring the Bharat Ratna upon him. He would be the second scientist to receive it after Sir CV Raman. The nation was giving Dr Kalam its highest civilian honour.

CHAPTER 18

A NEW DAWN

After the 1998 general elections, Atal Bihari Vajpayee became the Prime Minister of India; George Fernandes was appointed the Defence Minister. Brajesh Mishra, principal secretary to the PM, called Dr Kalam and Dr Chidambaram to the Prime Minister's residence the day after Holi. They were served tea and then taken to meet the Prime Minister, who smiled and said "*Samay aa gaya hai* (The time has come)."

In 1996, during his brief 13-day tenure in office, Prime Minister Vajpayee had spoken to Dr Kalam and Dr Chidambaram about his decision to conduct nuclear tests. They were now free to choose the time to carry out the tests.

Dr Chidambaram shared a good rapport with Dr Kalam although he was five years younger. After completing a PhD in Physics from the Indian Institute of Science in 1962, he had joined the Atomic Energy Establishment, Trombay, under Dr Homi Bhabha. (The centre was renamed the Bhabha Atomic Research Centre or BARC after Dr Bhabha died in 1966.) Dr Chidambaram had been part of the first nuclear test on 18 May 1974, at the Pokhran Test Range in Rajasthan, with Indira Gandhi as the Prime Minister.

After the meeting with the PM, he informed Dr Kalam that his daughter was getting married on 27 April that year. Keeping this in mind, Dr Kalam suggested Buddha Purnima, which fell on 11 May, as the day for the nuclear test. They sounded out their close aides, and everyone agreed wholeheartedly that this was a good idea.

On 2 May, Anil Kakodkar, the Director of BARC, lost his father; he left to perform the last rites and returned immediately as there was no time to mourn.

The 58 Engineer Regiment of the Indian Army's Corps of Engineers had been in control of the Pokhran Range. They had dug three vertical tunnels over several months, using the nights to escape the spy satellite images. Of the many dry, abandoned wells that lay in the vicinity, some had been selected to be deepened and expanded into 50-metre-deep shafts. The site had been prepared to a state where a nuclear test could be conducted in as little as 10 days. It had been maintained in this condition of constant readiness for more than a year.

Following a rigorous secrecy protocol, about a hundred scientists and technologists from BARC and DRDO were provided with Army fatigues and fake military identities. Dr Kalam was codenamed "Prithviraj" after the *Prithvi* missile, and he was called "Major General." Dr Chidambaram was "Natraj," another name for Lord Shiva.

Nuclear reactions—fission (in a fission device) or a mix of fission and fusion (in a thermonuclear device)—give an atomic weapon its destructive power. Both processes generate huge amounts of energy from relatively tiny amounts of material. The planned series of experiments would detonate six devices. A thermonuclear weapon was sealed inside a 200-metre-deep tunnel termed the White House. At the bottom of a 150-metre-deep tunnel codenamed Taj Mahal, a fission device was set in place and sealed. The Kumbhakaran shaft held a sub-kiloton device. The other three 50-metre shafts, for the second test series, were NT 1, 2 and 3 (abbreviated from Nava Tala or new wells).

The three gentlemen—Kalam, Chidambaram and Kakodkar—stood close to the test site on the night of 10–11 May 1998. Apart from the wind, there was complete silence. Almost simultaneously, each of them uttered Dr Bhabha's name. Dr Kalam said that had it not been for Dr Bhabha, they would not have been there that day. It felt as if a divine force had given vision to human minds, and a hidden hand had guided people to work on specific missions. Many great missions span multiple generations, each generation doing its bit to leave behind a body of work that is eventually completed by those who come after them.

At dawn, heavy winds shifted the desert sands—the same wind would carry the explosion's dust towards Pokhran town. Dr Kalam recalled a phrase he had read somewhere in his youth—one must wait for something that deserves the wait. The tests could be run when the wind died down at about 3.00 p.m.

The Prime Minister was in contact through a protected hotline from the test site. Dr Kalam spoke to him and received his approval. The first three devices exploded at exactly 3:43:44 p.m. IST on 11 May 1998. Their combined power raised an area roughly the size of a cricket ground several metres above the earth, producing billowing clouds of dust and sand. Later in the evening, with all the tension spent, Dr Kalam enquired if there was some filter coffee. Everyone immediately endorsed the request. So, it wasn't champagne but filter coffee that was used to toast the successful test!

When the results were announced, they created a sense of joy and pride among many Indian people. The international media were sceptical, however, and talked more about the failure of satellite surveillance! Two days later, the two sub-kiloton devices lowered into NT 1 and 2 were detonated. Dr Chidambaram ordered the device in NT 3 to be pulled out. He thought the scientists had got all the data they needed, and there was no need to waste a device.

The Prime Minister and Defence Minister came to Pokhran on 20 May. The Defence Minister, George Fernandes, jokingly told Dr Kalam that it was good that the spy satellites hovering over Pokhran had not captured his shining hair!

Meanwhile, *Agni*-II was also ready. Capable of carrying a nuclear warhead as a payload, *Agni*-II became an all-solid-propellant system by replacing *Agni*-I's liquid propulsion stage with a solid propellant motor. The missile's Re-entry Vehicle (RV) was merged with a Post Boost Vehicle (PBV). It was tested from Wheeler Island (renamed Abdul Kalam Island in 2015) off the Orissa coast on 11 April 1999. The mobile launcher was a converted rail wagon with its roof pulled open to let two oversized hydraulic pistons lift the missile to the vertical launch posture. The missile travelled 2,100 miles down-range.

Dr Kalam's task had been completed gloriously. He handed over his responsibilities to Dr VK Aatre, former head of the Naval Physical and Oceanographic Laboratory (NPOL), Kochi, and then Chief Controller (R&D).

When Dr Kalam visited the Prime Minister to bid farewell, Vajpayee smiled and remarked, "*Aap kahi nahi ja rahe ho* (You aren't going anywhere!)." The next day Brajesh Mishra informed Dr Kalam that a new Office of the Principal Scientific Adviser (PSA) to the Government of India had been established, at cabinet minister-level rank, and he had been named the first incumbent.

The PSA's office was set up at the Vigyan Bhavan Annexe, part of a conference venue on Maulana Azad Road. Dr Kalam asked YS Rajan to be his scientific secretary; he also had his private secretary, Harry Sheridon, transferred from DRDO to the new office.

He was uncertain how the new office would perform in the first several weeks, and Dr Kalam held wide-ranging consultations to figure out the PSA's functions. Some questions he asked were: Do the national laboratories and organizations miss out on anything? Is there a missing link in the benefits of science and technology reaching people? Who are the people desperately in need of assistance? Are the seven hundred thousand villages connected to the mainstream?

Prof. PV Indiresan helped Dr Kalam find the solution. The former Director of IIT Madras had created a rural economy model. When Dr Kalam met him at an event, he enquired if the bureaucrats had taken his advice. Prof. Indiresan responded that bureaucrats take the advice they want and nothing else! Dr Kalam sighed and said that altering the system was difficult, but that would not stop them from doing their job. He asked Prof. Indiresan to visit Delhi; they could pool resources to find a way in which villages could support themselves. They realized that offering some urban facilities in rural regions would enable India to overcome the challenges of fast urbanization. This mission was named PURA (Provision of Urban Amenities to Rural Areas).

Many villages in India are in remote locations and are often too small to be able to afford even fundamental utilities; they cannot maintain schools, clinics, markets and other services. PURA provided a means to overcome this problem. In PURA, one village was not seen as a separate unit; instead, a cluster of interconnected villages, with a combined population of thirty to fifty thousand, was considered large enough to provide many fundamental urban services. Many business leaders and corporates found this concept appealing.

On 30 September 2001, Dr Kalam flew in a helicopter from Ranchi to Bokaro to attend a meeting of the Science and Technology Council of the newly formed state of Jharkhand. Jharkhand's Minister of Science and Technology, Samaresh Singh, was with him. While descending, the helicopter's rotor malfunctioned, and it fell to the ground from roughly 100 metres. Everyone on board escaped with minor injuries, miraculously. The next morning, however, Dr Kalam read in the newspaper that a plane carrying the young leader Madhavrao Scindia and a team of journalists had crashed on the outskirts of the Mainpuri area of Uttar Pradesh, killing everyone on board.

Back in Delhi, Dr Kalam met the Prime Minister and requested that he be relieved from government duty. "Sir, I have finished seventy orbits around the sun. May I now retire to rest?" he said. The Prime Minister offered him a ministry post, but Dr Kalam did not accept. After a few minutes during which unspoken words hung in the air, the Prime Minister remarked, *"Jaisi aapki marzi* (As you wish)."

It took Dr Kalam about a month to wind up in Delhi. Several organizations approached him about joining them. He eventually went to his alma mater, Anna University in Chennai, to teach.

Vice Chancellor Prof. A. Kalanidhi offered Dr Kalam the position of Professor of Technology and Societal Transformation and provided him with an office and a room in the guest house. The guest house had no mess; breakfast would come from the Postgraduate Hostel in a tiffin box. To make up for this, Prof. Kalanidhi insisted that Dr Kalam's meals come from his own home, and this loving gesture overcame Dr Kalam's hesitation.

The vast and verdant Guindy campus, which covers over 100 hectares and borders the Adyar River on the north, seemed like paradise. Dr Kalam would spend his free time with the students, listening to their aspirations and responding to their enquiries. Linguistically and culturally, he was close to his roots in Rameswaram. He was genuinely happy and enjoying himself. This was an excellent way to conclude his odyssey, he believed.

On his first weekend in Chennai, Dr Kalam had visited Kanchipuram. The Shankaracharya of Kanchi had called farmers from hundreds of villages to launch a knowledge-empowered rural development programme based on the PURA concept. When the meeting ended, both acharyas—Swami Jayendra and Swami Vijayendra—had a private meeting with Dr Kalam. Swami Vijayendra told Dr Kalam that through his work he had realized the presence of the same *atman* (soul) in all living beings. Go and spread compassion, he advised.

On 10 June 2002, Dr Kalam received a message from Dr Kalanidhi's office that the Prime Minister needed to speak with him and he should come to the Vice Chancellor's office immediately. He was perplexed. He had not heard from any government functionary for more than a year now!

When Prime Minister Atal Bihari Vajpayee came on the line, he formally offered Dr Kalam the post of President of India. Dr Kalam was silent. He thanked the Prime Minister and asked for an hour to consider this proposal. The Prime Minister said he hoped for a yes and not a no.

By the evening, Dr Kalam's candidacy for President was revealed at a joint press conference led by George Fernandes, the Defence Minister; Pramod Mahajan, the Parliamentary Affairs Minister; Chandrababu Naidu, the Andhra Pradesh Chief Minister; and Kumari Mayawati, the Uttar Pradesh Chief Minister. The Anna University campus celebrated that evening! Hundreds of students came out to show their appreciation. Police security showed up the following morning for the presidential candidate. Dr APJ Abdul Kalam had now expanded beyond science and technology. He was now truly a public figure.

The following day, Pramod Mahajan phoned Dr Kalam to discuss a suitable time for him to submit the presidential nomination. Dr Kalam told him that astronomy, and not astrology, drives the planet.

In New Delhi, Defence Minister George Fernandes welcomed him at the airport. To everyone's surprise, Dr Kalam opted to stay, once again, at the DRDO guest house in the Asiad Village.

On 18 June 2002, Dr Kalam's nomination papers were filed. Led by Sonia Gandhi, the Congress Party submitted the first nomination papers. Prime Minister Vajpayee, Home Minister Lal Krishna Advani, External Affairs Minister Jaswant Singh and Defence Minister George Fernandes filed the second batch of nomination papers for the National Democratic Alliance. The strong political support for Dr Kalam's candidacy was not unchallenged; octogenarian freedom fighter Lakshmi Sahgal submitted her presidential election nomination papers as the Left Front's candidate.

The electoral college to select the President of India comprises members of parliament and the legislative assemblies of the states and union territories. Letters signed by Dr Kalam were sent out to MPs and MLAs.

He took a detour while he travelled in the south to visit Rameswaram on 9 July. His eldest brother, APJ Maracayer, set up a prayer session with ACM Noor-ul-Huda, the imam of the local mosque.

Later, Dr Kalam walked to the home of his classmate PLV Shastri, now a priest. That night, Maracayer told Dr Kalam that their mother had wanted to name him Aarif because she had seen him as enlightened, informed and committed to Allah. She had hoped to give her son a strong inner drive to motivate others for a better cause. Their father, however, had named him after the most revered Muslim of their time, Maulana Abul Kalam Azad. His elder brother believed Dr Kalam had proved both his mother and father right.

On 25 July 2002, the outgoing President of India, KR Narayanan, brought Dr Kalam to the central hall in Parliament. Vice President Krishan Kant and Lok Sabha Speaker Manohar Joshi welcomed him. Dr Kalam's brother and other relatives were sitting in the front row. Dr Kalam stopped briefly to speak with them, but understanding the gravity and solemnity of the moment, he continued walking to the dais.

Justice BN Kirpal, the Chief Justice of India, administered the oath of office as Dr Kalam was sworn in as the eleventh President of India. And in the glorious tradition of Indian democracy, as the new President, his first duty was to give a send-off to the outgoing President.

VI
LEADING INDIA
[2002–2015]

CHAPTER 19

FOR THE PEOPLE

For the swearing in, Dr Kalam's family visiting from Rameswaram spent time at the DRDO Development Enclave Guest House. On Dr Kalam's request, Harry Sheridon, Dr Kalam's erstwhile private secretary, rented a private bus to transport the visitors for all their sighseeing. Dr Kalam had insisted that no official vehicles be used; he also bore the expense of their stay and meals.

It is customary for every government office to display photographs of the President and the Prime Minister of India. With Dr Kalam, two issues came up: his hairstyle and his attire. Worn for comfort and utility, his distinctive pale blue shirt and sports shoes were unsuitable for his new position. So he switched to wearing a "bundgala," a jacket buttoned up to the neck. One of the most famous tailors in Delhi was called to create the new wardrobe. He came to take measurements. Before the swearing-in ceremony, the tailor and his staff arrived with three perfectly made bundgala suits. Dr Kalam put on a new dark suit; it looked very good on him—the coat lay square on his shoulders, and the length and drop were precise. The man himself, however, was far from pleased. Dr Kalam complained that the suit was suffocating him and he couldn't breathe. The tailor and his team appeared perplexed; for their part, they had performed their duties flawlessly, and to their trained eyes, the suit was a great fit.

Their renowned customer, Dr Kalam, had been designing things his entire professional life. Why would he feel shy in the realm of couture? He knew precisely what had to be done. He asked the tailor to make an inch-wide slot in the neck. A new design for the "bundgala" emerged during the process. It began to be known as the "Kalam suit": a bundgala suit with an open neck—a contradiction in terms! He stubbornly refused any sort of change to his hairstyle. But trimming the wild silver hair finished the change. Gone was the appeal of a philosopher-scientist with unkempt hair; in its place came the demeanour of a world leader.

Following the Bhuj earthquake in 2001, many thousands of lives had been lost; hundreds of thousands of individuals were made homeless. A massive reconstruction drive had been undertaken. In his role as

Principal Scientific Adviser, Dr Kalam had engaged in rehabilitation initiatives.

Just five months later, the state was rocked again when the communal violence of 2002 broke out. An already broken and suffering Gujarat, still recovering from the destruction caused by the earthquake, was crippled by the violence.

As the new President of India, Dr Kalam chose to visit Gujarat as his first responsibility. In muted voices, senior officials, including from the Prime Minister's Office, suggested he make another visit as his first. But Dr Kalam was in no mood to change his mind.

Gujarat's Chief Minister, Narendra Modi, received President Kalam at the airport and accompanied him throughout the visit, which included nine riot-stricken sites and three relief camps. President Kalam spoke to the people he met and relayed to the chief minister the steps he felt were needed to address their concerns. He held Modi's hand to convey a clear message to the people. Dr Kalam also visited Bhuj before returning to Delhi.

Dr Kalam had always shunned birthday celebrations, especially his own. But now that he was a public figure, this would not be simple. Being away from the capital helped him escape any planned formalities. On 15 October 2002, he decided to attend the Buddha Mahotsav celebration at the Buddhist monastery in Tawang, Arunachal Pradesh. On reaching Guwahati airport, he boarded an IAF helicopter to cross the enormous 14,000-foot-high Sela Mountain.

President Kalam visited the Gaden Namgyal Lhatse monastery of the Gelug school of Vajrayana Buddhism. The monastery's name can be roughly translated as "the spot selected by the horse is the heavenly paradise of total triumph." The horse is in the human body, and the triumph is over the mind and senses. Dr Kalam met Rinpoche, the Abbot. They shared an immediate rapport, and any language barrier dissolved when they held each other's hands.

The same evening, Governor Arvind Dave and Chief Minister Mukut Mithi hosted a dinner. There was much excitement over the dinner; in fact, there was no big venue in Tawang to accommodate the more than 200 guests, so a big tent was put up, and many bonfires were built to keep everyone warm. Governor Dave was known to Dr Kalam from the time of the Pokhran tests, when he had been the Director of the Research and Analysis Wing. The President called him Dave *Sahib*, in the old style.

In 2002, the holy month of Ramadan started on 5 November. As was the tradition (or *rivaaz*) in Delhi, the president, prime minister, political leaders, ambassadors, businesspeople—anyone of any significance—would host iftar celebrations. The media had turned these iftar parties into spectacles: marking out those who attended and those who did not. Many people looked forward to a big iftar celebration with President Kalam in Rashtrapati Bhavan. He, however, had other thoughts. He told his secretary, PM Nair, not to throw a feast for well-to-do individuals but rather to assist orphanages with food, clothes and blankets. The budget for this was rupees twenty-five lakh. He gave Nair a cheque for rupees one lakh out of his savings and left all the planning to the officials.

In January 2003, President Kalam was invited for the Dehing Patkai Cultural Festival in Assam. He inaugurated the Chukafa Harmony Arch constructed to commemorate the Ahom King Sukaphaa's entry into the Kamrup country, south of the Brahmaputra River. Ending the era of warring warlords, Ahoms would rule for six centuries. Dr Kalam developed a rapport with Governor Srinivas Kumar Sinha. A retired general, Governor Sinha, told him that his father had been the Inspector General of Police of Bihar, and his grandfather had been the first Indian Inspector General of British India. President Kalam would meet Sinha again in Kashmir in 2007.

Later, on the eve of Republic Day, he addressed the nation for the first time as President of India. In his address, Dr Kalam started with a call to build a knowledge society. He discussed a second green revolution, providing urban amenities to villages, and using e-governance to eliminate corruption and delays. He let down those hoping for a homily on secularism, socialism and moral values. President Kalam eloquently described how the world had changed from an agricultural civilization, where manual work was the most crucial element, to an industrial society, where the management of technology, capital and labour had the competitive advantage. He explained that we were now in the information age, where connectedness and software products had propelled a section of the economy of certain countries, including our own. A new society was developing in the twenty-first century, where information was the leading production resource rather than money and labour. The next morning, *The Telegraph* hailed President Kalam's speech as a "blend of politics, science and economics."

President Kalam's first official foreign trip began on 19 October 2003. Over seven days, he visited the United Arab Emirates, Sudan and Bulgaria. He became the first Indian president to visit Sudan. He addressed the Sudanese Parliament. His message was straightforward. Indians had built the steel suspension rail bridges in Khartoum and Atbara. Indian officials had overseen the first Sudanese parliamentary elections in 1953, and the Sudan Block at India's National Defence Academy stood as testimony to this friendship.

From his time at the DRDO, Dr Kalam was aware of Bulgaria's established strengths in mathematics, physics, computer hardware and precision manufacturing. Indo-Bulgarian cooperation had been ongoing in many fields since the Soviet era. Presidents Parvanov and Kalam suggested collaboration in computer hardware and software. Outside the Western sphere, Indian knowledge of software and Bulgarian capability in hardware manufacturing infrastructure stood out as an excellent combination. However, this had not happened. Dr Kalam tried to demonstrate to the establishment the need to capitalize on historical bonds and pursue future opportunities with old friends.

President Kalam also visited the historic Rila Monastery and had an interaction with Bishop Joan, who apprised him that the hermit St Ivan of Rila, who had founded the monastery, had lived in a cave, without any material possessions, away from the monastery. His students, who had come to the mountains to receive an education from him, had built the great complex.

As President Kalam explained later: "This Christian monastery is the biggest Bulgarian revival, spiritual and cultural centre, with a 16,000-volume library including 134 manuscripts from the 15th to 19th centuries. This holy site played an important role in the spiritual and social life of medieval Bulgaria. Destroyed by fire due to invasion at the beginning of the 19th century, the complex was rebuilt later and is now surrounded by a big fort. While being in that divine environment, amidst the Reverend Fathers aged between 80 and 90, I felt like praying. I went to the altar and asked permission of the Reverend Bishop Joan to recite a part of the prayer of St. Francis of Assisi. All the people present in the monastery repeated the prayer.

The Prayer of St. Francis of Assisi

Lord, make me an instrument of Your peace;
Where there is hatred, let me sow love;
And where there is injury, pardon;
And where there is doubt, faith;
And where there is despair, hope;
And where there is darkness, light;
and where there is sadness, joy.

The silent message in this prayer was felt by the Reverend Bishop, who blessed me by saying, 'You work for world peace'. My friends, may this beautiful divine message of love enlighten our life to work for universal peace."

President Kalam visited Tirupati on 20 November 2003. In a nearly thirty-minute extempore speech at Sri Venkateswara University, he elaborated on what he saw as his "law of development" to bring India into the privileged club of industrialized nations. He proposed a three-dimensional approach—cost-effectiveness, quality and on-time supply—to make Indian products competitive in the international market.

Later, Chief Minister N Chandrababu Naidu escorted him to the Sri Venkateswara Swamy Temple atop the Tirumala hills. At the Ranganayakula Mandapam, the temple's priests recited the Vedasirvachanam, a blessing. They spoke in Tamil. Dr Kalam requested the priests to perform an Asirvachanam to benefit the country and its people. Sitting on the ground, he ate the *prasadam* in a leaf bowl and placed some money in the *hundi*.

On 5 January 2004, President Kalam addressed the ninety-first session of the Indian Science Congress in Chandigarh. Nearly 4000 scientists from India and abroad were in the audience. By this time, Dr Kalam had mastered using various platforms to communicate what was on his mind. On this day, he cautioned against the notion that technological solutions could overcome all problems. Technology, he said, is never independent of societal or structural dimensions. Technology is only relevant when it is considered in terms of those who use it.

Dr Kalam said, "One of the problems with some of our laboratories is that they will always say, 'I have already done it.' I would call this the laboratory syndrome. Many underestimate the 'last mile' problems in taking the technology from the laboratory to the field. Technological development is complete only when the technology is transferred, absorbed and applied to the needs of people."

After his speech, Dr Kalam actively engaged with the scientists. No previous leader had inspired such excitement within the scientific community. Dr Kalam was frank in informing a group of biotechnologists that his support for biotechnology as the solution to agriculture and human health challenges was not blind. He told them he was trying to create appropriate checks and balances to control advances in the field. He said the top 10 multinational corporations controlled over 80% of the pesticide industry and had a 53% market share in the world medicines sector. The top 10 firms in the food retail sector were running 57 per cent of the global market. He asked, "Where are we?"

At the 12th National Children's Science Congress at Guwahati, President Kalam gave the children his "thinking mantra," which would eventually be a consistent element of his addresses in student forums.

Thinking is progress.
Non-thinking stagnates the individual, organization and country.
Thinking leads to action.
Knowledge without action is useless and irrelevant.
Knowledge with action brings prosperity.[1]

President Kalam urged children to realize that the human brain is a special gift. Curiosity and thought are the only ways to access the wonders of the cosmos. He claimed that thinking should become one's capital asset, independent of life's highs and lows. He told them, "Look at the sky. We are not alone. The universe is friendly to us and conspires only to give the best to those who dream and work."

In 2004, general elections were set to take place. In his second speech to the country, President Kalam spoke about the Lok Sabha election on the eve of Republic Day. He urged every political party to explicitly outline their vision, action plan and strategies for turning India into a developed nation by 2020. President Kalam urged the political parties to go beyond government criticism on the development front. He urged them to present their vision for growth and a substitute action plan. He said the least the political parties could do was run candidates with a clean record for the following Lok Sabha election.

Referring to the nearly forty-four crore young people of our nation, President Kalam stated that India at the start of the twenty-first century was a young country and that young people desired to live in a developed and corruption-free nation. He claimed a developed India had to be established in time to avoid social instability. His former DRDO coworker, R Swaminathan, now working as his aide, asked him if politicians would listen to what he had been saying. Dr Kalam replied that he had to speak out and that it was not his concern if it was not accepted. He said he was duty-bound to do his part and he would do it without the fear of becoming unpopular.

---

[1] President of India. Dr. A.P.J. Abdul Kalam. Address at the 12th National Children's Science Congress, Guwahati. https://presidentofindia.nic.in/dr-apj-abdul-kalam/speeches/address-12th-national-childrens-science-congress-guwahati

On 2 April 2004, President Kalam visited the Base Camp, Siachen Glacier. He surprised everyone by raising concerns about the personal payload of food for seven days, water, weapons, ammunition and sufficient reconnaissance equipment. Each soldier had to carry this. The President called for a 50% reduction in the weight of the gear through the use of advanced materials and food processing technology.[2]

On 18 April 2004, on the eve of the Lok Sabha election, President Kalam spoke out again. He urged voters to use their democracy 'positively' to choose those who would lead the country for the next five years. In his Doordarshan and All India Radio address, President Kalam stated, "By casting your vote for a candidate who in your opinion can represent you in the Lok Sabha, you are sowing the seeds for the creation of a prosperous India, a happy India, a safe India, a secure India, and above all, an India with nobility." In modern India, this was the first time a president had made such a call before an election.

The results declared on 13 May 2004 were a rude shock to the party in power. The number of people who voted for Congress and the BJP remained almost the same as in 1999; however, the Congress increased its seats by thirty-one, while the ruling BJP's seats decreased by forty-four, leading to its defeat.

President Kalam hosted a farewell function for the outgoing Prime Minister and his cabinet colleagues on 15 May 2004. Prime Minister Vajpayee was all praise for President Kalam, saying, *"Jab jab main Kalam sahib se milta tha, man aanandit ho jata tha* (Whenever I met Dr Kalam, I felt happy and energized)."

On 22 May 2004, President Kalam administered the oath to Dr Manmohan Singh as the Prime Minister of India, in Ashok Hall, Rashtrapati Bhavan.

---

[2] President of India. Dr. A.P.J. Abdul Kalam. Address at Base Camp, Siachen Glacier. https://presidentofindia.nic.in/dr-apj-abdul-kalam/speeches/address-base-camp-siachen-glacier

CHAPTER 20
RESOLVE

If Dr Kalam had been an unusual choice for the office of President, Dr Manmohan Singh was also an unusual choice to be Prime Minister. His qualifications remain unmatched by any other Prime Minister in modern Indian history. Dr Singh had held several critical government positions as a technocrat before he was selected to be the Finance Minister in PV Narasimha Rao's government. He was the opposition leader in the Rajya Sabha during the NDA government from 1998 to 2004. As a government official, he had held distinguished offices as Chairman of the University Grants Commission (UGC) and as Governor of the Reserve Bank of India. In the best way, President Kalam and Prime Minister Singh were seen as a break from the past.

The President of India usually has relatively little range independently, but the President's office is a position of pride and respect and a Prime Minister cannot easily brush this aside. The President is the head of state, while the Prime Minister and the Council of Ministers carry out the executive functions. The President must be updated on the activities and operations of all decisions made by the government.

In 2004, Dr Kalam was invited to speak at the Pan-African Parliament in Johannesburg, South Africa. En route, he stopped at Tanzania.

Dr Kalam used the forum to speak about connectivity, which he believed was the biggest developmental hurdle in the vast African continent. He unveiled a Pan-African Internet network that combined fibre optics and satellite communication. It would usher in a new era of e-governance, e-commerce, geological resource mapping and weather monitoring in the region. Universities and hospitals in India would be connected to their African counterparts in an exchange of knowledge. India committed USD 150 million towards capacity building.

Next came Dr Kalam's meeting with one of his heroes, Nelson Mandela. Mandela held Dr Kalam's hand and walked a few steps with him. When Dr Kalam mentioned Mahatma Gandhi, Mandela teasingly said that his country had transformed a barrister into a saint, but he had been killed in India. Dr Kalam also discovered how Africans had defended their way of life against brutal colonial powers. Resistance was rooted in the hearts of the people. It manifested in different forms—from the most violent to peaceful but stubborn resistance.

On the eve of Republic Day, in 2005, Dr Kalam began his address to the nation on a philosophical note. "Everyone has inside of him or her, a piece of good news. The good news is, that you don't know how great you can be!" Children smile naively as they bloom, but these smiles gradually disappear as they enter their teens. Fears like what they must do after their education, to find work, for example, steal their smiles, he said. No leader had ever spoken like him. He had risen to a higher spiritual plane. But every development comes with a test, and soon, he would have his.

In April 2005, Pakistani President Pervez Musharraf came to India. President Kalam hosted a lunch for him. The two leaders had a half-hour meeting during which President Kalam surprised the former military general with a slide presentation.

Dr Kalam went to Russia on a state visit. On reaching Moscow, Dr Kalam was getting ready for bed at around 2.00 a.m. when he received a communication from New Delhi regarding the dissolution of the Bihar legislative assembly. This had been decided by the Union Cabinet. Elections held earlier in the state had created a hung assembly and no government had been formed even after several months. He spoke to Prime Minister Dr Manmohan Singh and signed the consent. The next morning, the news of the dissolution at night created political outcry. The Central Government's power over the States remains a contentious issue in Indian politics. But, even more than that, analysts questioned why President Kalam did not put such an important decision on hold until his return and after broader discussion.

Later, both houses of parliament ratified the declaration, and new elections would establish a new assembly. The events led to many questions, however. Did the President have any option but to sign? Could he not have delayed the decision, or asked the government to wait till he returned? But if he had returned it for reconsideration, he would have had to cite specific grounds, and what grounds could he have cited from Moscow? Can waiting for a political impasse to resolve itself be the prerogative of the President of India? Dr Kalam acted by the book. What if the book itself was wrong?

President Kalam's tone and content progressively evolved from suggestion to recommendation, appeal to exhortation, and exuberance to doubt. On 1 July 2005, at the National Doctors' Day Award Ceremony, he spoke of the commercialization of medicine. Dr. Kalam stated that medical developments should reach the impoverished rather than be limited to expensive hospitals catering to affluent customers. He said righteousness is essential in whatever we do, whether social life or politics. Building a strong family, country and globe depends on virtue. We must provide a solid basis on which everyone operates, he reiterated.

On 15 October 2005, Dr Kalam turned seventy-four. For his birthday, he decided to go to Hyderabad to meet a group of Tanzanian children who had had surgery for congenital heart defects at Care Hospital; they had been flown in by Air India free of cost after Dr Kalam's call to help them. Dr Kalam lovingly patted each child's head and gave them all a package of gift-wrapped sweets he had brought from Delhi.

On 25 January 2006, the Supreme Court criticized the Bihar Governor for suggesting that the state assembly be dissolved. The court found that the dissolution was a *mala fide* use of the governor's authority to prevent opposition parties from claiming a stake in forming the government. Dr Kalam took the decision upon his conscience.

In his Republic Day address to the nation in 2006, Dr Kalam mentioned the story of a child, Abdul Qadir. When dacoits waylaid a caravan in the desert, he announced he had forty gold coins concealed in his jacket. Upon finding them, the surprised robber asked him why he had confessed this. Abdul Qadir answered that his mother had told him to always be honest, even at the expense of his life. Here, it was just forty gold coins, he said, but the promise he had made to his mother was priceless. The moral of the story was that it is not pragmatism but principles that would lead to sustainable progress.

The next month, Dr Kalam became the first President to sail underwater in a submarine. He boarded *INS Sindhurakshak* in Visakhapatnam, accompanied by Admiral Arun Prakash. A naval officer, Commander Pravesh Singh Bisht, mentioned to Dr Kalam that he had always considered the Navy as his mother. He said that seeing Dr Kalam was as if he was seeing his father meeting his mother: it seemed Dr Kalam could trigger such emotions by his presence.

In March 2006, Dr Kalam was pleased to see the isolation of India's atomic energy programme by the international community finally come to an end, during the visit of US President George W Bush. Energy generation and weapon development were clearly demarcated and a commitment was made to follow International Atomic Energy Agency (IAEA) standards. The United States would hereafter assist in civil nuclear energy generation and cooperate with the Nuclear Suppliers Group (NSG) to allow all necessary atomic energy material supply. There was criticism of the deal by the Left Parties and the Samajwadi

Party. But after Mulayam Singh met Dr Kalam, he changed his position and supported the government in Parliament.

The eighty-eighth convocation of the Banaras Hindu University (BHU) presented another opportunity to statesman Kalam. He was well-versed in the cultural connection between Kashi and Rameswaram. In 1991, he had presided over the convocation of the Indian Institute of Technology in BHU. On that occasion, the Raja of Kashi, Vibhuti Narayan Singh, introduced him to the audience. Since Vibhuti Narayan Singh had passed away in December 2000, Dr Kalam rolled out his plan for the evolution of an enlightened citizenship as a tribute to him.

On 3 March, at the BHU, President Kalam declared that taking the initiative is the hallmark of humans. He named the capacity to enquire, innovate, have technical skills, have entrepreneurial dealings and moral leadership, and extolled that education must build these skills. He said that if we develop these five capacities in our students, we will produce enlightened citizens who have self-direction, self-control, and are lifelong learners who can respect authority and appropriately question it. A good student must cultivate confidence to change and improve things and imbibe the spirit of "we can do it."

Having worked lifelong on technological projects, Dr Kalam was conditioned to view his visits as opportunities for bilateral cooperation—what can India learn from more developed nations? What can it give to less developed ones? In Myanmar, he ensured the signing of three agreements in the petroleum, space and education sectors. President Kalam visited the iconic Shwedagon Pagoda. He seemed spellbound by the tall golden structure.

He also visited the grave of Bahadur Shah Zafar, the last Emperor of India, who died there in exile. He wrote a poem lamenting his exile, and expressing his agony, despair and helplessness. Dr Kalam lit a candle near the tomb and sat in prayer. He wrote in the visitors' book, "O, Emperor of India. I came here today to recite Surah Fatiha. I have offered flowers and lit a candle here. It is not the tomb of a destitute; it is the mausoleum of the Emperor of India. May your soul rest in peace."

President Kalam initiated the Indradhanush series of concerts at the Rashtrapati Bhavan to honour great music artists. On 4 March 2006, President Kalam invited the Bharat Ratna Bismillah Khan, a shehnai maestro, to perform at the Mughal Gardens in Rashtrapati Bhavan. President Kalam persuaded him to stay in Rashtrapati Bhavan for three days. This event turned out to be the last public appearance of the shehnai maestro, who passed away later that year.

Meanwhile, another storm was brewing for Dr Kalam. A petition was filed with the Election Commission to disqualify the Rajya Sabha Member of Parliament and actor Jaya Bachchan of the Samajwadi Party because she held a public office of profit, which is prohibited by law. This opened a can of worms—the membership of Congress leader Sonia Gandhi was also challenged. Parliament passed a law with retroactive effect, presumably to clear the lawmakers of disqualification charges, exempting fifty-six public offices. When the Parliament (Prevention of Disqualification) Amendment Bill, 2006, came to President Kalam for his assent, he sent it back without signing it, and advised a parliamentary review. This created a furore.

Parliament returned the bill to Dr Kalam without making any changes. To everyone's surprise, President Kalam did not immediately sign it into law but waited 17 days for Parliament to address the matter. Rumours swirled that the President would sit over the bill until his term ended the following year, causing a political crisis. Dr Kalam signed the bill on 18 August 2006. He went through a severe moral quandary during this time. The idea of resigning without signing the bill also crossed his mind. But this would have caused a political crisis that Dr Kalam would have abhorred.

A little before this crisis, on 8 June 2006, President Kalam realized his childhood dream of flying an aircraft. He co-piloted the Sukhoi-30-MKI fighter plane alongside Wing Commander Ajay Rathore from Lohegaon Airport in Pune. He flew at one-and-a-quarter times the speed of sound at an altitude of 24,000 feet. The flight also involved manoeuvres, giving him first-hand experience of the combat plane's capabilities.

Dr Kalam was not a politician in many ways. He had never pursued public office. The President's office came to him due to certain political dynamics. Undoubtedly, he tackled his presidential responsibilities with a zeal and diligence that could hardly be exceeded. But he was never linked to his position. Dr Kalam grew much more resolved about the purpose of human life. In a year, he would break away from the gravitational pull of public affairs and let his spirit soar, he resolved.

CHAPTER 21

INNER ILLUMINATION

President Kalam invoked a powerful question in his last address to the nation on the eve of Republic Day in 2007. His call to the people of India was reminiscent of US President John F Kennedy's inaugural address to his nation forty-six years earlier, where he had implored his people to ask not what your country can do for you but rather what you can do for it. Dr Kalam asked: "What can I give?" Dr Kalam found the source of all corruption in the question "what can I take", and believed that thinking of giving back would provide the solution.

Dr Kalam had Russian President Vladimir Putin beside him during the Republic Day parade. India and Russia have a strategic connection that has functioned effectively, and their relationship is deep and broad in the field of missile development. Given Dr Kalam's work with the Russian space and defence agencies, having the Russian president by his side was a suitable conclusion to his life in public office.

On 21 February 2007, Dr Kalam gave an inspiring lecture to the directors of the DRDO. Using the stories of five Nobel winners, he outlined the five aspects of a useful scientific career: ideals, lifetime dedication, a universal perspective, turning obstacles into possibilities, and a generous mindset.

He narrated several instances that supported these qualities. In 1954, Sir CV Raman was among the inaugural Bharat Ratna award winners. President Dr Rajendra Prasad invited him to be his guest at Rashtrapati Bhavan, but he politely declined the invitation, as his PhD student was in the final stage of writing his thesis and needed his presence. Here was an academic who sacrificed a grand event linked to the country's most prestigious accolade to fulfil his obligation to his student. Giving value to your work over everything else is a trait of the greats.

In 1947, physicist Dr Subrahmanyan Chandrasekhar was guiding Tsung-Dao Lee and Chen Ning Yan. Chandrasekhar, who worked at Yerkes Observatory in Lake Geneva, Wisconsin, often drove 100 miles to Chicago to mentor and teach his students every week, sometimes in challenging weather conditions. These two pupils took home the

Nobel Prize in Physics in 1957. Science is a relay race in which one generation passes the baton to the next.

German physician Prof. Bert Sakmann came to understand that engineering concepts may help one understand living things. Working with electrical and computer engineers, he defined the fundamental mechanism of vision and the presence of ionic channels in cell membranes. This revealed the enigma of diseases, including diabetes, epilepsy, heart ailments and some neuromuscular diseases. Prof. Sakmann showed the borderless, transcendent character of science.

Dutch scientist Prof. Paul Crutzen won the Nobel Prize in Chemistry for proving that the chemical components of nitrogen oxides hasten the depletion of stratospheric ozone, which shields the Earth from the Sun's UV radiation. From early on, Crutzen was plagued by hardship. His family circumstances were difficult, and World War II and mandatory military service interrupted his studies. He turned his difficulties into opportunities and showed how a determined mind could triumph over obstacles.

Finally, he mentioned Prof. Norman Borlaug. Dr Kalam had presented Dr Borlaug the first MS Swaminathan Award for Leadership in Agriculture in 2005. Dr Borlaug named his colleagues in the audience as his collaborators, asking them to stand up and receive the applause. The magnanimity of sharing success with your team and giving credit to your colleagues is the hallmark of a good scientist.

It was at this event that Dr Kalam first spoke about courage; it would later become a constant theme in his lectures to the youth.

Courage to think differently,
Courage to invent,
Courage to discover the impossible,
Courage to travel on an unexplored path,
Courage to share the knowledge,
Courage to remove the pain,
Courage to reach the unreached,
Courage to combat problems,
And succeed
Are the unique qualities of the youth.[1]

---

[1] President of India. Dr. A.P.J. Abdul Kalam. Address at the DRDO Directors Conference, DRDO Bhavan, New Delhi. https://presidentofindia.nic.in/dr-apj-abdul-kalam/speeches/address-drdo-directors-conference-drdo-bhavan-new-delhi

Throughout his life, Dr Kalam demonstrated courage. He was not made for bluster, and maybe because of this, as well as his sensitivity and concern for others, people didn't notice his steely determination. Most recently, in his stand-off with Parliament in the office-of-profit controversy, he had demonstrated his courage. More often, individuals would see his concern for others, which was shown in the development of civilian spin-offs of defence technology for the betterment of society.

On 24 February 2007, President Kalam visited ailing Field Marshal SHFJ Manekshaw, affectionately known as Sam Bahadur, at the Military Hospital, Wellington, near Ooty. President Kalam spent some quiet time with India's distinguished military hero. He held Manekshaw's hand and sat by his bedside.

Once out of the room, he spoke to Sam Bahadur's attendant Subedar Bikram Singh Thapa. Dr Kalam inquired about his coming a considerable distance from his regiment. Subedar informed him that the 5th Gorkha Rifles had been under Sam Bahadur's leadership in 1950 and that the regiment was duty-bound to care for him for the rest of his life. President Kalam wrote in the hospital's visitors' book: "Military Hospital, Wellington is always contributing the best. Please take care of our great wealth, our only Field Marshal Manekshaw."

When Josep Borrell Fontelles, the twenty-second President of the European Parliament, visited him in October 2006, President Kalam agreed to speak before the European Parliament.

He left for Europe on 24 April 2007, on a five-day visit to France and Greece. Dr Kalam paid a visit to the Space University in Strasbourg, a worldwide higher education institution committed to advancing research in outer space for peaceful purposes. Prof. Michael Simpson, President of the International Space University, informed Dr Kalam about the 3-I concept, which called for an *Interdisciplinary, Intercultural* and *International* setting to train and educate space professionals and postgraduate students.

At a talk at the university, President Kalam praised India's emergence on the world stage of space science and technology. Supported by over 500 enterprises and universities, and its 14,000 scientific, technical and support personnel spread across several research centres, India can create any satellite launch vehicle to position meteorological, communications and remote sensing satellites in various orbits.

Almost all daily life today involves space applications. India has a constellation of six remote sensing and ten communications satellites that enable tele-education (10,000 classrooms), tele-medicine (200 hospitals), meteorology, disaster management assistance, natural resource surveying and communication. Through a public–private partnership approach, our nation creates 100,000 public service facilities nationwide to give rural people credible information. Village Knowledge Centres provide a range of services, including advice on public health, agricultural techniques, and access to government services—an avatar of PURA envisioned by Dr Kalam.

Dr Kalam spoke with the students following his talk. An Indian student working on a master's degree in space studies asked Dr Kalam how long it would take for the first Indian woman to land on Mars or the moon. Dr Kalam answered that three of the astronauts who had been on space missions had been of Indian origin: Rakesh Sharma, Kalpana Chawla and Sunita Williams. Of the three, two were women. Therefore, Indian women's prospects of arriving on the moon or Mars were excellent, he believed.

President Kalam was at the European Parliament outside Strasbourg's city centre the following day. His address started with a Tamil saying from the Sangam era, roughly from the 3rd century BCE to the 3rd century CE. The quote implied that the world is one huge family. He added that European civilization has a special position in human history. From its origins, contemporary European science had caused quantum leaps in technology. But Europe had also been a stage for hostilities for hundreds of years, including the two World Wars. The European Union had been created against this background and with these forces in mind to promote peace and prosperity for the continent.

Dr Kalam mentioned that he had brought a message from India to start three important Indo-European missions that could contribute to global peace and prosperity. Drawing from India's history and the European Union's dynamics, he suggested the following initiatives. "The first task is the evolution of an enlightened society, in which citizens have a system of values, leading to a prosperous and peaceful world. The second idea is creating energy independence. Normally, people talk about energy security. I am talking about energy independence: a three-dimensional approach to energy choice that aims to achieve a clean world. The third aim is a World Knowledge Platform to bring together the core skills of the European Union and India in certain areas to provide solutions to critical issues like water, healthcare and capacity-building."[2]

---

[2] European Parliament. (2007, April 25). Verbatim Report of Proceedings. https://www.europarl.europa.eu/doceo/document/CRE-6-2007-04-25-ITM-010_EN.html?redirect

Near the conclusion of his forty-five-minute address, Dr Kalam read aloud a poem he had written titled "The message from Mother India to the European Union." The poem reflected the essence of European topography and the daring, creative and meticulous attitude of those who lived here.

A beautiful environment leads
To beautiful minds.
Beautiful minds generate
Freshness and creativity.

Created explorers of land and sea.
Created minds that innovate.
Created great scientific minds everywhere.
Why?

Gave birth to many discoveries.
Discovered a continent and unknown lands.
Ventured into unexplored paths.
Created new highways.[3]

The poem then shifted to Europe's historical conflicts, where many bloody wars had been fought in the name of faith, and colonial campaigns carried out upon nations across the globe.

In the minds of the best
Worst was also born.
Generated seeds of battle and hatred.
Hundreds of years of wars and bloodshed.

Millions of my wonderful children
Lost in the land and sea.
Tears flooded many nations.
Many engulfed in oceans of sadness.[4]

President Kalam set the European Union as the ideal embodiment of human possibilities after defining the two polarities—the greatest of minds and the worst of acts.

---

[3] Ibid.
[4] Ibid.

Then came the vision of the European Union.
Took the oath
Never to turn human knowledge
Against ourselves or others.

United in their thinking
Actions emanated
To make Europe prosperous
And peace bound the European Union.

Those glad tidings captivated
The people of the planets of my galaxy.
O, European Union, let your mission
Spread everywhere, like the air we breathe.[5]

President Kalam's method of holding the mirror in front of over seven hundred leaders from twenty-eight European nations was remarkable. Parliamentarians applauded him several times and stood up to meet him when he completed his speech by saying "namaskar" with folded hands. President Hans-Gert Pottering of the European Parliament called the speech exceptional, a kind of speech they hadn't witnessed before.

Back in India, the government announced Pratibha Patil, the Governor of the state of Rajasthan, as their candidate for the presidential election. This was after they had determined that President Kalam was not seeking a second term in office. He was urged to run by the All India Anna Dravida Munnetra Kazhagam (AIADMK) under J Jayalalithaa, the Samajwadi Party under Mulayam Singh Yadav, the Telugu Desam Party (TDP) under Chandrababu Naidu, and the Indian National Lok Dal (INLD) under Om Prakash Chautala, but he declined.

In 2007, Pratibha Patil was elected as the twelfth President of India. Dr LM Singhvi, eminent Indian lawyer and legislator, declared in *The Tribune* that President Kalam was finishing his term amidst nationwide love for his academic ability and kind human traits. He would be remembered as the president of the people, he said. He held the venerable office and structure of the president with remarkable distinction, free of personal axes to grind. His spiritual and moral powers should be used to rouse India and fulfil its spiritual, cultural,

---

[5] Ibid.

economic and social goals. He wrote: "The nation needs the sanity and equanimity of Kalam, the austere and ascetic citizen."[6]

Dr Kalam left Rashtrapati Bhavan with two pieces of luggage; leaving all the gifts he received as the President of India. No personal articles were added to his belongings in the five years. He flew to Chennai on the evening on 25 July 2007, escorted by Anna University Vice Chancellor Prof. D Viswanathan. For Dr Kalam, living lean had always been the right way.

---

[6] Singhvi, LM. (2007, July 24). Welcome Citizen Kala. *The Tribune.* https://www.tribuneindia.com/2007/20070724/edit.htm#5

CHAPTER 22

BEACON

Dr Kalam continued to be highly sought after even after stepping down from his position as the President of India. He appeared to be thriving at an age when most people slow down, and he exhibited no outward symptoms of a decline in his health. His father had been active well into his nineties, and his older brother APJ Maracayer had been in good shape at the same age, so he had inherited good health, it seemed. More so, the most beloved President of India was motivated by a sense of purpose. His nearly limitless energy came from his sense of obligation towards the country and, by extension, the world.

Dr Kalam could now devote his time and energy to encouraging children to achieve their full potential—something he loved doing the most. On 28 July 2007, during the sixth convocation of the International Institute of Information Technology (IIIT) in Hyderabad, he declared his intention to teach part-time, to a standing ovation from the students. He had formally dedicated this institute to the nation on 15 March 2003.

Projects involving social welfare also attracted Dr Kalam. On 30 July 2007, the governing board of the Emergency Management and Research Institute (EMRI) appointed him Chairman Emeritus. Since August 2005, EMRI has been offering free, world-class emergency response as a non-profit organization.

On 15 August, in the presence of over a thousand enthusiastic students, Dr Kalam raised the national flag at IIIT Hyderabad, to commemorate sixty-five years of Indian independence. Afterwards, accompanied by Chief Minister Dr YS Rajasekhara Reddy, Dr Kalam offered the citizens of Andhra Pradesh the "108" emergency free ambulance service. He firmly believed in the model of public–private collaboration and that it should be replicated throughout. The private sector cannot shrink from its public responsibility and must contribute to the service of society, he said.

In April 2009, Dr Kalam visited Seattle. Earlier, in November 2002, Bill Gates had visited India—the CEO of the most prominent software firm in the world meeting a visionary "techie" President. Things had been chilly at that meeting when President Kalam had started pushing for open-source software. But since then, open-source software had flourished, and internet on mobile phones had changed the game. William H. Gates, Bill Gates's father, presented Dr Kalam his book, *Showing Up for Life*. "You are a living testimony of the book's theme," Gates Sr. said.

On 24 April, Dr Kalam was shown around Seattle's Boeing Everett Factory by Dinesh Keskar, Boeing International Trading's Vice President. Situated on a hundred acres, this plant has a constructed area measuring 4 billion cubic feet. Joseph "Joe" Sutter, the "father of the 747," who oversaw a design team of 4500 people at Boeing, was eighty-eight years old when he met him. To his joy, internationally renowned musician Dr Kanniks Kannikeswaran performed before Dr Kalam.

Walking your talk is never easy, but for some people, it comes effortlessly. Dr Kalam accepted the first Sitaram Jindal Foundation (SJF) award—on condition that he would donate the cash to organizations of his choice. With the foundation's approval, Dr Kalam donated twenty-five lakh rupees each to four charities on the same day he received the one-crore-rupee award, all while requesting that the news remain confidential.

The Samajwadi Party swept the Uttar Pradesh assembly elections in March 2012. Mulayam Singh Yadav's son, Akhilesh Yadav, became the chief minister of the most populous state in India. At thirty-eight, he was the state's youngest chief minister. He convened a conference with the support of the *Hindustan Times*, and invited Dr Kalam to provide a vision for development in Uttar Pradesh. Dr Kalam developed an instant rapport with the young chief minister, an engineering graduate with a master's degree in environmental engineering from the University of Sydney, Australia.

In his talk, Dr Kalam said that Uttar Pradesh is a resource-rich state. He asked if there was a way to raise the per capita income of 26,000 rupees to 100,000 rupees. One out of five of the country's 100 million youth call Uttar Pradesh home. By tapping into the skills of the youth of Uttar Pradesh, Dr Kalam predicted that eight out of every hundred skilled job opportunities might happen in Uttar Pradesh. In hindsight, the "Skill India" Mission, launched nationally in 2016, was based on his ideas from that day.

There was still a lot of talk, among his fans and some political leaders, about bringing Dr Kalam back to Rashtrapati Bhavan. Pranab Mukherjee was nominated as the candidate for the 2012 presidential elections by the ruling United Progressive Alliance. The opposition parties wanted Dr Kalam to contest. The media fuelled conjecture about Dr Kalam's possible comeback to the presidency. Dr Kalam finally spoke out on 18 June 2012, and said he would not run for president. Pranab Mukherjee was elected the thirteenth President of India.

The prospect of delivering a keynote speech at the 2012 Beijing Forum was something Dr Kalam looked forward to. Since the translation of two of his works into Chinese, *Wings of Fire* (2002) and *Guiding Souls* (2007), he had had a desire to visit the nation. The development of China as a global force in the previous thirty years had fascinated him, and the civilization's durability filled him with wonder. The Beijing Forum took place at Peking University; it was a global gathering to find ways to support better education and social change across the globe.

On 2 November 2012, Dr Kalam delivered the keynote address, joined by several renowned speakers, including former Prime Minister of the Republic of Korea Ro Jai-bong and UN Secretary-General Ban Ki-moon. As part of his goal of creating a habitable planet, Dr Kalam addressed the management of water, energy, healthcare and education—issues facing seven billion people. Dr Kalam was aware that Ban Ki-moon was among the first leaders to identify global warming as a key issue. He had famously said that Climate Change matched his fear of a Nuclear Winter as the leading existential threat on the horizon.

On 24 May 2013, the National Space Society of the United States presented Dr Kalam with the Wernher von Braun Memorial Award, at the 32nd International Space Development Conference in San Diego, California. On this occasion, Dr Kalam spoke about von Braun's 1973 visit to India and recalled his liaison officer role.

By this time, Dr Kalam looked upon himself as a soul on a sojourn and reflected upon his experiences as part of his spiritual evolution. He would say that the right way of living involves expanding one's consciousness with generosity and not constraining it within identities.

The Edinburgh India Institute at the University of Edinburgh invited Dr Kalam in May 2014. A collaboration was established with the National Centre for Biological Sciences, University of Delhi, the Tata Institute of Fundamental Research, the National Institute of Ocean Technology, and the Indian Institute of Science. Indian students were in great demand, and this arrangement would link the most promising talent with the best opportunities.

In fact, Dr Kalam knew that Prafulla Chandra Ray, who founded India's first chemical enterprise, had studied at the University of Edinburgh in the late nineteenth century.

Dr Kalam was accompanied to different labs by Vice Chancellor Sir Timothy O'Shea, who mentioned that James Clerk Maxwell, Charles Darwin and Alexander Graham Bell had all walked here. He bestowed an honorary Doctor of Science degree on Dr Kalam. This would be his forty-eighth doctorate, coming from among the oldest universities in the world! It was to be the last.

On the afternoon of 27 July 2015, Dr Kalam took his seat on a flight to Guwahati. His mentee Srijan Pal Singh accompanied him. Dr Kalam wore his trademark "Kalam" suit. The drive to IIM Shillong took an additional two-and-a-half hours, due to the rainy weather. Mindful of the waiting audience, his next stop was the lecture hall, skipping any refreshments and rest. Hundreds of students erupted in a raucous welcome for Dr Kalam as he entered the auditorium.

"A *Liveable Planet Earth* is the subject I've settled on. Dear friends ..."

As he said this, Dr Kalam collapsed in front of a shocked audience. One instant he was speaking, and then he stumbled and became silent forever. His dying moments were unremarkable. Many assumed he had fainted. This was classic Dr APJ Abdul Kalam—captivating the crowd in his subdued voice one moment, and then gone the next. One of India's most adored scientists, statesmen and visionaries had died. It was 27 July 2015, 6:30 p.m. As open and transparent as his life was, so was his death.

The Union Cabinet proclaimed a national mourning period of seven days. Dr Kalam was flown to New Delhi by the Indian Air Force draped in the national tricolour. Even though he was not one for spectacles, as a patriot, he would have loved to have the national flag draped over him. At the airport, Prime Minister Modi was present to receive the mortal remains. Thousands of people, including lawmakers from all parties, bureaucrats, friends and citizens, gathered to pay their respects as Dr Kalam's body was placed in state. Long lines formed well after midnight.

On 30 July 2015, Dr Kalam was laid to rest with military honours in Rameswaram. The final salute was given by Prime Minister Narendra Modi.

What do the millions of people who love, respect and cherish Dr Kalam do to bring his spirit into their lives? Looking back on his life, from his final plea for a more liveable planet and a mindful and responsible citizenry, to his early years, we can perceive three foundations—imagination, piousness and faith. From these three emerge righteousness, integrity and courage.

In his later years, Dr Kalam wanted to develop a movement to make our planet more liveable, developing technologies to reduce the consequences of climate change, produce more food, and enjoy a clean environment. Corporations and the enormous wealth they have created must be used to create an equitable world where no human being sleeps hungry and no youth has to wait to earn a livelihood.

Perhaps the fruition of this idea would be the ultimate tribute to Dr APJ Abdul Kalam.